PALESTINIAN CITIZENS IN ISRAEL

Alternative Histories: Narratives from the Middle East and Mediterranean

Series Editor: Sargon Donabed

This series provides a forum for exchange on a myriad of alternative histories of marginalised communities and individuals in the Near and Middle East and Mediterranean, and those of Middle Eastern or Mediterranean heritage. It also highlights thematic issues relating to various native peoples and their narratives and – with particular contemporary relevance – explores encounters with the notion of 'other' within societies. Often moving beyond the conventional state-centred and dominant monolithic approach, or reinterpreting previously accepted stories, books in the series examine and explain themes from inter-communal relations, environment, health and society, and explore ethnic, communal, racial, linguistic and religious developments, in addition to geopolitics.

Books in the series (published and forthcoming)

Sayfo: An Account of the Assyrian Genocide
'Abd al-Masih Nu'man of Qarabash
Translated and annotated by Michael Abdalla and Łukasz Kiczko

Tunisia's Andalusians: The Cultural Identity of a North African Minority
Marta Dominguez Diaz

Palestinian Citizens in Israel: A History Through Fiction, 1948–2010
Manar H. Makhoul

Armenians Beyond Diaspora: Making Lebanon their Own
Tsolin Nalbantian

Museums and the Art of Minorities: Cultural Representation in the Middle East and North Africa
Edited by Virginie Rey

Shia Minorities in the Contemporary World: Migration, Transnationalism and Multilocality
Edited by Oliver Scharbrodt and Yafa Shanneik

Protestants, Gender and the Arab Renaissance in Late Ottoman Syria
Deanna Ferree Womack

edinburghuniversitypress.com/series/ahnme

PALESTINIAN CITIZENS IN ISRAEL

A HISTORY THROUGH FICTION, 1948–2010

Manar H. Makhoul

EDINBURGH
University Press

Edinburgh University Press is one of the leading university presses in the UK. We publish academic books and journals in our selected subject areas across the humanities and social sciences, combining cutting-edge scholarship with high editorial and production values to produce academic works of lasting importance. For more information visit our website: edinburghuniversitypress.com

Edinburgh University Press Ltd
The Tun – Holyrood Road
12 (2f) Jackson's Entry
Edinburgh EH8 8PJ

First published in hardback by Edinburgh University Press 2020

Typeset in 11/15 Adobe Garamond by
Servis Filmsetting Ltd, Stockport, Cheshire

A CIP record for this book is available from the British Library

ISBN 978 1 4744 5927 3 (hardback)
ISBN 978 1 4744 5928 0 (paperback)
ISBN 978 1 4744 5930 3 (webready PDF)
ISBN 978 1 4744 5929 7 (epub)

CONTENTS

List of Tables vi
Acknowledgements vii
Note on Transliteration x

Introduction 1
1 Palestinian Novels in Israel, 1948–1967 15
2 Postmodernisations, 1967–1987 67
3 Palestinian Novels in Israel, 1987–2010: United by Alienation 139
Reflections: Evolution of Palestinian Identity in Israel 208

Bibliography 214
Index 227

TABLES

ACKNOWLEDGEMENTS

I would like to extend my deepest gratitude to Professor Yasir Sulieman, my supervisor at the University of Cambridge between 2007 and 2011, for his involvement in the publishing of this book from its first stages as a doctoral dissertation. *Shukran*, Yasir, for your support, patience and guidance during the research period, and later for encouraging me to publish the book with Edinburgh University Press.

I would like also to thank Dr Oren Barak, who supervised my work for my MA thesis at the Hebrew University of Jerusalem, for his relentless support and encouragement. Professor Avraham Sela, who was my first lecturer at the Hebrew University, has been a great role model in my early years in academia. His stimulation and support during those years are unforgettable. Dr Anat Lapidot was the person who encouraged me to apply to Cambridge University. Her faith in me for so long was extremely motivating. I am grateful for being able to work with her at the Van Leer Jerusalem Institute after my return. I would also like to thank Dr Shukri Arraf, a dear friend of my family, who was always available for telephone enquiries from Cambridge, generously offering his wealth of knowledge and expertise. Special thanks to Sayyed Kashua, whose extraordinary writing has brought me to the study of literature in search of identity. I have been following the writing of Sayyed since 1999, and my MA thesis on him led to the research proposal leading to this book. Many thanks also to Hanan Musa for assisting in getting hold of many of the novels when I did not have time to go back to Israel. Last, but not least, I would like to thank Kath Farrell for her impeccable copy-editing of the thesis under the tight timetable of the last few months.

The development of my dissertation into this book would have not been possible without the support I received during my postdoctoral fellowship at the Minerva Humanities Centre in Tel-Aviv University. I am grateful for the enormous encouragement and support I received from Professor Rivka Feldhay and Dr Raef Zreik. The project they are leading, Humanities in Conflict Zones, and their respective research groups at the centre have been fertile intellectual grounds for developing innovative research. It would be impossible to mention every member at the centre, but I would like to particularly mention a few who had a profound impact on me. I am indebted to my friend and colleague Dr Zahiye Kundos, who encouraged me to apply for this fellowship. I have known Zahiye since our undergraduate studies at the Hebrew University, and it is a great honour to partner with her professionally. Dr Gal Hertz's unceasing support for everyone in the project is an enormous energiser. Gal and Zahiye are a great source of inspiration and hope. The Programme for the Study of Jewish-Arab Culture at Tel-Aviv University is another ground-breaking intellectual enterprise that I am proud to participate in. Professor Galili Shahar has been a great mentor since I joined the programme. Together with Dr Almog Behar we developed this research project into a successful course in the Department of Literature, further expanding the scope of its analysis. Also, thank you, Almog, for suggesting my name to teach a course based on this research in Sapir Academic College, back in 2015, becoming my first academic post after my graduation. My gratitude also goes to Dr Maram Masarwi, Dr Yusri Hazran, Dr Tom Pessah, Dr Manar Mahmoud, Dr Avital Barak and Dr Ran Segev.

Apart from the professional and academic support of all of the people mentioned above, and many more, working on this book would have not been possible without the unconditional support, love and encouragement of my family: my father, Halim, who read each and every paper I ever wrote, and to whom this book is dedicated; my amazingly loving and supportive mother, Salwa; Dima, Ibn-Sina, Amid and Suha, Lubna and Jens (who also read and commented on earlier chapters of the book); Reem, Steve – thank you all for being there for me.

Indeed, my 'Cambridge experience' would have been completely different, and frankly unimaginable, without my dear friends there: Yonatan Mendel, Ellah Yedaaya, Bruno De Nicola, Marta Dominguez, Ronald Klingebiel, Jessica Johnson, Prajakti Kalra, Siddarth 'Montu' Saxena, Khaled Hroub, Kholoud Amr, Heba Mostafa, Simon Ryle, Mariam Tanwir, Shahzad Shafqat, Tarik Mouakil, Louise Burdloff, Therese Cregan, Sharif Hamadeh, Tilde Rosmer, Ignacio Sanchez, James Weaver, Juliette Touma, Ghusoun Bisharat (thank you also for lending me two books for more than four years), Isabelle Humphries, Camilla Greene, James Greene, Nicky Sherrot, Clara Vigdis, Layla Younis, Maha Younis and Antoine Raffoul.

Special thanks to my friends at home: Gideon Herscher, for his relentless help with preparing the application to Cambridge. Without the generous help of Gidi's father, Dr Uri Herscher, who helped me secure funding for the first year, landing in Cambridge would have been seriously difficult. I feel indebted to both of you. Avi Krauz provided me with crucial mental support for many years in Jerusalem and Cambridge. Special thanks are for my friend and colleague Dr Wael Abu-Oxa. For many years, Wael has been a great friend and a fierce opponent in innumerable debates. He has been a source of great inspiration and motivation.

Thank you all.

NOTE ON TRANSLITERATION

Following house style, Arabic names and terms have not been transliterated in the main text. However, properly transliterated forms of novel titles can be found in the tables following each chapter.

Names of authors with published works in English will be spelled according to the published spelling, as is the case with Atallah Mansour, Shukri Arraf and Fouzi El-Asmar.

For transliteration of Hebrew I have followed the Academy of the Hebrew Language's 2006 transliteration guidelines.

In memory of my father, Halim
(1 February 1946 – 5 March 2019)

INTRODUCTION

Palestinian citizens in Israel constitute a special community.[1] They are the remnants of Palestinian society who, after the 1948 war, were to become citizens in the newly established state of Israel. Although they remained in their homeland, this society has undergone massive transformations in almost all aspects of life. The 1948 war, which for the Jewish-Israelis was a war of independence and for the Palestinians a Nakba, a catastrophe, made the Palestinians in Israel a minority, where they were a majority before the war. Palestinians in Israel not only had to adapt to their new status as a minority, they also had to adjust to a new political reality and, no less importantly, to the encounter with a new cultural environment.

The main concern of this study is to investigate and understand the process of change in, and the transformation of, the Palestinian national discourse from 1948 until recent years (the time frame of this study is 1948–2010). In other words, my research aims at understanding the underlying forces that evolved the discourse of Palestinians from that of a liberation movement up to 1948 to that of a discourse that now calls for civil equality with the Jewish-Israelis. This political orientation contrasts with the national discourse of the rest of the Palestinian nation that lives outside Israel (in the West Bank and Gaza Strip – under Israeli military occupation, the neighbouring Arab countries and the rest of the world), and maintains its struggle for emancipation against Israel, sometimes by force. Moreover, understanding the political orientation of Palestinians in Israel cannot be separated from the cultural aspects of their experience in Israel. For more than six decades, Palestinians in Israel have been exposed to Israeli-Western culture and have been directly influenced by it.

In this Introduction, I will address several aspects regarding this study and its methodology. This book aims to outline and understand the *evolution* in Palestinian identity in Israel over six decades after 1948. The initial assumption, then, is that identities are in constant change and adjustment to social, political and economic environments. However, despite the use of 'evolution', this book does not follow the theoretical lead of social Darwinism. From the viewpoint expressed here, evolution of Palestinian identity does not aspire to arrive at a 'higher' or 'advanced' stage of development. My use of 'evolution' refers solely to the free, undesigned form in which Palestinian identity has been transformed since 1948. Similarly, I have not used the term 'development' because it implies progression towards a 'better' state. The term 'transformation' is also unsuitable because it downplays the interconnectedness of the transformations in Palestinian identity. Evolution is a term that contains the transformations in identity in a historical, chronological form, preserving the different compiling layers of identity. Literature, as I will show in the following chapters, is an excellent device for registering transformations in Palestinian identity.

What do we know about Palestinian identity in Israel? What are the existing research approaches that address this community? To answer these questions, the discussion that follows will outline the shortcomings and limitations of existing methodologies, offering an alternative, yet complementary methodology that will be carried out in this book. The introduction to the main scholarly approaches in the study of Palestinians in Israel will not be an exhaustive review, but rather a survey of the central arguments and methodologies of each approach. 'Purpose-made' comprehensive reviews on the sociology of Palestinians in Israel exist elsewhere (Nakhleh 1977; Kimmerling 1992; Yiftachel 1992; Rosenhek 1998).

The Sociology of the Palestinians in Israel

There are two major phases in the sociology of Palestinians in Israel.[2] The earlier phase, extending until the 1970s, was dominated by proponents of modernisation theory. In the study of Palestinian integration, or the lack of it, in Israel, this theory presupposes, as its name suggests, Palestinian 'backwardness' comparatively with Israeli society. In order to 'solve' this cultural imbalance, Palestinians are expected to modernise, thus laying the responsibility of integrating into Israel on them (Rosenhek 1998: 561). Such an approach is explained by some (e.g. Kimmerling 1992) to be a result of Israeli sociology considering itself, in its early years, as being part of the Israeli establishment. As will become apparent in Chapter 1, the modernisation approach as adopted by Israeli sociology and the establishment is also evident in Palestinian discourse until 1967. The modernisation of Palestinians in Israel had a profound effect on Palestinian identity. This is so because this process, supposedly leading to their integration into Israeli society, meant the erasure of the conflictual history between Palestinians and Jewish-Israelis, focusing on the cultural backwardness of the former as the reason for the lack of peace.

Another characteristic of some of the works of Israeli sociologists is related to the fact that they see transformations in Palestinian political activity in terms of 'Israelisation' and 'Palestinisation' (or 'radicalisation'). On the face of it, the term 'Palestinisation' presupposes that the Palestinians in Israel are not Palestinians, while in fact it means their political 'radicalisation' from the Israeli point of view regarding expressions of Palestinian solidarity across the borders (Landau 1969; Stendel 1996; Rekhess 1989, 2002). Without going into detailed criticism of each of these works, in terms of Palestinian identity evolution in Israel, the terms 'Israelisation' and 'Palestinisation' (let alone 'radicalisation') convey a binary process of 'either/or', depending on the political context in Israel or in the Middle East. This is a simplistic, let alone politicised, way to convey the political and cultural processes taking place in Palestinian society over decades. Surely, Palestinians in Israel are simultaneously subject to a wide array of cultural, political and economic processes that cannot be simply portrayed in such binary terms.

Modernisation approaches have been subject to critical scrutiny by many (see: Nakhleh 1977; Sa'di 1992, 1997), and in the 1970s were replaced by a theory that focuses on analysing the power relationship between Jewish-Israelis and Palestinians in terms of majority and minority. According to this approach:

> [t]he position of Palestinian citizens in Israeli society is described as one of structural subordination, stressing the inequality which characterises their situation in terms of class, social status and political power [...], and the relationships between them and the state apparatus are conceived in terms of control, domination and exclusionary institutional practices. (Rosenhek 1998: 564)

One of the earliest studies exemplifying this approach is Ian Lustick's *Arabs in the Jewish State* (1980a), in which he discussed the system of control that limited and manipulated the Palestinians inside Israel. Lustick suggests that Israel's control over its Palestinian citizens is maintained through a three-fold system of segmentation, dependence and co-optation. Alternatively, Sammy Smooha (1990) proposed a model of 'ethnic democracy' to describe the relations between Jews and Palestinians in Israel. In an ethnic democracy, one ethnic group dominates other groups while granting political and civil rights to individuals and minority groups. Israel is defined as the state of the Jews, and Hebrew is its dominant language. Its institutions, national holidays, symbols and national heroes are all Jewish. The state's ethnic minority, the Palestinians, can struggle to gain further rights and equality through the democratic means available to them.

As'ad Ghanem (1998), however, opposes the inclusion of the democratic element in defining Israel. For him, an ethnic democracy is not a full democracy, since there is an inherent contradiction between the two concepts. Similarly, Yoav Peled (1993) suggests that Smooha's binary model, which combines two contradictory elements (the ethnic and the democratic), cannot explain the Palestinians' status in Israel. He offers a triple-element model, which combines three concepts: republicanism, liberalism and ethno-nationalism. According to Peled, there are two types of citizenship in Israel: republican citizenship for Jews, and liberal citizenship for the Palestinians. Thus, whereas both Jewish-Israelis and Palestinians officially enjoy equal rights, it is in fact only the Jewish-Israelis who can contribute to defining the national 'common good'.

The above-mentioned models have two common characteristics. Firstly, they describe the physical-institutional structure of Israel in which the Jewish majority has control over: allocation of natural resources (land, water and so on); designation of budgets; defining the parameters of economic development; administration of the education system; enforcement of law; and definition of the common good and the national interest. Secondly, the 'structure' of the conceptual/ideological analysis in all of these models is similar. Ideologically, Israel is a state that is of and for the Jewish people: its institutions reflect the spiritual interests and the culture of the Jews. The Israeli ethos is Jewish, and the state was built through the Judaisation of the physical and cultural space. As a result, the study of the *structure* of the relationship between Israel and the Palestinians tells us more about Israel, and less about Palestinian identity. In other words, Israeli sociology provides limited understanding regarding processes internal to Palestinian society in Israel. The lack of an 'internal prism' in the study of Palestinian society in Israel has been noted before (Bishara 1993; Ghanim 2009). This book is one step in overcoming this deficiency as it deals with Palestinian identity in Israel from a Palestinian perspective.

Criticism of the modernisation approach has not been exclusive to academia. Since 1967, Palestinian novels have reflected a Palestinian re-evaluation of their modernisation within the Israeli-Zionist context, as will be discussed in Chapter 2. Contrary to the academic viewpoint, novelists did not focus on the structure of Palestinian–Israeli relations but emphasised the various implications of modernisation for Palestinian society. Moreover, novels between 1967 and 1987 (the time frame of Chapter 2) offer a reassessment of the relationship between Palestinians, on the one hand, and Jewish-Israelis and Israel as a state on the other. Also here, the focus is not on structure as much as it is on ideology: Zionism is an exclusive ideology, which inherently erases Palestinian existence and disallows Palestinian integration into Israel. Palestinian novels, thus, express a sense of a missed opportunity to achieve coexistence in Israel. In addition, novels convey a Palestinian 'doubly contradictory' identity – one that signals that Palestinians in Israel are neither 'completely' Palestinian, nor 'utterly' Israeli. Such a theme, elaborated in detail in Chapter 2, challenges formulations of Israeli sociology in terms of 'Palestinisation' or 'Israelisation' processes.

The deficiencies in the analysis of Palestinian identity in Israel in Israeli sociology seem to be related to issues of methodology. The use of polls seems to be a prominent choice (see the following sample: Tessler 1977; Seliktar 1984; Rouhana 1997; Ghanem 2002; Lowrance 2005). In most polls, the respondents are asked to answer a set of questions regarding their personal and collective experience in Israel. In most cases, they are also given a range of preset identifications to choose from. Although polls are helpful in indicating general political orientations in Palestinian society (similar to monitoring voting patterns), they tell us little about what being a 'Palestinian-Israeli' really means, and whether it means the same thing for all respondents. What does it really mean in terms of understanding Palestinian identity if, say, 37 per cent of respondents say they are 'Palestinians', while 22 per cent say they feel more like 'Palestinian citizens in Israel'? Is the 'Palestinian' component of both types of identification similar to both groups of respondents? Does it automatically mean that respondents who choose to be identified as 'Palestinians' are more politically 'radical' than those who choose to include an Israeli identification? Does such identity choice refer to national or cultural identification? Similar criticism regarding the use of polls is raised by other researchers (Rouhana 1993; Ghanim 2009).

Another strand of sociology of Palestinians in Israel is related to settler- and postcolonial approaches. These approaches offer another critical outlook onto the Zionist-Israeli case in Palestine, and bring to the fore questions of occupation, ethnic, racial, class and gender discrimination. Postcolonial theory analyses and conceptualises the complex relations between the colonising and the colonised, and addresses the history of oppression and resisting the values of the 'civilising mission' (Young 2001: 11). Postcolonial critique has been applied extensively in the study of Palestinians in Israel in the past two decades in studies ranging from literature (Hannan Hever), sociology (Yehouda Shenhav) and to architecture (Haim Yacobi). However, Areej Sabbagh-Khoury concludes that postcolonial critique in Israel has been dominated by Jewish-Israeli scholars (Sabbagh-Khoury 2018: 392), and presents the case of the emerging settler–colonial criticism in Israel in the past decade or so and examines its development in the context of Israeli academia. She explains the renewed interest to be a result of transformations in Palestinian discourse in Israel since the mid-1990s (for an extensive survey on contemporary settler–colonial studies in Palestine, see: Sabbagh-Khoury 2018; R. Barakat 2018).

The primary distinction between colonialism and settler colonialism lies in the intentions and aspirations of the colonisers. Settler colonisers take over a territory already inhabited by an indigenous population, employ different strategies of expulsion, extermination and erasure aiming to change the demographic balance in favour of the colonisers. Moreover, settler colonialism aims to create a new political entity, rather than stay connected to the metropolis – as is the case with colonialism. Ultimately, the settler coloniser aims not to exploit the indigenous, but rather to replace them altogether – becoming the indigenous themselves (Degani 2015: 3; Sabbagh-Khoury 2018). The following chapters show several manifestations of Israeli settler colonial characteristics. For example, the erasure of Palestinian indigeneity and replacing it with a Jewish-Israeli one has been carried out through a modernisation project during the 1960s – as is evident in Chapter 1. This erasure has been at the centre of Palestinian writing in the 1970s and the 1980s – as is discussed in Chapter 2.

Postcolonial and settler colonial studies are important in characterising the relationship between Israel, the Jewish-Israeli society and the Palestinian citizens in Israel. However, this research is not bound to these approaches. This is so for a number of reasons. Firstly, colonial studies, like the latter phase in Israeli sociology and sociology of Palestinians in Israel, is drawn to the *structure* of the relationship between Israel and the Palestinian citizens (e.g. see: Rouhana and Sabbagh-Khoury 2014). As a result, Barakat concludes that 'regardless of intentions, employing the [settler-colonial] analytic can and has led to a Zionist centred reading of the narrative of Palestine' (R. Barakat 2018: 2). This focus on Israel is further expressed in 'the possibility that Zionism and Israel become the objects of research from the viewpoint of their Palestinian victims' (Sabbagh-Khoury 2018: 392). In other words, while characterising this relationship is important, the focus, the point of departure, remains Israel. Barakat offers an alternative approach 'to read Palestinians as the makers of Palestinian history as opposed to Palestinians as a part of a Zionist narrative', an outlook similar to the premise of this research project.

Secondly, colonial studies seem to be interested in different modes of resistance to colonialism (Rouhana and Sabbagh-Khoury 2014). However, this research is interested in the broader Palestinian discourse, that which includes resistance but is not limited to it. Chapter 1 is a prime example of this, outlining different modes of Palestinian adaptation to the new reality after 1948, including adopting a modernisation discourse. Palestinian modernisation novels written in the 1960s cannot be considered 'resistance literature' as depicted by Ghassan Kanafani in relation to Palestinian poetry in Israel in that period. This point will become clearer when I discuss existing research on Palestinian literature below.

Literature and Nationalism

In order to overcome the shortcomings of sociological research on Palestinians in Israel, focusing on structure and system, hence Israel, while giving little attention to Palestinian voice, there was a need for an approach that provides an internal prism into Palestinian national and political orientations and discourse. Analysing literature seems to be a useful way to achieve this goal. Benedict Anderson considered the novel was the prime carrier of nationalist meaning in the literary field (Anderson 2006). Nevertheless, while Anderson ascribed a central role for the novel in Western nationalism, researchers of literature and national identity called for 'a revision' of his assertion in the context of the Middle East; pointing out the role of poetry in Arab nationalism and therefore the importance of considering the historical and cultural specificity of the region (Suleiman 2006a: 5). Either way, our premise is that there are aspects of national identity expressed in literature, prose as well as poetry that are more difficult to reach through other methods or research approaches. Following the same rationale, Edward Said claims that literature cannot be separated from the social and political domains of the writer, hence we can extract from the literary work important insights about the cultural and political environment within which the author lived:

> To lose sight of or ignore the national and international context of, say, Dickens's representation of Victorian businessmen, and to focus only on the internal coherence of their roles in his novels is to miss an essential connection between his fiction and its historical world. And understanding that connection does not reduce or diminish the novels' value as works of art:

> on the contrary, because of their *worldliness*, because of their complex affiliation with their real setting, they are more interesting and more valuable as works of art. (Said 1994: 13; italics in original)

Literature not only reflects reality because of its 'worldliness', but as Suleiman indicates, 'no account of Arab nationalism would be complete without understanding the contribution literature made, and still makes, to its articulation or to its role in group mobilisation' (Suleiman 2006b: 208). In other words, literature both reflects and contributes to shaping national discourse and identities.

The choice to study Palestinian literature to understand national identity stems from considering the complexity and interconnectedness of the social, political, economic and cultural processes on human behaviour. In light of this, the task of analysing Palestinian national discourse through reading of novels calls for an interdisciplinary, or even what Johnson calls 'anti-disciplinary', methodology. This is so because 'cultural processes do not correspond to the contours of academic knowledges, as they are. No one academic discipline grasps the full complexity (or seriousness)' of any given field (Johnson 1986: 42). Moreover, this research builds upon the general criticisms of critical theory, poststructuralism and postmodernism in the sense that it does not adhere to any particular methodology or approach. Doing so would run the risk of limiting the analysis to a certain set of parameters (Agger 1991). Reading texts that have been written over sixty years ago in a highly unstable social and political reality requires an eclectic, interdisciplinary and intertextual analysis. The spectrum of topics embedded in the literary texts here is vast, thus my approach allows for multiple perspectives, or discourses, to be voiced from Palestinian novels.

Palestinian Literature

There has been a long-held interest in Palestinian literature (used in this instance in its broadest sense, referring to literature in its various forms produced by Palestinians everywhere in the world) as an indicator or 'thermometer' of Palestinian identity, both inside and outside Israel (Kanafani 1966, 1968; al-Qasim 1979, 1991; Abbasi 1983; Harlow 1987; Abdel-Malek and Jacobson 1999; S. K. Jayyusi 1999; al-Usta 2002; Shalhat 2003; Suleiman and

Muhawi 2006; Ghanayim 2008; Abu-Remaileh 2010, 2014; Abu-Manneh 2016). These works encompass a wide range of disciplines and orientations. I do not intend to present a 'literature review' of such works, due to lack of space, and as critical engagement with relevant studies is provided in the body of the book.

It is possible to identify a number of characteristics of scholarly research on Palestinian literature. First, traditional research on Palestinian literature focuses on form, technique, structure and aesthetics, giving little contextualised attention to nationalism, identity and literature. For example, in his PhD thesis on Palestinian literature in Israel, Mahmud Abbasi 'makes use of formalistic critical methods since it is mainly concerned with contents' (Abbasi 1983). As a result, such research enumerates themes or characteristics in literature, without addressing their implications, what they reflect, in terms of identity evolution (Elad-Bouskila 1999; al-Usta 2002).

A second characteristic of research on Palestinian literature is related to the Palestinian literary canon. Because the Palestinian literary canon crosses borders, including authors from within and outside Israel, research on Palestinian literature overlooks local particularities that could shed a different light on Palestinian identity. Another related characteristic of literary criticism of Palestinian literature relates to studies that focus on single works (e.g. al-Qasim 1979, 1991; al-Usta 2002). Such studies provide in-depth analysis of the literary work from different perspectives. This, however, provides little in terms of identifying general trends or patterns in literature. However, there are attempts to deal with this literature in a non-traditional way, such as Ibrahim Taha's (2002) communication model (for more on Palestinian literature, see: Kayyal 2008). However, one can wonder, if the study of Palestinian literature and identity is so established, why do we need new research?

The premise of this book is that if we want to understand the evolution of discourse and identity among Palestinian citizens in Israel, we need to focus on their literature vis-à-vis the existing sociological research on this group. This decision has several implications on the research. Firstly, the geographic delimitation addresses the above-mentioned lack of an internal prism in Palestinian identity transformation in Israel. Secondly, in order to encompass the broadest spectrum of representations, this book analyses the complete corpus of seventy-five Palestinian novels published in Israel between 1948 and 2010. By incorporating the widest possible array of narratives, this study avoids the bias of canonisation. Canonisation refers to the selection of masterpieces (in art and literature) that represent a national ethos and identity. This process is inherently political:

> Academics, publishers, critics and those in control of the various channels of communication partake in this process of canon formation which, by its very nature, is always in a state of becoming. Men and women of letters participate in this cultural-cum-political process as members of the elite or counter-elite in their own communities, but the nature of their participation is contingent on the historical contexts and the political trajectories in which they find themselves. (Suleiman 2006a: 2)

In other words, focusing on the canon would predetermine our research to parameters according to which these *selected* literary works were chosen.

The third particularity of this book in relation to established research on Palestinian identity and literature in Israel lies in the fact that this research follows the evolution, or transformation, in Palestinian identity in Israel over sixty or so years. An analysis relating to Palestinian literature and identity usually tends to focus on one, or a few, literary texts. While such 'micro' research may provide deep insights into individual works, the inclusion of the majority of literary works in a macro study allows the tracking of transformations, taking the temporal dimension into consideration. However, due to the large number of novels, on the one hand, and the limited space in this study, on the other, it is impossible to give individual attention to each of the novels. In the discussion below, I draw on a representative sample while referring to novels sharing the same themes to elaborate on issues related to Palestinian identity in Israel. This does not mean, however, that novels in the same group are thematically identical. I have grouped the novels based on shared characteristics relating to the Palestinian discourse in Israel. Based on this, the sample, or samples, presented in the book are those that contain the broadest common characteristics in the group.

Finally, I do not claim that the groups of novels are a definitive portrayal of Palestinian discourse in Israel, but they provide certain indications regarding its evolution. Despite the intention to include as wide a spectrum of representations and opinions as possible, by avoiding canonisation, this study does not claim to represent an ultimate 'truth' about Palestinian identity in Israel. Novels represent the opinions and orientations of only a portion of Palestinian society in Israel, constituting, for instance, those members of society with a certain level of education. Moreover, Palestinian novelists in Israel are predominantly male. The four female Palestinian novelists in Israel (Fatma Dhyab, Asya Shibli, Raja Bakriyya and Adaniyya Shibli) constitute a very small minority (8 per cent) of the total number of surveyed authors (forty-eight), while their eight novels make up a mere 11 per cent of the total seventy-five.

In addition to the demographic composition of the authors, the limited space in this book governed the range of discussed topics. The volume of topics that require further analysis in these novels is enormous. As we will see throughout the book, novels provide an extraordinarily fine 'documentation' of Palestinian life in Israel, calling for further research and examination. I will, in due course, refer in a few places to different issues that require further consideration. Indeed, we need further research into Palestinian identity in Israel that represents more groups or sections in this society.

This book is divided into three chapters, reflecting significant transformations in the life of Palestinians in Israel (1948–67, 1967–87 and 1987–2010). The first period stretches from 1948 until the 1967 war, a period dominated by the military rule years (imposed until 1966). This was a crucial period for Palestinians in Israel, as these were years of adaptation to the new reality created during and after the 1948 war and the establishment of Israel. Palestinians who remained in Israel became a minority in a matter of a few months, having the social, cultural and political fabric of their society completely shattered as a result of the destruction of hundreds of villages and the consequent exodus of the majority of Palestinians. Palestinian novels in this period provide a documentation of some of the events of the Nakba[3] (in Haifa), as well as some aspects of Palestinian life during the military rule. However, novels in this period register the powerful effects on Palestinians in Israel of modernisation discourse, which became prevalent during the 1960s.

The second period stretches until the outbreak of the first Intifada in 1987, witnessing major social and political transformations in Palestinian society in Israel. Above all, as indicated earlier, Palestinian novels reflect

Palestinian efforts to deal with the implications of their modernisation in Israel. Themes regarding social differentiation (individualisation, break-up of family structure and abandoning social and religious institutions) are paramount. Moreover, the renewed contact with the Palestinians in the newly Occupied Territories (the West Bank and Gaza Strip) placed Palestinians in Israel in a perplexing situation. Despite the social reunification of both parts of the Palestinian nation, living on both sides of the Green Line, the two parts mutually acknowledged their distinctive political orientations, thus resulting in excluding Palestinian citizens in Israel from the Palestinian national struggle.

The post-1987 period includes the years of the Intifada, the subsequent peace process, its failure and the eruption of the second Intifada in the 2000s. This is a politically distinctive period in the life of Palestinians inside (and outside) Israel, in which they start to consider their future in light of a peace process that excludes them from the solution of the Palestinian problem. The first Intifada had a significant impact on Palestinians in Israel, in terms of their sentimental identification with Palestinians in the Occupied Territories and their violent resistance against Israeli occupation. Although Palestinians in Israel did not take part in the uprising, they have undergone a profound transformation in their identification, and begin to associate themselves with the Palestinian national struggle. This tendency continues during the years of the peace process between Israel and the Palestine Liberation Organization (PLO), a process that excluded the Palestinians in Israel from the resolution of the Palestinian problem, further inducing them to consider their future collective status in Israel.

Notes

1. There are many names for the 'Palestinian citizens in Israel', usually referred to as 'Israeli Arabs' or 'Israel's Arab minority'. However, most of these identifications are politically and ideologically charged (Makhoul 2018a). My use of 'Palestinian citizens in Israel' in this book aims to avoid, as much as possible, ideological or political references by being descriptive, that is, to refer to that portion of the Palestinian nation which remained in Israel after the 1948 war, and later obtained citizenship. Nevertheless, the term 'Palestinian citizens in Israel' itself can be misleading, because it suggests equality through citizenship. This confusion is a result

of Israel's distinction between citizenship and nationality, creating a hierarchy between the two. There is no Israeli nationality, but a Jewish nationality. This hierarchy has been legally established initially through the Law of Return (1950), and later corroborated through additional legislation and court rulings, aiming to ground Israel as a state for the Jews, according to which '[e]very Jew has the right to come to this country as an oleh [immigrant]'. This categorisation provides Jewish nationals civil and political rights that are higher than those holding Israeli citizenship (for further discussion on this, see: Handelman 1994).

2. Not limited to disciplinary boundaries, 'the sociology of Palestinians in Israel' is used here in its broadest sense, that is, the works of sociologists, political scientists and historians who study Palestinian life in Israel. This broad interpretation of the term also refers to the scholars themselves, who may be Palestinian, Jewish-Israeli or belong to any other nationality.
3. On the history of the term 'Nakba' in the Palestinian context, see: Ghanim 2011.

1

PALESTINIAN NOVELS IN ISRAEL, 1948–1967

The 1948 War and Military Rule

The events of, and years immediately following, the 1948 war had a tremendous effect on the Palestinian community. The social fabric of Palestinian society was dramatically and irreversibly altered as a result of the mass exodus, culminating in traumatic loss of family members, many of whom were never to be seen again. Military rule[1] following the war entailed harsh and repressive policies against Palestinians who stayed on to become citizens of Israel. These policies brought about the loss of sources of livelihood, loss of property due to confiscation and put severe restrictions on movement.

The 1948 Nakba was, in fact, the peak of a process that had begun earlier, with active hostilities starting in November 1947, after the adoption of the Partition Plan at the United Nations. As violent clashes broke out between the Palestinians and the Jewish settlers, the Zionist leaders realised the magnitude of the historic opportunity before them. They decided in early 1948 to adopt a more offensive approach (Shlaim 2000: 31). Carrying out an offensive approach meant the expulsion of Palestinians from many areas of Palestine, starting with the urban centres. This first phase of the 1948 war, which was in fact a civil war, resulted in the uprooting of about

250,000 Palestinians (Pappé 2007: 40). It was only after the termination of the British Mandate, on 15 May 1948, that the Zionist movement could proclaim the establishment of Israel, and it was then that the Arab armies entered Palestine. This date marked the beginning of the second phase of the war, which ended with the signing of Armistice Agreements in January 1949 (W. Khalidi 1985: 35; Pappé 1997: 40).

In 1950, Israel declared military rule to control the Palestinian population within its borders, continuing the military control of Palestinian territories held during the war. For nearly two decades, the sole means of communication between Israel and the Palestinian population would remain the army or the police. To encompass all aspects of the administration, military officials were granted extensive powers, both executive and judicial:

> These regulations give the authorities extensive and extremely rigorous powers, and their enforcement can destroy individual freedom and individual rights to property almost completely. They cover every aspect of life, from control over the freedom of speech, movement, and the press, to the regulation of the possession of arms, the expropriation of property, and the control of means of transportation. (Jiryis 1976: 16)

The origins of the military rule were in the British Mandatory Defence (Emergency) Regulations of 1945 (which reached back to the 1936–9 revolt) and the Israeli Emergency (Security Zones) Regulations, 5707, of 1949 (Jiryis 1976: 9). The military rule was enforced in all areas populated by Palestinians. These were the Galilee, the Triangle and the Negev. For a short time, military rule was also enforced in the cities of Ramlah, Lydda (Lod), Jaffa and Ashkelon (formerly Al-Majdal). However, since it was impossible to enforce military rule in these mixed cities, it was lifted in July 1949 (Jiryis 1976: 9; Ozacky-Lazar 2002: 104, 111; Pappé 2006: 154–5).

Military rule served various objectives beyond the declared 'security' justification. It was essentially a tool to control the Palestinian population inside Israel, to take over the remainder of their lands and villages. The military rule also aimed to prevent the return of any Palestinian refugees to their homes. Short-term uses of military rule included the regulation of the Palestinian labour force according to the needs of the Israeli market (as in the present case of the Palestinians of the West Bank and Gaza Strip), and a political tool in the hands of the ruling party, Mapai, on election days (Jiryis 1976: 15; R. Khalidi 1988: 37; Korn 2000: 159; Kook 2002: 69; Ozacky-Lazar 2002: 104; Masalha 2007: 258–9).

In this chapter I will outline the evolution of Palestinian identity in Israel during the years of the military rule until the outbreak of the 1967 war, as manifested in novels published between 1948 and 1967 (see Table 1.1 at the end of this chapter for the complete list of novels). Palestinian identity in Israel went through three stages, presented in three sections below. The first stage entails initial adaptation to life under Israeli rule. Here we see remnants of the Palestinian national discourse before 1948 and the first signs of evolution in the years after 1948. The second stage provides evidence for major transformations in Palestinian discourse: abandonment of the national dream of statehood; the call for modernisation of Palestinian society in Israel; as well as a drive for peace and coexistence with the Jewish society of Israel. The third stage involves another transformation in Palestinian identity in Israel: a re-evaluation of the Palestinian relationship with Israel and hopes of a joint future, as expressed in the second stage.

Caution and Adaptation in the Early Years

This section will outline a cautious Palestinian attitude, as well as adaptation, towards life in Israel as portrayed in the first two novels to be published after 1948.[2] These two novels, published in 1958 and 1959, voice the remnants of Palestinian discourse prior to 1948, and a discourse that begins to adapt to the new reality Palestinians encounter in Israel. The narratives of the two novels represent a yardstick with which we can compare later novels in the period 1948–67. *Mudhakkarat Laji' aw Hayfa fi-l-Ma'raka* (*A Refugee's Memoirs or Haifa in the Battle*, 1958), by Tawfiq Mu'ammar, the first novel in our survey, deals exclusively with the events leading to the occupation of Haifa, detailing the expulsion of its inhabitants in April 1948, through the eyes of the protagonist, Ghalib Abd al-Karim. The title of the novel provides important clues as to its political orientation.

The title is composed of two parts connected by the conjunction 'or' (*aw*). The first part indicates that the novel is the memoir of a refugee. This refugee is Palestinian, since the second part of the title states that the novel talks about Haifa in the battle. There seems to be an implied causal relationship between the two parts of the title: becoming a refugee is a result of a battle raging in Haifa. The implied relationship between the two parts of the title is prompted by the use of the conjunction 'or' (*aw*). *Aw* equalises the two sections of the title, suggesting that either of them could be a title for the novel. The battle (*al-maʿraka*) to which the title refers is the one that took place during the 1948 war in Palestine. The use of the definite article (*al-*) reflects the commitment of the author to the Palestinian cause, since for Muʿammar there is only one battle – the battle over Palestine – that one (a Palestinian) could write about. Seen from this angle, it is possible to say that the act of writing the novel reflects the historical engagement of Muʿammar in the battle for the memory of Haifa, Palestine and the events of the 1948 war (for a paratextual analysis of this novel, see: Makhoul 2018b).

With regards to understanding transformations in Palestinian identity in Israel during the first period (1948–67), *Mudhakkarat Lajiʾ aw Hayfa fi-l-Maʿraka* marks an initial adaptation in Palestinian identity after 1948. To show this I will analyse two excerpts: the first reflects Palestinian national discourse regarding the 1948 war in Haifa, while the second illustrates adaptation in Palestinian discourse in Israel.

The following quotation exemplifies Palestinian national and historical narrative of the events of the 1948 war in Haifa. Although it is not my intention to discuss in detail the Palestinian historical narrative, the following excerpt helps us to understand the evolution of Palestinian discourse in Israel during this period, by providing impressions of, or testimonial to, the occupation of Haifa as viewed by the protagonist:

> Nahb ʿāmm shāmil lam tashhad lahu hādhihi al-madīna mathīlan fī aḥlak ʿuṣūriha wa-ashadduhā hamajiyya wa-barbariyya. Marrat ʿalā hādhihi al-bilād fī tārīkhihā al-ṭawīl miḥan wa-nakabāt wa-taʿrraḍat li-maʾāsi alīma wa-waylāt, wa-taʿāqabat ʿalayhā aqwām wa-duwal kathīra, wa-ijtāḥathā juyūsh ghāziya min kull ḥadb wa-ṣawb nasharat al-mawt wa-l-damār fī kull makān [...] wa-lam yaḥduth an shahidat hādhihi al-bilād damār akthar shumūlan wa-nahban awsaʿ niṭāqan wa-tamzīq shaml wa-ibāda ashaddu hawlan wa-faẓāʿa, mimmā shāhidathu fī hādhihi al-fatra min al-tārīkh, fī hādhihi al-ḥiqba min ḥiqab al-qarn al-ʿishrīn fī ʿahd al-dawla al-barīṭāniyya

al-muntadiba 'al-ḥalīfa' wa-l-duwal al-ʿarabiyya al-sabʿ wa-fī ẓill hayʾat al-umam al-muttaḥida wa-munnaẓẓamāt ḥuqūq al-insān. (p. 110)

A complete and total pillage, unprecedented in this city's darkest and most savage and barbaric periods. Many disasters and catastrophes took place in this country's long history, and it faced torturous calamities and horrors, and it was ruled successively by many peoples and countries, and it was invaded by occupying armies from all directions, spreading death and destruction everywhere [...] but this country has not witnessed more exhaustive destruction, more extended pillage, social destruction and annihilation that are more horrific and catastrophic than it has witnessed in this period of history, in this stage of the twentieth century under the Mandate of Britain, our 'ally', and the seven Arab countries, while under the auspices of the United Nations and human rights organisations. (p. 110)

The account of the 'complete and total pillage' (*nahb ʿāmm shāmil*) and of the battle over Haifa are comparable to historical accounts of the occupation of Haifa (Pappé 2007; W. Khalidi 2008). In fact, Muʿammar indicates in the introduction to the novel that he personally witnessed the events of the war in Haifa. As will be seen later in this section, the author declares that the aim of this novel is to document the occupation of Haifa for the benefit of future generations. This aim is evident in the language of the novel, which uses terms such as historical era (*ḥiqba*), international ally (*ḥalīfa*), the British Mandate (*al-muntadiba*) and the United Nations (*hayʾat al-umam al-muttaḥida*), as well as referring to human rights organisations (*munaẓẓamāt ḥuqūq al-insān*).

In contrast to historical narrative and language, novelistic description allows for the expression of emotions such as shock and anger. For the protagonist, the expulsion of the indigenous Palestinian population of Haifa, estimated at 70,000 individuals (Lustick 1980b: 132), is comparable to the darkest (*aḥlak*), most barbaric (*hamajiyya wa-barbariyya*) catastrophes (*nakabāt*) that assaulted the country during its long history. The description moves from dealing with the particular case of Haifa, to encompass the entire country. The many catastrophes (*nakabāt*), invasions (*ijtiyāḥāt*), hardships (*miḥan, maʾāsi, waylāt*), destructions (*damār*) and exterminations (*tamzīq shaml, ibāda*) that struck the country throughout history do not compare to the Zionist crimes in the 1948 war, thereby making the war by implication the worst *nakba* (catastrophe) of all. Moreover, in this description the narrative aims to tell not only about the Palestinian predicament but also to stress the cruelty of the occupying army.

The political-historical discourse voiced in the above excerpt, and generally in the novel, extends to ridiculing the allies of the Palestinians during the war, especially Britain, but also the seven Arab countries that took part in the war. His ridicule is directed at international institutions, such as the United Nations and human rights organisations, all of which failed to protect the Palestinians from the cruelties of the Zionist army. The 'barbarity' in the opening of the excerpt contrasts with the 'human rights' that close the paragraph. This contrast implies, in an ironic way, that the Palestinians did not have true allies to protect them. Their so-called allies have, on the contrary, turned their backs on them, leaving them an easy target for the Zionist occupation. The main British character in the novel, Major General Hugh C. Stockwell, who was the British commander in Haifa,[3] is portrayed at the beginning of the novel to be a true friend of the Palestinians, helping them in their struggle against the Jewish forces in the city. At a later stage of the plot the Palestinians discover that Stockwell was in fact collaborating with the Zionist movement, playing a decisive role in the fall of Haifa and the expulsion of its Palestinian population. The incorporation of individuals, such as Stockwell, who actually took part in the events of the 1948 war, as characters in the plot aims to assert the novel as a historic documentation of the events of the war.

In the general historical debate over the events of the 1948 war, the discourse presented in *Mudhakkarat Laji' aw Hayfa fi-l-Ma'raka* resembles the Palestinian narrative rather than the Israeli one (e.g. see: Said 1979; W. Khalidi 1988; Shlaim 1995; Falah 1996). The reason I point out the similarity between the Palestinian historical-national and literary narratives is to establish the latter as the 'point of departure' of Palestinian discourse in Israel after 1948. The documentation of the Palestinian narrative on the events of 1948 in Haifa is explicitly stated by the author in the introduction to the novel. Mu'ammar says that the objective of this novel is to document (*tadwīn*) and to publicise (*nashr*) the events that took place in Haifa and Palestine in 1948 'in order for them to be a lesson to our children and grandchildren'. This statement reflects the commitment of the author to the Palestinian national struggle from two points of view: firstly, it is a struggle over the memory of the 1948 war and Palestine. Secondly, this memory is important for the future Palestinian generations, upon whose shoulders the continuing struggle over Palestine rests. In other words, for Mu'ammar this struggle is still under way, and he takes part in it through the act of writing. Thus, by using the collective first-person plural (our), he expresses his commitment to the education of future Palestinian generations concerning setbacks faced by the Palestinians in the 1948 war.

The importance of preserving the memory of the 1948 war and the loss of Palestine in it are of great importance for Mu'ammar. In fact, apart from his explicit statements in this regard, the implicit motivation for writing this novel derive from his fear that Palestine, its history and memory, will be forever lost. In what follows we will see that although *Mudhakkarat Laji' aw Hayfa fi-l-Ma'raka* resembles the Palestinian historical narrative on the events of the 1948 war, it also reflects some initial transformations in Palestinian discourse inside Israel. After 'declaring' his motivation to document the events of the 1948 war for the benefit of future generations, Mu'ammar's following statement conveys only a tentative attitude to the publication of the novel, expressing a more cautious Palestinian perspective during the first years inside Israel after 1948:

> Wa-ammā bi-sha'n mawḍū' al-qiṣṣa wa-l-ra'y alladhī tu'abbir 'anhu fīmā yata'allaq bi-l-asbāb allatī dafa'at al-'arab ilā al-raḥīl fa-innahū ra'y shakhṣiyy a'taniqhu wa-ajhar bihi bi-quwwa 'amalan bi-ḥurriyat al-qawl wa-l-fikr allatī nan'amu bihā fī isrā'īl. Wa-arjū an tataqabbal al-suluṭāt al-isrā'īliyya hādhihi al-qiṣṣa bimā yattafiq wa-hādhihī al-ḥurriyya, wa-biraḥabat al-ṣadr wa-ṭūl al-anāt allatī ta'awwadnā an nalmasahā fī sulūkihā ḥiyāl mā yuqāl wa-yuktab bi-sha'n maṭālibinā wa-qaḍāyānā mustashhidan bi-l-kalima al-khālida allatī ba'ath bihā foltīr al-'aẓīm ilā jān jāk rūsū qabl mi'atay sana yaqūl lahu fīhā: 'innī wa-inn kuntu lā uwāfiq 'alā kalima wāḥida mimmā taqūl ghayr annī sa-udāfi' ḥattā al-mawt 'an ḥaqik fī qawl mā turīd an taqūl'. (al-muqaddima)

As for the subject of the story and the opinion it expresses regarding the reasons that led the Arabs to depart, it is a personal opinion that I hold and

> declare loudly pursuant of the freedom of expression and thought that we enjoy in Israel. And I hope that the Israeli authorities accept this story in accordance with this freedom, and the open heart and patience that we have become accustomed to in her behaviour towards everything that is said and written regarding our demands and issues, quoting the eternal message that the great Voltaire sent to Jean Jack Rousseau two hundred years ago, saying, 'I don't agree with what you say but I will defend to the death your right to say it'. (Introduction)

This excerpt expresses two criticisms of Israel: one explicit, the other implicit. First, Mu'ammar affirms that the narrative (*mawḍū ʿ al-qiṣṣa*) and the opinion (*ra ʾy*) present in this novel relate to the Zionist military brutalities during the 1948 war and the driving of the Palestinians out of their country (*al-raḥīl*). The second, implicit, criticism is found in his hope (*arjū*) that Israel accept (*tataqabbal*) this critical novel. In order to enable acceptance of the novel and its criticism, the author 'invites' Israel to follow the example of civil rights proponents such as Voltaire. This invitation implies that Israel violates civil rights principles. In other words, if Mu'ammar was confident about the existence of freedom of expression and thought in Israel, he would not have referred to it in the first place.

In spite of the criticisms, the excerpt reflects a cautious, attenuated attitude towards Israel. This is evident in several places: first, the use of the word *rahīl* (departure, migration) to refer to the Palestinian flight during the 1948 war scales down the political, or indeed military, causes for their departure. A second example can be seen in the use of the word *arjū*, which can either mean 'I expect' or 'I exhort'. Each meaning represents a different attitude: if we take *arjū* to mean 'I expect', this suggests a strong stance on the part of the author. If we take it to mean 'I exhort', it conveys a more submissive attitude. A third example of the cautious attitude of this novel is evidenced in the seeming contradiction between, on the one hand, praising the patience of Israel (*ṭūl anāt*) towards 'all which is said and written' about Palestinian 'demands and issues' (*maṭālibinā wa-qaḍāyānā*), alongside, on the other hand, the implicit suggestion that Israel is the target of criticism, due to its practices against the Palestinians. Israel, then, may grant freedom of speech, but her other policies remain unwelcome and subject to extensive critical 'talking and writing'.

The cautious attitude in *Mudhakkarat Laji' aw Hayfa fi-l-Ma'raka* indicates three things: firstly, that Mu'ammar, the narrative he promotes and Israel stand in complete opposition to one another, manifesting their conflictual relations. Secondly, it recognises that the balance of power between Israel and its Palestinian citizens is in favour of Israel: Palestinians in Israel can demand rights from the state, but they cannot impose their will on it, since Israel with its commanding power can either accept or reject their demands. This balance of power is evident in the shift from singular to plural in the excerpt: singular verbs refer to actions for which the author is responsible ('it is a personal opinion' (*ra'yun shakhṣiyy*); 'that I follow' (*a'taniqhu*); 'and express loudly' (*wa-ajharu*); 'I hope' (*arjū*)). Plural verbs refer to responsibilities or actions of Israel ('the reasons that forced the Arabs to flee' (*al-asbāb allatī dafa'at al-'arab ilā al-raḥīl*); freedom that 'we enjoy' in Israel (*nan'amu*); 'we are used to' (*ta'awwadnā*); 'our demands and issues' (*maṭālibinā wa-qaḍāyānā*)). The subordinate Palestinian citizens in Israel enjoy freedoms that Israel grants; they also have demands from superior Israel.

Thirdly, the cautious and attenuated writing of history in light of the balance of power between the Palestinians and Israel highlights the aforementioned importance Mu'ammar attributes to the memory of Palestine. Seen from this prism, it is possible to speculate as to the reasons driving him to publish his two novels in such proximity to each other after one decade of living under Israeli rule. In other words, an understanding of the importance of memory and documentation arises in the event of realising that memory and history are starting to diminish. Thus, it appears, Mu'ammar takes upon himself the task of documenting the events of the 1948 war, as well as Palestinian life under military rule, in his second novel.

In the second novel, *Bit-hun* (*It Will Be Alright*, 1959), Mu'ammar no longer alludes to freedom of speech and thought in Israel, nor does he speak about the events of the 1948 war. He focuses on Palestinian life in Israel during the military rule. The plot describes the bus journey of Abu Salim, an animal merchant from Nazareth who is on his way to Haifa to buy a cow. Abu Salim forgets his travel permit at home and is in a state of panic throughout the entire journey, in fear of the police searches at roadblocks. The attempts of the bus passengers to assuage the fears of Abu Salim lay the ground for a discussion on a wide range of problems facing Palestinians under the military rule. The following excerpt, taken from the introduction, outlines the themes that the novel handles:

> Hādhihi al-qiṣṣa tashraḥ ḥālat al-ʿarab fī isrāʾīl fī baʿḍ nawāḥī ḥayātahum baʿd iḥdā ʿashara sana min qiyām al-ḥukm al-isrāʾīliyy fī bilādihim, wa-hiya tuʿālij bi-ṭarīqa wāqiʿiyya mā yaʿtawir al-ʿarab min makhāwif wa-yaktanif mustaqbalahum min ghūmūḍ wa-mā yataraddad ʿalā alsinatihim fī kull āwina … min qaḍāyā al-aḥkām al-ʿaskariyya 'wa-taṣārīḥ al-khurūj' wa-ḍarībat al-dakhl, wa-l-ʿamal wa-l-ʿummāl, wa-l-waẓāʾif al-ḥukūmiyya, wa-arāḍī al-nāṣira al-muṣādara, wa-l-lājiʾīn, wa-bi-nawʿ khāṣ hādhihi 'al-siyāsa' al-mutaʿannita allatī mā bariḥat tuntahaj ḍiddahum fī iṣrār mundhu qiyām al-dawla wa-l-latī in istamarrat ʿalā mā hiya ʿalayh sa-tuʾaddī, walā shakk, ilā awkham al-ʿawāqib. (al-muqaddima)
>
> This story explains the state of affairs of the Arabs in Israel from a number of aspects of their lives, eleven years after the establishment of the Israeli rule in their country, it realistically addresses the most important fears of the Arabs, the ambiguity that shades their future, and the concerns they speak about all the time … [starting] from the issues of the military regulations and 'travel permits', income tax, work and labour, the bureaucratic positions, the confiscated lands in Nazareth, the refugees, and especially this obstinate 'policy' that continues to be implemented consistently since the establishment of the state and which would, if continued, lead to severe consequences. (Introduction)

Bit-hun deals with what Muʿammar referred to in the introduction of *Mudhakkarat Lajiʾ aw Hayfa fi-l-Maʿraka* as 'our demands and issues' (*maṭālibinā wa-qaḍāyānā*), mentioned in the preceding excerpt above. With regards to Palestinian national identity, the way in which these issues are presented convey: first, a struggle that has been 'attenuated' from an initial endeavour of national liberation, to a variety of subsequent 'issues' (*qaḍāyā*), a point that will be discussed later in this section. Secondly, this attenuation occurs through a normalisation of the relationship between Israel and the

Palestinians based on the imbalance of power between them: the ambiguity (*ghumūḍ*) and fears (*makhāwif*) regarding the future of Palestinians in Israel reflects their powerlessness. Such a discourse is embedded in the title of the novel, *Bit-hun* ('it will be alright'), which suggests a two-sided message: (1) things are bad at the moment (of writing); and (2) it is to be hoped that things will improve in the future. In other words, the use of the term *Bit-hun* is intended to alleviate stress and frustration, without guaranteeing improvement of the situation. It is both an expression of hope in the future and an admission of powerlessness.

Moreover, the attenuation of Palestinian discourse is evident in the terminological transformation used by Mu'ammar in reference to the Palestinian–Zionist conflict in comparison to his earlier novel. This is important as the impression based on the excerpts used here may be misleading. In the *quoted* excerpts from the two novels, Mu'ammar refers to Palestine as 'the country' (*al-bilād*), rather than 'Palestine'. Another example is related to referring to the Palestinian citizens in Israel as 'Arabs'. However, a closer look at the works of Mu'ammar reveals some transformations in his terminological references. For example, Mu'ammar opens the introduction to *Mudhakkarat Laji' aw Hayfa fi-l-Ma'raka* by saying that the novel 'addresses important aspects of the "Palestinian war" (*al-ḥarb al-falasṭīniyya*) and the Arab struggle (*al-kifāḥ al-'arabiyy*)'. In addition to this, the opening sentence of the novel starts with the protagonist asking 'who of us, the Palestinian refugees (*al-lāji'īn al-falasṭīniyyīn*), does not remember the bloody events (*al-ḥawādith al-dāmiya*) of the early months of 1948 which preceded the departure of the Palestine Arabs (*raḥīl 'ārab falasṭīn*)?'.

In comparison to this, the introduction to *Bit-hun* (quoted above) indicates that the novel is about the 'situation of the Arabs in Israel (*ḥālat al-'ārab fī isrā'īl*)'. The attenuation in *Bit-hun* is evident in self-censorship in what relates to the use of the word 'Palestine', which has come to be a politically charged term in Israel. Although Mu'ammar uses the word 'Palestine' to refer to the geographical area, he never refers in *Bit-hun* to Palestinian citizens in Israel as 'Palestinians' in the same way he did in the earlier novel. In fact, in *Bit-hun*, Mu'ammar most frequently uses the term 'Israeli Arabs' or 'the Arabs of Israel'. The closest he comes to associate Palestinian citizens in Israel with 'Palestine' is when he says, once, 'we, the people of Palestine (*iḥnā ahl falasṭīn*)' (p. 49). While *ahl* in Arabic translates to 'people' in English, it conveys the meaning of 'residents', or 'those who live in Palestine'. In other words, 'we, the people of Palestine' is an attenuated, denationalised way of saying 'we, Palestinians'. This is so because '*ahl falasṭīn*' refers generally to those who live in the geographical area of Palestine.

The attenuation of the Palestinian discourse in Israel is evident in its fragmentation in various military rule regulations, taxation, labour and land confiscation. Although Muʿammar depicts Israeli policies against the Palestinians in collective terms, these are 'individual' issues for both Palestinian and Israeli sides, meaning that, in dealing with any of these issues, Palestinians in Israel have to appeal individually to particular Israeli authorities. For example, the struggle to redeem a confiscated piece of land had to be done individually. It was only in the 1970s that the Palestinian struggle against land expropriation became a collective matter, culminating in Land Day (*yawm al-arḍ*). As a result of having to deal with Israeli authorities, the Palestinian struggle in Israel became one against discrimination.

Azmi Bishara arrives at a conclusion regarding Palestinian discourse in this period (1948–67), according to which Palestinians in Israel developed an awareness of 'discriminated-against people [*mekupaḥīm*], which is difficult to define as national awareness' (Bishara 1993: 9). To put it bluntly, people who are fighting a national struggle for liberation do not complain about discrimination. Discrimination is fought against by citizens. In other words, since the multiplicity of problems that Palestinians had to deal with indicates that they started to perceive themselves as a discriminated-against people, this also suggests that they had accepted that they were part of the state. Therefore, in order to deal with their problems in Israel, Palestinians had to work within the framework allowed by the 'system' – that of the Israeli authorities.

Working within the state apparatus (*waẓāʾif ḥukūmiyya*), as mentioned in the above excerpt, is especially important in this regard as it marks two things: first, Muʿammar highlights that Palestinians are discriminated against in terms of employment in the state apparatus. More importantly, it indicates that Palestinians wish to take part in the governance of the country: to be part of the Israeli system. This desire stems from previous experience when, during the British Mandate, Palestinians and Jews were incorporated, at least in theory, into the Mandate system, which had a unified police force as well as other state apparatuses. Muʿammar sees military rule as a temporary measure (an issue that will be discussed in analysing the following excerpt), which Israel should terminate in order to allow the Palestinians to rule their country (*bilādihim*). This impression is strengthened by the language that Muʿammar employs, which equates Israeli rule in Palestine (*al-ḥukm al-isrāʾīliyy fī bilādihim*) with the British Mandate, seeing the Palestinians, nevertheless, as the true owners of the land who, due to their weakness, are unable to rule it.

This view is further amplified as Muʿammar could not comprehend why the incorporation of Palestinians into the Israeli ruling system could not be implemented in Israel, even eleven years after its establishment. The fact that Israel does not do so, in addition to the continuation of harsh military regulations, deems Israel obstinate (*mutaʿannita*). Muʿammar warns that the continuation of such an attitude against the Palestinians will lead to severe consequences (*awkham al-ʿawāqib*), which implies that the Palestinians will be unable to tolerate such discrimination over a long period. This warning indicates, moreover, that the incorporation of Palestinians into Israel should be an Israeli interest, in order to pre-empt potential unrest.

Another dimension of the attenuation discourse presented in *Bit-hun* relates to the fact that the novel focuses on the problems of Palestinian citizens in Israel. For example, the refugee problem is the only issue that relates to the wider Palestinian problem (listed last in the above excerpt and given less attention in the plot, relative to the other issues). This attenuation marks the beginning of a distinction among Palestinians in Israel between themselves and Palestinians outside Israel. As a matter of fact, Palestinian novels published in Israel continue to 'exclude' Palestinians outside Israel until the late 1980s. I will discuss this exclusion further in Chapters 2 and 3.

The following quotation can help explain the political vision voiced by Muʿammar regarding Palestinian integration in the Israeli system. In the excerpt, one of the passengers on the bus clarifies to Abu Salim his opinion regarding the policies that Palestinians have faced in Israel:

> Lā taẓun yā abū salīm innī mutaḥāmil ʿalā isrāʾīl, fa-anā urid lahā al-khayr wa-an takūn bi-l-fiʿl adāt li-l-bināʾ wa-l-taqaddum wa-mawṭinan li-l-ḥurriya wa-l-dīmuqrāṭiyya wa-mithālan ḥayyan li-kul umma nāhiḍa mutaḥarrira fī-l-ʿālam, wa-lākin ḥukkām isrāʾīl khayyabū al-āmāl wa-khānū al-amāna

> al-marbūṭa fī aʿnāqihim wa-jaʿalū isrāʾīl bi-l-nisba li-sukkāniha al-ʿarab al-aṣliyyīn wa-aṣḥāb al-ḥaqq al-awwal fīhā dawla yuḍrab bi-ẓulmihā al-mathal wa-maʿqilan li-l-ṣahyūniyya al-mutaṭarrifa, wa-l-taʿaṣṣub al-aʿmā, wa-l-iḍṭihād al-dhamīm wa-l-karāhiya al-ʿunṣuriyya illi istawradūha maʿhum min būlūnyā wa-rūsya al-qayṣariyya mukhālifīn wa-munāqiḍīn mā taʿahhada bihi dustūr al-dawla al-ṣāḍir fī al-khāmis ʿashar min ayyār ʿām 1948 min daʿwat al-shaʿb al-ʿarabi fī isrāʾīl ʻli-yaʾkhudh naṣībahu fī iqamat al-dawla ʿalā asās al-raʿawiyya al-mutasāwiya wa-ʿalā asās al-tamthīl al-mulāʾim fī kāffat muʾassasātiha al-muʾaqqata wa-l-dāʾimaʼ. (p. 52)

> Don't think, Abu Salim, that I have a grudge against Israel, I wish her good and that she becomes actually a vehicle for construction and progress and a home for freedom and democracy and a living example to every developing free nation in the world. But the rulers of Israel since 1948 have disappointed, and betrayed the responsibility on their shoulders and made of Israel for its indigenous Arab inhabitants, and the holders of the first right on it, a state that is an example for injustice and a home for extremist Zionism, blind racism, despicable discrimination and racist hatred that they have been imported with them from Poland and Tsarist Russia, thus contradicting the constitution of the state, which was declared on 15 May 1948 calling the Arab nation in Israel to 'take its role in establishing the state based on equal citizenship and on proportional representation in all its temporary and permanent institutions'[4]. (p. 52)

Muʿammar offers a discourse that combines contradictory elements of continuity and change: maintaining the pre-1948 Palestinian narrative, on the one hand, and adapting to the post-1948 changing political environment, on the other. These contradictions manifest the tense transformation in Palestinian discourse during this period. One example is the contrast between viewing the Palestinians in Israel as those natives (*sukkān aṣliyyīn*) who have the primary right (*al-ḥaqq al-awwal*) to the country, while still quoting the statement in the Declaration of Independence that calls for their incorporation into the Israeli system.

In discussing the preceding excerpt, I referred to Muʿammar viewing the military rule as temporary, pondering the obstinate refusal of Israel to incorporate Palestinians into its institutions. In the above excerpt Muʿammar sees that since the Palestinians are the natives, having the primary right over Palestine, they should be the ones ruling it. However, with the attenuation of their national discourse, Palestinians see that they should be, at least, absorbed into the state-building process (*fī iqāmat al-dawla*) in Israel, in 'all its temporary and permanent institutions' (*kāffat muʾassasātihā al-muʾaqatta wa-l-dāʾima*). Although Muʿammar criticises the Israeli rulers (*ḥukkām isrāʾīl*) for not fulfilling the promises of the Declaration of Independence, his criticism implies acceptance of the idea of incorporating Palestinians into the Israeli state and an abandonment of the Palestinian endeavour for a state of their own.

A second example of the contradictory discourse voiced by Muʿammar in the above quotation is evident in his view of both Israel and of Zionism as racist and full of animosity towards the Palestinians, listing the injustices of Israel (*ẓulm*), its blind racism (*taʿaṣṣub aʿmā*), oppression (*iḍṭihād*) and hatred (*karāhiya*), on the one hand, while, on the other, seeking good (*khayr*) for Israel, and envisioning her as a rising and enlightened country (*nāhiḍa*), a term usually referring to the *nahḍa*, the Arab enlightenment. This contradiction conveys the message that although the speaker does not view Israel as an enlightened democracy 'at the moment', he hopes that it will become so one day. The discourse is therefore about how Israel should be: a just and non-racist state. Israel as an enlightened democracy could be a place in which the Palestinians would want to live. The quotation from the state constitution (*dustūr*, actually referring to the Declaration of Independence), moreover, suggests acceptance of the political situation. Moreover, it indicates that the speaker wishes to be incorporated into the state whose 'constitution' he quotes.

The above excerpts show that Palestinians began to view themselves as citizens of Israel, conceding their weakness and normalising their status inside Israel. Later novels in this period mark a further normalisation of Palestinian life inside Israel, as the discussion in the following section will reveal.

Modernisation Novels

The six novels upon which this section is based provide a discourse of modernisation among Palestinian citizens in Israel during the 1960s. Modernisation is the source of a long academic and historical debate, and is usually referred to in two ways. The first denotes a historical process, where modernisation describes the transformation process from 'traditional' to 'modern' societies. The historical-analytical reference aims to analyse this transformation in Western societies in light of philosophical and scientific developments since the Enlightenment. American political scientist Ronald Inglehart traces the 200-year-old modernisation theory to the writings of Karl Marx, Max Weber and Daniel Bell (Inglehart 1997: 7). Moreover, scholars try to identify the common characteristics of this process in different societies, based on their unique circumstances. Stuart Hall, for example, distinguished four encompassing features of modernisation: secular power; economics based on money; dynamic social stratification; and rationalist and secularist interpretation of the world (Holub 2001: 285).

The second reference to modernisation lay in the thinking of the American political elite during the early years of the Cold War. According to this view, the USA emerged from the Second World War as a superpower seeking to dominate the international arena. The prominence of the Soviet Union, promoting communism in Eastern Europe and in postcolonial countries, posed a challenge to American domination. In order to counter Soviet prominence in developing countries, the American political elite encouraged research on these societies, aiming to promote 'economic development and political stability in the Third World, so as to avoid losing the new [decolonising] states to the Soviet communist bloc' (So 1990: 17).

The two 'histories' do not necessarily contradict each other. Eisenstadt talks about the 'original' modernity in Europe, and the idea of convergence that proponents of modernisation theory led in the 1950s and 1960s. Convergence refers to the belief that 'modernisation would wipe out cultural, institutional, structural and mental differences and, if unimpeded, would lead to a uniform modern world' (Eisenstadt and Schluchter 1998: 2–3). Moreover, from the viewpoint of political thought, modernisation theory, as Inglehart indicates, has been established in Western thought for many years. It refers to the belief that economic, cultural and political change 'go together in coherent patterns that are changing the world in predictable ways' (Inglehart 1997: 7). This definition is also true with regard to the 'second' history mentioned above. The contemporary historical context in which 'new' modernisation theory was established, does not 'deny both the antiquity and continuity of the notion of development in Western thought [...] nor a tradition of concern with "growth" and "improvement" on the part of many social observers and participants including colonial administrators' (Bernstein 1971: 142). The point I am trying to make here is that the construction of modernisation theory in the mid-twentieth century is a direct result of ideological-political motivations (Bernstein 1971; Tipps 1973; Latham 1998), and that the two facets – the ideological-political and academic – of modernisation theory are difficult to separate.

The link between ideology and academia, in relation to modernisation theory, exists also in the Zionist-Israeli case. In a comprehensive study, Palestinian historian Ahmad Sa'di outlines the development of modernisation discourse in Zionist thought. Sa'di indicates that modernisation discourse has existed in Zionist thought since its inception: 'Statements concerning the modernising role of Zionism vis-à-vis the Palestinians can be traced back to the first encounter between representatives of the two parties' (Sa'di 1997: 26; see also: Peres 1970). Moreover, during the 1950s, the American and Israeli governments seem to have held similar ideological-political motivations. The history of the establishment of departments of sociology in Israeli universities by proponents of modernisation theory is very similar to the history of the establishment of similar departments (political science and sociology) in American universities in the same period. Israeli sociologist Baruch Kimmerling writes about the establishment of the first sociology department in Israel and its ideological motivation:

> The 'Research Seminar' on immigration was transformed into a Department of Sociology at the Hebrew University. It was founded as an institute that perceived itself to be an integral part of the nation-building process of the universalistic version of the Zionist vision. (Kimmerling 1992: 448–9)

Without discussing too deeply the different strands in Zionist thought, the 'universalistic version of the Zionist vision' refers to seeing Zionism as an ideology that contains universal values, or a mission, which relates to all humankind rather than particularly to the Jewish people. Proponents of the universalistic Zionist vision 'emphasised the duty to act according to the moral laws of Judaism, which they interpreted as being universal moral laws objectively applied' (Kidron 2003: 100). Nevertheless, this universalistic approach echoes the belief of convergence that Eisenstadt mentioned earlier in reference to extending modernisation to cover the whole world. Nonetheless, it is possible to establish the connection between Zionist scholars who saw Zionism as an ideology that needed to be 'objectively applied', and the development of a Zionist-Israeli civilising mission, aimed at the indigenous Palestinians, to which Sa'di has referred above. In the Introduction, I have referred to the shortcomings of Israeli modernisation theory as an explanatory tool to Palestinian life under Israeli rule, and the transformation that took place in Israeli sociology in the 1970s (for an extensive discussion on the evolution of Israeli sociology, see: Bishara 2011).

Palestinian modernisation should be seen in light of this ideological and analytical context in Israel. In other words, 'modernisation' here is not an analytical devise, it is rather an empirical finding, a critical characterisation of Palestinian discourse in this period as expressed in this group of novels, conjuring Palestinian and Zionist discourses while taking into consideration the particular political, ideological and social context in Israel in the 1960s. While modernisation theory has been used in Israeli sociology in the same period, the discussion offers a critical reading of modernisation discourse promoted by Israeli sociologists with an aim to understand their implications on Palestinian identity in Israel.

In what follows I will analyse Palestinian modernisation discourse in novels vis-à-vis Zionist-Israeli modernisation discourse, as reflected in both ideological-political and academic spheres. However, rather than focusing the discussion in this section on the process of modernisation itself, tracing the history of Palestinian modernisation in Israel, I will concentrate on the implications of modernisation on Palestinian identity in Israel. I will do so by discussing two exemplary modernisation novels.

Wa-Baqiyat Samira (*And Samira Remained*, 1962), by Atallah Mansour, marks an additional transformation in the Palestinian discourse during the military rule period, focusing primarily on social aspects. It is the earliest novel to address that initial contact with the Jewish-Israeli society, and the confusion that it created among Palestinians.

The two-part novel tells the story of Riyad and Samira, the inhabitants of a Palestinian Galilean village. The first part of the novel (thirteen chapters), entitled 'Sons of the Village' (*awlād balad*), focusses on Riyad's life in the village, at school and in the fields grazing with the family cows. After graduating from the elementary school, Riyad moves to Haifa where he becomes a 'messenger' in the British-run post office. Riyad has a single persistent memory of Samira: it relates to the time he saw her, a few years back, when she was a young girl, in the company of her neighbour Ali, who tried to woo her. Riyad remembers the images of this memory after his coerced marriage with her. Riyad cannot contain his jealousy of Ali, that his wife may have loved another person before him, and decides to return to Haifa on his own soon after the wedding. As the 1948 war intensifies in the city, Riyad becomes a refugee in Lebanon. He decides to remain there, where he marries another woman. The second part of the novel (nine chapters), entitled 'Why All This?' (*limādhā kull hādhā?*), focusses on Samira since the occupation of Haifa and the disappearance of Riyad. The chapters here describe Samira's adaptation to Riyad's absence, as well as to life in Israel. Samira meets Jewish-Israelis when she works in an Israeli farm and attempts to adapt to their different culture. At the end of the novel, Samira aborts Riyad's baby, the moment she hears about his second marriage.

There are two main dimensions that need to be elaborated in this novel: the political and the social. The political discourse has generated a debate among critics (see: Ghanayim 2008), and marks another attenuation in the Palestinian discourse in Israel. For example, chapter 12, entitled 'Storms' (*zawābi'*), describes Riyad's stance on the fighting in Haifa:

> Fa-ḥaṣara ihtimāmahu wa-i'tinā'ahu bi-salāmatihi al-shakhṣiyya … mu'allilan nafsahu bi-amal murūr al-zawba'a wa-'awdat al-amān. (p. 82)

> He focused his attention to his personal safety … hoping that the storm would pass, and security be restored. (p. 82)

In other words, the attenuation is evident in describing the 1948 war in terms of a natural disaster, which means that there is no way to influence its progression, and one can only deal with its outcomes. This contradicts the narrative presented by Tawfiq Mu'ammar, whose protagonist in *Mudhakkarat Laji' aw Hayfa fi-l-Ma'raka* took an active role in defending the city. In contrast, Riyad not only abstained from taking a position regarding the war, he did not think that defending Haifa relates to him, since: 'he did not see any reason to die for in Haifa' (pp. 88–9).[5]

Riyad's lacklustre political stance on the war in 1948 has been disapproved of by critics, pointing out that his sense of belonging was to his village, not to Haifa or Palestine (Ghanayim 2008: 31–3). Nonetheless, without applying any value judgement on the novel, one could say that it portrayed a certain portion of Palestinian society at the time, that had their sense of belonging to their village and lacked any awareness or interest in national affairs, even if this is not convenient to national literary critics. In this particular novel, Riyad's detachment from Haifa is apparent in the anaemic description of the city, especially when compared with the vibrant and colourful portrayals of his childhood in the village. This is also true when compared with Muʿammar's depiction of the city and the lively depiction of the battles in it.

Nevertheless, *Wa-Baqiyat Samira* is important because it marks a major transformation in the Palestinian discourse in this period: it brings to the fore questions that have been posed to the Palestinian community in Israel by its encounter with Jewish-Israeli society after the 1948 war. This first encounter constituted what Ghanayim called, borrowing from Adonis, 'the shock of modernity' (Ghanayim 2008: 37). Atallah Mansour, the author of *Wa-Baqiyat Samira*, says in his 2013 autobiography that he aimed to achieve two goals with publishing the novel:

> First was the straightforward argument that our society oppresses its women. Second, I was trying to draw a more complicated analogy between Samira's condition and that of the Palestinian people. (Mansour 2013: 145–6)

To put it succinctly, the combination between the social and the political refers to the modernisation process that the Palestinians underwent within a Zionist-Israeli political structure in this period. These two dimensions will dominate Palestinian discourse, in various ways, for many years. Moreover, *Wa-Baqiyat Samira* reflects confused and perplexed positions regarding the question of modernisation and its impact on the Palestinian community.

On the one hand, the novel criticised certain aspects of traditional Palestinian norms and traditions. For example, the novel depicts Riyad as a jealous and backward husband. Another example relates to Riyad's father forcing him to marry Samira, portraying this marriage as 'A Given' (*amr wāqiʿ*), as indicated in the title of chapter 9; and later the expectation that he publicly proves Samira's virginity to the village inhabitants:

> Laqad tazawwaj irdāʾan li-wālidayhi … wa-ʿāshar zawjatahu irdāʾan li-l-nāss!! Wa-shaʿar wa-kaʾannahu yurīd an yataqayyaʾ … innahā tanām al-ān ilā janbihi … kutlat laḥm muhmala … hādhā huwa al-zawāj!! (p. 74)

> He married to please his parents … and slept with his wife to please the people!! He felt he wanted to puke … she is asleep now next to him … an abandoned lump of meat … this is marriage!! (p. 74)

It is possible to say that Samira's abortion at the end of the novel is a symbolic abortion of the patriarchal social structure. On the other hand, chapter 20, entitled 'Between Two Perspectives', demonstrates the clashing emotions and thoughts that the encounter with the Jewish-Israeli society generates:

> Takhruj [samīra] maʿ jamāʿa min al-nisāʾ taʿmal maʿ jamāʿa min al-yahūd yuṭliqūn ʿalā anfusahum ism 'kībūts'… innahum min al-rijāl wa-l-nisāʾ, wa-ʿilāqatahum bi-baʿḍahum baʿḍan tuthīr fī samīra ʿawāṭif mutaḍāriba.. innaha tāra tashʿur bi-l-ḥasad … wa-ukhrā bi-l-istighrāb. (p. 119)

> [Samira] joins a group of women [from her village] to work with a group of Jews who call themselves 'kibbutz' … they are men and women, and their relationships generates contradicting emotions in Samira. One moment she feels envy … the other moment she feels wonder. (p. 119)

Mansour presents the kibbutz in a very simplistic way: a group of Jewish people who call themselves 'kibbutz', rather than a form of settlement, both as colonial-Zionist or the ideological-leftist. Moreover, what matters to Samira are the social relationships between the members of the kibbutz, especially those relating to women's independence and freedom. The following dialogue is between Samira and Hadasa, a Jewish-Israeli member of the kibbutz who was seen by Samira kissing a man in public:

> Inna hadāsa tataḥaddath ʿan al-rajul wa-kaʾannahu milk lahā … wa-kaʾanna li-l-marʾa ḥaqqan fī-l-tafkīr bi-aʿmāl al-rajul wa-ʿiqabahu idhā lam yahtamm bihā … āh lā … innahā lā tastaṭīʿ al-tafkīr bi-hādhihi al-ṣūra … inna hadāsa tuthīru fīhā al-ḥiqd ʿalā zawjihā … āh … ʿalayhā an taṣfaʿ hādhihi al-shirrīra ʿalā wajhihā. (p. 132)

> Hadasa speaks about the man as if she owns him … as if the woman has a right to evaluate the actions of the man and to punish him if he did not

> give her attention … aah no … she cannot think this way… Hadasa makes her feel anger at her husband … aah … she has to slap this evil woman on her face. (p. 132)

The conversation with Hadasa shakes the social and familial structures that Samira knows, and leads to an emotionally violent reaction in her. Samira is torn inside, she claims freedom one moment, and the other she wishes Riyad was next to her to restore the familiar social order (Ghanayim 2008: 38). Adel al-Usta sees that this novel leans towards the Jewish lifestyle (al-Usta 1992: 81–3), because the conversation between the two women ends with Hadasa having the final say.

Nevertheless, despite the apparent 'leaning' towards the Jewish-Israeli lifestyle, *Wa-Baqiyat Samira* does not call for a comprehensive modernisation to Palestinians in Israel. This novel reflects, above all, the confusion and uncertainty regarding the future of Palestinians in Israel as a result of the social and cultural differences between the two communities, as is evident in the final scene of the novel. This scene combines the images of Riyad and Hadasa in Samira's imagination:

> Inna ʿalāmāt al-istifhām al-kathīra tataṣārʿ fī dimāghiha al-ladhī tawaqqaf ʿan al-tafkīr min ḥawl al-amr […] wa-tughmiḍ ʿaynayhā bi-shidda wa-taṣrukh
>
> Yā allāh … shū ʿmilt anā min al-ʿāṭil?
>
> Yā allāh … shū ʿmilnā min al-ʿāṭil!! (p. 145)
>
> Many question marks are clashing in her head, which stopped thinking as a result of the enormity of the situation. […] She closes her eyes and screams:
>
> 'Oh God … what wrong have I done?'
>
> 'Oh God … what wrong have we done!!' (p. 145)

The transformation from the singular to the plural ('what wrong have *we* done!!') marks Mansour's intention to symbolise the Palestinians in Israel through Samira. Nevertheless, the novel does not offer any solutions to the many question marks in Samira's head, leaving them open. In other words, while it is possible to understand Samira's wonder ('what wrong have

I done?') to Riyad's abandoning her without any explanation, there is an issue with turning to the plural. If the novels lean towards the Jewish-Israeli lifestyle, as indicated above, why is Samira crying the fate of the Palestinians? Is she crying the dismantling of the traditional and familiar family structure as a result of being exposed to another culture? In sum, this novel outlines the collective question marks in the minds of Palestinians in this period, without offering solutions.

In comparison, *Qalb fi Qarya* (*A Heart in a Village*, 1963), by Mahmud Kana'na, offers a comprehensive depiction of the modernisation discourse among Palestinians in Israel in this period. *Qalb fi Qarya* tells the story of Hasan, a Palestinian citizen in Israel who is brought up in a Palestinian village in the 1960s. At first Hasan is a criminal and vandal who is despised throughout the village. However, after spending only a few months in an Israeli kibbutz he returns to his society a reformed person. The excerpt below depicts the transformations that Hasan had undergone, in his personality, attitude and role within society:

> Naʿam innahum yaqūlūn lahu kull yawm bi-anna ʿalayhi masʾūliyya ʿuẓmā: hiya iḥyāʾ al-zirāʿa al-ḥadītha fī-l-qarya al-ʿarabiyya. Hiya bināʾ mujtamaʿ ʿarabī jadīd fī qurānā. Naʿam innahu ḥasan, ḥasan al-haddām al-sāriq qabla ayyām maʿdūdāt, hādhā al-sharīd al-rafīq fī ʿiṣābat al-ashrār yuntashal min baynahum bi-yadd al-ʿināya li-yuṣbiḥ al-ān ḥajaran asāsiyyan lahu qīmatahu fī bināʾ ṣarḥ tilka al-muhimma al-insāniyya. Huwa nafsahu yafīq min ghaflatihi wa-sudurihi li-yarā nafsahu jisran akīda ʿalayhā yaʿbur rakb al-iṣlāḥ wa-l-taqaddum al-sāʾir min al-qarya al-yahūdiyya al-zirāʿiyya ilā al-qarya al-ʿarabiyya, li-yuhdī lahā ṭuruqan jadīda fī nuẓum al-intāj wa-nuẓum al-taʿāyush fī mujtamaʿ ṣāliḥ lā tufsiduhu al-khilāfāt mujtamaʿ lahu fī iqtiṣādiyyātahu mā yakfal lahu al-niʿma wa-l-rafāhiya al-latī ḥurimat minhā al-qarya al-ʿarabiyya qurūnan ṭawīla. (p. 55)

> Yes, they tell him every day that he's been given a great responsibility: reviving the modern agriculture in the Arab village. It is the building of a new Arab society in our villages. Yes, it is him, Hasan. Hasan, the vandal thief of yesterday, this vagabond member of a villain gang, is lifted from among them by the divine hand, to become now a valuable cornerstone in establishing the structure of this humanistic mission. He himself awakes from

> his sleep to see himself a stable bridge upon which the process of reform and progress passes, and which is progressing from the Jewish agricultural village to the Arab village, to provide it with new methods of production systems and coexistence in a healthy society that is not corrupted by disputes, a society that has an economy that ensures its prosperity and luxury, from which the Arab village was deprived for long centuries. (p. 55)

Hasan has been chosen by divine providence (*yad al-ʿināya*), seemingly embodied in the kibbutz's agricultural instructor, to comprehensively reform (*iṣlāḥ*) and modernise Palestinian villages in Israel. In line with the modernising task, the discourse in this novel is collective, as indicated in the use of first-person plural in *qurānā* ('our villages'). The collective tone is also evident in its generic reference to 'the Arab village' (*al-qarya al-ʿarabiyya*) and 'the Jewish village' (*al-qarya al-yahūdiyya*). Moreover, the modernisation of Palestinian villages is multifaceted. It entails political, social, economic and technological transformations that are all interrelated. The end result of this reform and modernisation is boon and prosperity (*niʿma wa-rafāhiya*), of which the Arab village had, for many centuries, (*qurūn ṭawīla*) been deprived (*ḥurimat minhā*).

The above excerpt contrasts with the discourse presented in the first section by Tawfiq Muʿammar. On the one hand, Muʿammar calls for Palestinian participation in ruling their country (*bilādihim*) on equal grounds with the Jewish-Israelis. The basis of this proposition is that the Palestinians are the indigenous people and have the primary right to the country. On the other hand, according to the narrative presented in *Qalb fi Qarya*, Palestinian society is deemed poor, backward, primitive and burdened with disputes (*khilāfāt*); characteristics that do not qualify it to rule the country, an absent notion in the discourse of modernisation novels. The contrast between modernisation novels and the earlier works in this period (1948–67) will be examined hereafter, through discussing the way in which modernisation novels echo the main characteristics of modernisation discourse. In order to do so, I will first outline the main aspects of modernisation theory.

In a study on the ideological roots of American modernisation policy in Latin America during the Kennedy presidency, Michael Latham lists the four main principles that were incorporated into the analysis of modernisation thinkers:

> (1) 'traditional' and 'modern' societies are separated by a sharp dichotomy; (2) economic, political, and social changes are integrated and interdependent; (3) development tends to proceed toward the modern state along a common, linear path; and (4) the progress of 'developing' societies can be dramatically accelerated through contact with the knowledge and resources of modern ones. (Latham 1998: 200)

Although Latham focused his discussion on a particular period in American history, there is general agreement, among critics and proponents of modernisation alike, on the four tenets of the theory quoted above (Bernstein 1971; Tipps 1973; So 1990; Inglehart 1997; Rosenhek 1998). In analysing the preceding excerpt from *Qalb fi Qarya*, it is possible to identify different representations of these tenets in terms of the content and formulation of the argument.

Firstly, there is the dichotomous contrast between Palestinian and Jewish society. Palestinian society and villages are 'traditional', while Jewish-Israeli society and kibbutzim are 'modern'. According to the excerpt, Hasan is carrying the task of building a new Palestinian society (*binā' mujtama' 'arabī jadīd*),[6] to replace the old, decaying society. The word *tufsiduhu* may be interpreted in a number of slightly different ways. The root (*f-s-d*) in Arabic carries the meaning of 'corruption' or 'immorality'. *Fasād* in Arabic means 'corruption', of a financial or moral kind. Another word stemming from this root is *fāsid*, meaning 'corrupt', but also 'rotten' or 'decayed' (usually of food). The use of *tufsiduhu* in the excerpt conveys a closer meaning to the second interpretation – depicting Palestinian society as a rotten society (*mujtama' fāsid*) due to its numerous internal disputes (*khilāfāt*). This is evident also in depicting Hasan as a vandal and immoral person prior to being lifted by divine providence. In the same fashion, Palestinian agriculture is implied to be primitive through the stated need of modernisation (*iḥyā' al-zirā'a al-ḥadītha*). The Palestinian village is, thus, backward in contrast to the modern kibbutz.

Secondly, the reform and modernisation of Palestinian society needs to be carried out comprehensively on different fronts: political, economic and social. The interrelatedness of these components is clearly expressed in the excerpt, when the technological modernisation of Palestinian agriculture is linked to political coexistence between Palestinians and Jews in Israel. Note, for example, the pair *nuẓum intāj* and *nuẓum taʿāyush*. *Nuẓum* in Arabic means 'systems' or 'operating systems' and is usually used in technological contexts. In the context of the above excerpt, *nuẓum intāj* means 'systems of production'. It is possible to develop agricultural 'systems of production', but the term (*nuẓum*) does not 'fit' when used in the context of coexistence between asymmetrical groups in a divided society. The parallel between the technological modernisation of Palestinian agriculture, essentially to increase production with economic consequences, and political coexistence between Palestinians and Jews in Israel reflects the scale of the modernisation task that Palestinian society in Israel faces. Another expression of the interconnectedness of the different characteristics of modernisation is explicitly laid out in the final sentence of the excerpt, outlining the hoped-for results of this process: a moral society (*mujtamaʿ ṣāliḥ*), which is unspoiled (*lā tufsiduhu*) by disputes; a society which sets up an economy that ensures its prosperity.

Thirdly, the representation of Palestinian progress from a backward to a modern society is uni-directional: the 'process of reform' (*rakb al-iṣlāḥ*) proceeds from the Jewish kibbutz towards the Palestinian village (*al-sāʾir min al-qarya al-yahūdiyya al-zirāʿiyya ʾilā al-qarya al-ʿarabiyya*). The image of Zionist-Israeli modernisation progressing from the kibbutz towards the Palestinian village (note the construct *min ... ilā*) embodies in itself several characteristics of modernisation discourse: one, modernisation as a multi-faceted process (a point discussed earlier) – the word (*rakb*) means 'convoy', conveying the sense of multiplicity of participants, rather than 'process' (in a simple, standard, translation of *rakb al-iṣlāḥ* as 'process of reform').[7] In the same way that a convoy is made up of a number of participants, modernisation that progresses from the kibbutz towards the Palestinian village is seen to be made of a multiplicity of 'modernisations', listed afterwards in the excerpt: technological-economic (systems of production, prosperity); political (coexistence); and social (moral values). Two, despite being made of different 'components', or riders, a convoy acts as a coherent unit, with all its parts interrelating. In the same way, modernisation discourse is perceived as a bundle of different modernisations that, nonetheless, make up a whole unit. Three, the progression of Zionist-Israeli modernisation is inevitable. This idea is expressed in the use of *al-sāʾir* in the present tense. Modernisation is occurring in the present, and Palestinians have no choice or control over its progression. Modernisation, from a social evolutionary theory point of view, is a historic inevitability, since it 'constitutes a "universal pattern"' (see: Bernstein 1971; Tipps 1973).

Fourthly, modernisation discourse suggests that the modernisation of Palestinian society had been dramatically accelerated, after many centuries (*qurūn ṭawīla*) of stagnation, due to contact, post-1948, with Jewish-Israeli society. Even more, the above excerpt from *Qalb fi Qarya* suggests that the modernisation of Palestinian society in Israel is not initiated by Palestinians, but by Jewish-Israelis. Expressed in the passive, Hasan is 'lifted' (*yuntashalu*) by divine providence; he is reminded every day by his Jewish-Israeli instructors at the kibbutz (*yaqūlūn lahu kulla yawm*) that he bears a great responsibility (*mas'ūliyya 'uẓmā*) and carries a humanistic mission (*muhimma insāniyya*). It is due to such constant preaching that Hasan awakes from his sleep (*yafiq min ghaflatihi*) to realise the importance of the role handed to him. In other words, it is not mere 'contact' with this Jewish-Israeli society that ignited the modernisation of Palestinians; such transformations are the result of the direct and active interference of Israeli-Jewish people.

According to this logic, Palestinian society (or Hasan) would have remained 'asleep' in its immoral backwardness, had not the Jewish-Israelis initiated the modernisation of Palestinian society. This interpretation complements what I explained above regarding the inevitability of modernisation for Palestinians in Israel. This is a result of the fact that the Zionist movement, and later Israel, sought to present itself as a modernising agent in Palestine, and indeed in the Middle East (Said 1979: 12). Palestinian historian Ahmad Sa'di arrives at a similar conclusion in his study of Zionist-Israeli modernisation discourse:

> Two points [...] are focal to the Zionist discourse of modernisation: Firstly, the Zionists' self-perception as bearers of higher culture, and civilised values. As such they are endowed with a moral right and even with an obligation to spread civilisation among the natives. [...] Secondly, the argument of modernisation is established upon hierarchies and juxtapositions. (Sa'di 1997: 28)

I have outlined the 'hierarchies and juxtapositions' present in Palestinian modernisation discourse in the preceding discussion on the dichotomous formulation of the Palestinian modernisation narrative. In relation to the first point Sa'di raises, on the perceived role of the Zionist movement as a bearer of higher culture, a deeper look into the analogies used in the above excerpt from *Qalb fi Qarya* highlights the discursive characteristics of Zionist-Israeli modernisation. The narrative in the novel depicts Hasan to have been lifted, and awakened, by divine providence, to realise the historic role to modernise his society. This image of divine intervention is biblical in the sense that it connotes the goodness of the divine powers in guiding the lost souls on earth. Being asleep also implies the powerlessness of the sleeping person: his blindness, or ignorance, of what is happening around him. Such representation suggests blind imperviousness to knowledge, modernity or, to use a biblical term, 'light'. In short, Palestinians have lived, unaware, in darkness, for long centuries, until finally receiving blessing through the guidance of the Zionist movement (now Israel).

The narrative in *Qalb fi Qarya* provides more clues that underline the depiction of modernisation discourse as a historic inevitability. This is evident in the preceding excerpt from *Qalb fi Qarya* through the double use of the word 'yes' (*naʿam*). This serves both as assertion and confirmation of the drastic metamorphosis of Hasan, as a result of the kibbutz instructor and his intervention. In other words, seeing modernisation as a historic inevitability, Hasan feels compelled to defend his role as a bearer of a humanistic mission (I will analyse the meaning of defending modernisation discourse later in this section). In the following excerpt, Hasan replies to his friend, who speculates regarding the intentions of the kibbutz officials in inviting Palestinians to participate in training schemes organised there:

> W-hum dāʾiman bi-qūlū innu iḥnā ʿam byījūna shabāb min afrīqya w-min al-hind w-min amīrka, w-blād kthīri w-bitʿallamū hūn ʿindnā fī isrāʾīl fī-l-kībutsāt wa-l-munaẓẓamāt al-taʿāwuniyya al-thānyi, w-iḥnā minḥibb nʿallimhum hadūl al-aghrāb, kīf mā minḥib nʿallim shabāb al-qurā al-ʿarab illī hum muwʿṭinīn fī-l-dūli mithilnā mithilhum. (pp. 66–7)

> And they always say that young men from Africa and India and America come to us, and from many [other] countries, and they learn here in Israel in the kibbutzim and the other cooperative organisations, and we love to

> teach those foreigners, why would we not love to teach the Arab young village men who are citizens in this country just like us. (pp. 66–7)

This quotation exemplifies the adoption of Zionist-Israeli discourse by Palestinian individuals. Hasan presents a narrative that is repeatedly voiced (*dāʾiman bi-qūlū*) by the Jewish-Israelis in the kibbutz. The excerpt echoes the Zionist-Israeli self-perceived modernising mission: instructors in the kibbutz tell Hasan that they love (*minḥibb*) to educate both foreigners and Palestinians alike. Here, the Zionist-Israeli modernisation mission exceeds the boundaries of Israel/Palestine: Israel hosts people from Africa, India and the USA who come to train and be enlightened in its kibbutzim.

Modernisation, in 1950s and 1960s Israel, was a matter of policy. It also influenced its foreign policy. The following quotation from Natanel Lorch, an Israeli historian, sheds more light on this issue. In the article from which this quotation is taken, Lorch analyses the development of the relations between Israel and African countries until 1963 (coincidentally the date of publication of the article, as well as *Qalb fi Qarya*):

> Economically, [Israel] is a developing, not yet a developed, country; in some spheres far enough ahead of the African nations to provide useful lessons, but not so far as to have attained a stage beyond their reach, like the industrialised countries in both the Eastern and the Western bloc. As one African trainee, familiar with both Israel and a large industrial territory, has put it: 'There I have had an opportunity to study the history of development, in Israel I am studying development itself'.
>
> By and large, therefore, African visitors to Israel have gone away with a feeling of self-confidence in their ability to tackle their own problems within a reasonable time, whereas visits to more advanced countries may sometimes have produced intense depression, perhaps bordering on despair, at the vast gap that divides those countries from their own. It has been said that this self-confidence is Israel's principal export to Africa. On the whole, Israelis have lived up to the challenge which the mounting flow of visitors and trainees from Africa presents and have been able to make them feel at home. (Lorch 1963: 360)

A few points need to be addressed from this quotation: first, it manifests the linear, uni-directional and evolutionary process of modernisation. According to this logic, there are 'developed' countries (which have arrived at the higher levels of modernisation); and there are 'developing' countries (which have started a process leading to a single target: modernisation, though this has not yet been fully achieved). In the 1960s, Israel, according to Lorch, is a developing country, since it does not match the development levels of Western powers. Israel is ahead of African countries, however, in its *level* of progression. Lorch, and others (Ajami and Sours 1970), believe that it is Israel's intermediate position, in terms of its development, that attracts African countries to learn from it.

The reason for seeing Israel as an ideal model to learn from stems from modernisation gaps between the African nations and the developed countries, which seem to Lorch so vast that they lead to 'depression, perhaps bordering on despair'. This is an unsubstantiated claim, indicated by the use of 'perhaps' and the lack of any reference to research about African 'depression and despair' resulting from underdevelopment. Secondly, and related to this, Lorch does not tell us who said that 'self-confidence is Israel's principal export to Africa'. Such unfounded statements manifest, more, the ideological stance of the author, rather than a factual or empirical observation. This is further expressed in the unsubstantiated remark that Israel succeeded in making African visitors and trainees 'feel at home'. In short, Lorch does not provide the parameters according to which we might measure depression, despair, self-confidence or the sense of 'feeling at home', in the context of Israeli policy towards African countries in the 1960s. Nor does he demonstrate how he arrives at the conclusions he has outlined.

The ideological basis of the modernisation policy Israel promotes in African countries, and that Lorch seems to adhere to, or advocate, is summarised in the following quotation from a publication of the Israeli Ministry of Commerce and Industry from 1967: 'By assisting the African nations to progress more rapidly towards the benefits of modern technology their potential as a trading partner will be enhanced as well' (quoted in Ajami and Sours 1970: 407). This statement contains two characteristics of Israeli policy: one that relates to efforts to modernise African countries, and another that comprises the motivation for such a policy.

Despite the problems in the narrative presented by Lorch, this text is still relevant to our discussion on the preceding excerpt from *Qalb fi Qarya* in two respects: both factual and discursive. Factually speaking, the quotation provides evidence for the presence of African trainees in Israel during the period under consideration and placing the narrative of the novel in a historical context. Moreover, in terms of their discourse, the narratives of the novel and of Lorch match with regard to the training of Africans in Israel.

Moreover, from a discursive point of view, the mention of both 'developed' (USA) and 'developing' (India, Africa) countries in the quotation from *Qalb fi Qarya* serves to place Israel at the forefront of the modernised world, even if such a claim is denied by Lorch. It is worth noting, in this context, that the mention of trainees coming from India to Israel is interesting, since India did not establish diplomatic relations with Israel until 1992. This fact makes the arrival of Indian nationals in order to participate in kibbutz training programmes less likely, and the participation of India would certainly not have been on the scale of that of African countries.[8] It is difficult, due to lack of statistical data[9] on participants in training programmes, to completely deny or verify such claims. Nevertheless, it is not my intention to investigate the demographic composition of participants in training programmes in Israel, but to highlight the way in which the Zionist-Israeli modernisation was 'marketed' to, and absorbed by, Palestinian citizens in Israel.

India and Africa have been the subjects of Western colonial rule for hundreds of years. Having Israel involved in these regions places her on a par with Western colonial powers, in terms of their modernisation role. Moreover, seeing Israel at the forefront of Western hegemony places Palestinian citizens in Israel in the same position, or status, of underdeveloped nations, in need of Western aid and direction in order to achieve modernisation. I will return to this point later, after I briefly present another factual aspect regarding foreigners arriving to Israeli kibbutzim.

The quotation from Lorch is important in our analysis of the excerpt from *Qalb fi Qarya* since it helps distinguish between two guest populations in Israel: African or Asian trainees participating in designated development programmes, and Western participants, represented in the above excerpt by the USA (*amīrka*). Western individuals who come to spend a few months in Israeli kibbutzim are not included in development programmes. Western volunteers come to the kibbutz for a variety of reasons: to experience communal life, learn Hebrew, visit the Holy Land or find Jewish fulfilment (for more on volunteer tourism in the Kibbutz, see: Mittelberg 1988). The distinction between training programmes for 'Third World' countries and Western volunteer tourism is crucial, since it helps place Palestinian participants in kibbutz programmes in an ideological context. As Palestinian citizens in Israel were invited to take part in kibbutz training programmes, rather than participate as volunteer tourists, they are categorised along similar lines to the other 'underdeveloped' nations who trained there.

In *Qalb fi Qarya*, Western and non-Western participants in kibbutz life are all 'strangers' (*aghrāb*). The usual, more common, Arabic word for 'foreigner' is *ajnabi*. The terminological use of the Arabic word *aghrāb* is paralleled, even if coincidentally, in an article entitled 'Strangers in the Kibbutz' by Alison Bowes, as well as Mittelberg's above-mentioned book, *Strangers in Paradise*. Borrowing the terms 'stranger' from the German sociologist Georg Simmel, Bowes points to the main reason for the exclusion of strangers in the kibbutz:

> from the point of view of the kibbutzniks, the insiders, a kibbutz is a group of members, candidates and their children, run by the members as a commune. According to this definition, the volunteers are firmly outsiders, categorically different from the 'kibbutz'. (Bowes 1980: 665)

Such a firm categorical exclusion from the definition of a kibbutz applies also to Palestinian citizens in Israel, placing them on a par with other participants in training programmes. Since Palestinian citizens in Israel cannot be *ajānib* (foreigners) in their own country, the only word that can place them in the same category as foreigners in the kibbutz is *aghrāb*. Palestinians, like all other non-Jews, are inherently alien: strangers both to 'Israeliness' and to Zionism.

The exclusive attitude of kibbutz members towards Palestinian trainees has been expressed in a very similar way by Palestinian journalist and novelist Atallah Mansour in his autobiography, *Waiting for the Dawn* (1975). In the following quotation, Mansour, who participated in a kibbutz training programme, writes about the impossibility of Palestinian trainees integrating into the kibbutz:

> The Kibbutz, as we were always told, is a socialist institution, where all are equal. But we could not become real Kibbutz people since we had to go back to our community and solve its problems, they told us. And how are we to do this? By the recruitments of the Arab population to the Arab section in the Workers' Union party (Mapam), they replied. The party which invited us to participate in the salvation of our community had to be convinced about accepting us as members. Later on they were convinced, but, they still have a special section for Arabs even today. (Mansour 1975: 33)

The narrative that Mansour expresses is very similar to that conveyed in *Qalb fi Qarya*. For example, note the repeated indoctrination by kibbutz members ('we were always told') regarding the high values of equality that Zionism holds. Moreover, like Hasan, Mansour and other Palestinian participants were told they needed to go back to their villages in order to 'salvage' them. This sending away, according to the above quotation, was served as a pretext for an exclusivist discourse. It is interesting to note that the handed-over modernising mission is never expressed as a Palestinian initiative, but as a Zionist one. Mansour indicates, moreover, that the exclusion of Palestinians was institutionalised in the Zionist bodies that raised the flag of 'equality'.

The categorical exclusion of anybody who is not a member of the kibbutz contradicts the narrative, presented earlier by Lorch, that foreigners 'felt at home' in Israel. In terms of Palestinian identification, Palestinians who were supposed to be 'at home' (exemplified in the excerpt above through the use of *muwāṭinīn … mithlanā mithlahum*) were made to feel like 'strangers'. By depicting Palestinians as strangers in their homeland, which means erasing them as the natives, kibbutz members overturn the historical fact that the strangers were the Jewish-Zionist settlers who arrived in Palestine to colonise it. This discursive reversal of history completely dismantles the Palestinian historical narrative regarding the conflict over Palestine, expressed, for example, by Tawfiq Mu'ammar. Edward Said views this historic reversal in Palestine as one of the main objectives of the Zionist movement:

> Zionism aimed to create a society that could never be anything but 'native' (with minimal ties to a metropolitan centre) at the same time that it determined not to come to terms with the very natives it was replacing with new 'natives'. (Said 1979: 33)

With regard to the exclusion of Palestinians, if we return to the excerpt from *Qalb fi Qarya*, the labelling of Palestinian citizens in Israel, by the kibbutz instructor, as 'citizens' (*muwāṭinīn*) is notable. First, it suggests that Palestinians need enlightenment and modernisation in the same way that members of other, unenlightened nations do. Secondly, it proffers that Palestinians are, by the definition of Zionism, outside the boundaries of Israeliness, treated in the novel as guest members in the kibbutzim. From this point of view, by 'reminding' the Palestinians in Israel that they are 'citizens just like us' (*muwāṭinīn … mithlanā mithlahum*), the instructor also reiterates who has the power to determine belonging (both to the kibbutz and to the country), even if the Palestinians are the indigenous people of the land.

In light of the above, belonging to 'Israeliness' is not grounded in continued living on the land, but in ideologically belonging to Zionism (being Jewish). Saying that Palestinians and Jews in Israel are citizens alike (*mithlanā mithlahum*) gives, in fact, a false sense of equality. The erasure of Palestinians is performed by making them aliens, by making them outsiders in their own homeland. Palestinians who adopt Zionist-Israeli modernisation discourse inherently erase themselves. This is reminiscent of Shira Robinson's depiction of Israeli citizenship as a 'category of exclusion', even though her original use referred to Israel's efforts to prevent the return of Palestinian refugees by providing identification cards to the Palestinians who remained after the 1948 war (Robinson 2013). In the context of the discussion here, Israeli citizenship is utilised, domestically, to demark boundaries of belonging.

The erasure of Palestinian existence from Palestine has taken several forms. Ideologically speaking, the Zionist movement depicted Palestine as 'a land without people' long before the establishment of Israel, and the clearest physical manifestation of this approach was the ethnic cleansing ('demographic erasure') of the majority of Palestinian society from Palestine during the 1947–8 war and afterwards (see: Pappé 2007). Other aspects of erasure take place on social, political and linguistic levels. Suleiman (2004, 2011) provides an extensive survey of the socio-linguistic erasure of Palestinian history and existence by looking at names, toponyms and code names. Masalha (2008) depicts in detail the historical, political and ideological bases of the policy of erasure that Israel has carried out against Palestinian locations in Israel, as well as the Palestinian activities that counter it. The historic erasure of Palestinians, both physically and historically, is best summarised by Oren Yiftachel:[10]

> The act of erasure has been guided for decades by the mechanisms of the Jewish state, which seek to expunge the remains of the Arab-Palestinian society living in the country until 1948, as well as deny the tragedy visited on this people by Zionism. The act of erasure, which followed the violence, the flight, the expulsion, and the demolition of villages, is prominent in most major discursive arenas – in school textbooks, in the history that Zionist society recounts itself, in the political discourse, in the media, in official maps, and now also in the names of communities, roads, and junctions. Palestine, which underlies Israel, is continuously being erased from the Israeli Jewish body and speech. (Oren Yiftachel's foreword to Kadman 2015)

Erasure of Palestine and Palestinians by Israel has attracted the attention of many researchers from different disciplines in recent years. Most recently, Makdisi (2010) discussed the 'Architecture of Erasure' in Israel; in her doctoral thesis, Abigail Sone (2010) examined the 'Linguistic and Spatial Practice in a Divided Landscape', focusing on the erasure of Palestinian citizens in Israel in some respects; and the 'Erasure of Palestine' was also the theme of the 2009 Annual Conference of the Palestine Centre (the Jerusalem Fund for Education and Community Development) in Washington, DC.[11] The discussion in this section is a further contribution to these efforts, focusing on the erasure of the Palestinian as an individual and as a human being, from Jewish-Israeli space, rather than an abstract identity. Thus, as the erasure of Palestinians was part of Zionist discourse even before the establishment of Israel, the term 'erasure' refers not only to Palestinian citizens in Israel, but to all Palestinians. Those who remained in Israel, and those outside Israel. In this book I will focus on the responses of Palestinian citizens in Israel regarding their erasure, in various forms, by Israel.

As a result of the contradiction between Zionist ideological erasure and Palestinian actual existence, Palestinian citizens in Israel became 'present-absentees'. Although this label was originally, bureaucratically and politically coined to refer to Palestinian internal refugees in Israel, it is a good representation of wider Palestinian existence in Israel where 'the land on which they live is their homeland, but the dominant culture is not their culture and the country is not their country' (Muhawi 2006: 34). However, the term 'present-absentee' does not express the actual dynamics of Palestinian experience in Israel as described above. The 'absentee' aspect of the term should not convey passivity, because it is a continuous action applied to the Palestinians in Israel. Thus, a better way to describe Palestinian experience in Israel is through the phrases 'present-absentified' or 'present-erased' (*al-ḥāḍir al-mughayyab*). Palestinian citizens in Israel (the indigenous people of Palestine, living in Israel) are subjected to a process of alienation from their space, as a result of the ideological incorporation of modernisation and Zionism. This is so because belonging in Israel is ideologically bound to modernist Zionism.

The result of this erasure is that citizenship becomes the only form of belonging that Palestinians can hold onto, allowing a sense of fake equality based on the simple, almost lexical definition of 'citizens' as being 'members of the same country'. Palestinian citizenship, as it appears in modernisation novels, is devoid of any symbolic or ideological identification with Israel. In other words, this is a double-layer process in which the adoption of a modernising mode of thought denationalises Palestinian discourse in Israel. The first layer of Palestinian modernisation discourse is the call for Palestinians to modernise (with the aim of improving the chances of peaceful coexistence with the Jewish-Israelis). The second layer refers to strangeness of Palestinians in Israel (*aghrāb*), which is embedded in their ideological (and ethnic/racial) incompatibility with modernist Zionism. Thus, Palestinians resort to calling for coexistence between the two mismatching nations. This call for coexistence intrinsically requires the erasure of any political reality or identity that may disturb such a discourse.

Palestinian denationalisation in this period is evident in the fact that modernisation novels do not offer a definition of what a 'Palestinian citizen in Israel' is (notwithstanding the terminology they use to refer to this group). The only definition that arises from modernisation novels is a negative one, according to which Palestinians are non-modern and non-Israeli. Such a definition eliminates all the historical, cultural and social peculiarities of Palestinian society. In other words, modernisation novels are novels of erasure. As I will show below, though the plots of modernisation novels are clearly situated in Israel during the 1950s and 1960s, the 1948 war, its results, the military rule, the confiscation of land and the restrictions on movement are either completely absent, or, if mentioned, extremely diluted – or even explicitly detached from Palestinian reality.

Differences in modernisation levels, rather than the ideological exclusivity of Zionism, are seen in modernisation novels to be the reason for the discrepancy between Palestinians and Jewish-Israelis. This is clarified in the following excerpt. Hasan defends his participation in the training programme, deflecting accusations from village members who accuse him of becoming 'Jewish':

> Aṣīr yahūdī hādhā mustaḥīl li-annī ʿarabī w-baftkhir bi-ʿurūbti li-annu al-sharīf mā binkir aṣlu. Asāsan al-yahūd mā buṭulbū minnā innā nghayyir qawmiyyitnā walā biḥibbū al-shakhṣ yikūn ḍaʿīf la-ha-l-daraji! W-līsh aṣlan aṣīr yahūdī? W-mīn ḍāghiṭ ʿalayy aṣīr yahūdī?! Wallā iḥnā ʿayshīn fī-l-qurūn al-wusṭā wa-l-tamyīz w-maḥākim al-taftīsh[?] Ṭayyib hum al-yahūd mitdhakrīn innā ʿishnā iḥnā al-shaʿbīn maʿ baʿḍ aḥsan ḥayāt w-saʿāda fī-l-andalus w-kul tārīkh al-ʿarab. Lākin al-wāqiʿ innak mā fhimt shū baʿnī w-shū baqṣud. Al-muhhim bi-ṣarāḥā anā baḥkī innī wajadat innū al-shāb al-ʿarabi wa-l-shaʿb [al-ʿarabī] bighdar yʿīsh w-sahl yʿīsh maʿ al-shāb al-yahūdī wa-l-shaʿb al-yahūdī idhā kānū al-jihatīn min mustawā wāḥad. (pp. 74–5)

> That I become Jewish is impossible, because I am Arab and I am proud in my Arabness, because the noble man does not deny his roots. Not even the Jews ask us to change our nationality, and they don't like anyone to be so weak! And why would I want to become Jewish? And is there anyone who is pushing me to become Jewish?! Or do we live in the Middle Ages and discrimination and inquisition[?] Actually they, the Jews, remember that we lived, both nations, the best and happiest life in al-Andalus and throughout the Arab history. But in fact you did not understand my intention. I am saying that I found that the Arab man and nation can, easily, live with the Jewish man and nation, if they both were on the same level. (pp. 74–5)

This excerpt incorporates a number of characteristics in Palestinian modernisation discourse. Firstly, modernisation novels, echoing Israeli modernisation discourse, wrap ideological-political exclusion in a narrative about levels of modernisation. The final statement in the quotation, referring to the possibility of Palestinian and Jewish-Israelis living together, both as individuals and collectively, links this discussion to the preceding one on the perception of not Zionist ideology but differences in levels of modernisation as the barrier to coexistence. By saying that both the whole nation and Palestinian individuals could live alongside the Jewish-Israelis, if they were 'of the same level' (*min mustawā wāḥid*), gives a false meaning to the word 'equality', which, in Arabic, is *musāwā*. *Mustawā wāḥid* cannot, in Arabic, be used in a political context. *Musāwā*, which refers to political equality, is replaced by *mustawā*, which means 'level', referring to levels of progress and modernisation.

Secondly, and related to this, Palestinians are held responsible for the lack of coexistence with Jewish-Israelis. Note the use of the conditional 'if' (*idhā*) in the construction of the final statement in the excerpt: *if* Palestinians manage to arrive at the level of modernisation of the Jewish-Israelis, then both nations will be able to live together peacefully. It is the responsibility of Palestinians, therefore, to achieve this. The onus is on them, not the state, to achieve equality. Echoing a similar logic, Israeli sociology, which utilises modernisation theory in the study of Palestinians, perceives 'the internal characteristics of Arab society, and particularly its traditional nature, [to be] the principal factors preventing the political participation and socio-economic mobility of Palestinian citizens, causing in that way their marginal position in Israeli society' (Rosenhek 1998: 561). The discourse which blames Palestinian backwardness for their lack of integration in Israeli society is, according to Sa'di, common among 'Israeli politicians, administrators and academics' (Sa'di 1997: 35). We see here that it is also common among Palestinian modernisation novelists.

Thirdly, as indicated earlier, the depiction of lack of modernisation as the cause of lack of integration in modernisation discourse results in a Palestinian modernisation discourse that suppresses the political reality in Israel. Modernisation novels suppress this political reality for the sake of promoting the cause of peaceful coexistence with the Jewish-Israelis. For example, the way the final statement in the above excerpt is formulated – regarding the possibility that Palestinians and Jewish-Israelis might be able to live together if they were equal – downplays the fact that they are neither living with each other peacefully, nor in a state of equality.

Moreover, in the above excerpt from *Qalb fi Qarya*, Zionism is depicted as a movement that does not aim to impose its identity on the indigenous Palestinians, but, rather, is a liberal, not an exclusivist, movement. Through referring to the political or racial suppression of the Middle Ages (*al-qurūn al-wusṭā*), the Inquisition (*maḥākim al-taftīsh*) and discrimination (*tamyīz*), Hasan ignores the racially determined laws in Israel at the time of narration (during the years of oppressive military rule). Such repression of contemporary political reality is integral to Zionist-Israeli modernisation discourse. Critics of Israeli modernisation theory show how it fails to explain the Palestinian lack of integration into Israeli society due to its marginalisation of the political context. For Rosenhek,

> [t]here is no reference [by proponents of modernisation theory] to the policies implemented by the Israeli state, such as the operation of a military government on Palestinian citizens until 1966 and other exclusionary practices, as factors which contributed to the alienation of Palestinians from the state. (Rosenhek 1998: 561)

Fourthly, and as a result of the above, Palestinian modernisation discourse erases Palestinian identity. Palestinians in Israel do not attempt, according to modernisation novels, to assimilate into Israeli society. The by-default ideological exclusion of Palestinians from Zionism disqualifies them from such an attempt. According to the excerpt above, Palestinians do not want to become 'Jewish', asserting their Arab identity and their pride in it. Note that Hasan says 'Jews do not ask us to change our nationality' (*nghayyir qawmiyyitnā*). In other words, his pride in his Arab identity stems from Zionist exclusion in Israel. Palestinian pride, or self-confidence, to borrow Lorch's term, is expressed in the excerpt when Hasan says that Jews do not like Palestinians 'to be so weak' (*ḍaʿīf la-ha-l-daraji*).

Moreover, Hasan is proud of his *Arab*, not his Palestinian, identity. According to the Zionist narrative, here repeated by Hasan, there are two nations: Jewish and Arab. This narrative erases Palestinians as a national group competing with the Zionists. Hasan says that both nations (*iḥna al-shaʿbayn*), the Arab and the Jewish, can live together peacefully in the same way that Arabs and Jews lived together peacefully in al-Andalus. In al-Andalus, Jews lived peacefully with *Arabs*, not with Palestinians. The reference to Arabs and Jews living together peacefully in al-Andalus erases the contemporary historical context of Jewish occupation of Palestine and the establishment of Israel. Moreover, the sole focus on 'nationality' (*qawmiyya*) implies that Palestinians must change. These aspects have been discussed earlier in this section, namely, the various characteristics of modernisation.

Modernisation novels mark a complete transformation in Palestinian national discourse, in comparison to both novels by Tawfiq Muʿammar. Whereas Muʿammar criticises the Zionist brutalities during the 1948 war, calling Israel to grant the human rights of freedom of expression and thought, seeing Israel and Zionism as racist and discriminatory and viewing Palestinians as the indigenous inhabitants who possess the primary right to Palestine, modernisation novels discard all of this. They ignore the conflictual history between Palestinians and the Zionist movement and Israel. Moreover, Palestinian modernisation novels actually express gratitude for Israeli modernisation.

However, despite this political contrast between the discourse of Muʿammar and modernisation novels, it is possible to see that also the former reflected some modernisation tendencies. In addition to accepting the idea that Palestinian citizens in Israel should be incorporated into the state apparatus, there is evidence in the writing of Muʿammar about Israel seeing itself as a modernising agent. In the last quote from *Bit-hun*, the speaker expresses his good intentions for Israel, and that he hopes it 'genuinely be a tool for development and progress' (*an takūn bi-l-fiʿl adā li-l-bināʾ wa-l-taqaddum*) and be 'a role model for every rising nation in the world' (*wa mithālan ḥayyan li-kul umma nāhiḍa mutaḥarrira fi al-ʿālam*). Such a statement provides another example of Muʿammar's cautious, but critical, discourse. Here, this statement conveys Palestinian support of Israel, but not in its current racist form, as Israeli leaders have been disappointing (*khayyabū al-āmāl*).

Moreover, the attenuated tone in modernisation novels downplays the political reality, the restrictive policies imposed on Palestinians and even some key events in Palestinian life in Israel in this period. Let's take the case of the 1956 Kafr Qasim massacre as an example.[12] The Kafr Qasim massacre has been a defining moment in Palestinian life in Israel, particularly in shaping modes of political activism for years to come (see: Robinson 2003). Discussing the pivotal role the massacre had in shaping Palestinian discourse in these years, Sorek demonstrates how Palestinian political discourse was that of citizenship and integration (Sorek 2015: 46). Arriving at a similar conclusion, Robinson shows how 'the massacre and the responses it generated established a precedent for organised protest against civil inequality [...]' (Robinson 2003: 394). These conclusions resonate with the findings we have seen here so far. To put it succinctly, even though novels may have not addressed this particular event directly,[13] they do point to the key issues that shaped the socio-political outlook of this community. Novels provide an extensive depiction of the issues that concerned Palestinians in this period, starting with Mu'ammar raising the issue of memory of the occupation of Haifa and Palestine, through to life under the military rule and the multi-dimensional modernisation influencing the political, social and economic aspects of Palestinian life. Nevertheless, the primary question that lies at the basis of Palestinian discourse in Israel in this period relates to Palestinian adaptation and integration in Israel.

Nevertheless, although it may, at first, seem paradoxical, modernisation novels provide evidence that Palestinians in Israel during this period (1948–67) were worried about losing their identity. The fact that Hasan needs to defend his choices means that many people (such as his friend who questions him about Israeli intentions in inviting Palestinians to train in the kibbutzim) view Israeli modernisation with mistrust. The representation of such 'questioning' of modernisation is downscaled or dismissed without much consideration. Novels focus, instead, on the advantages of modernisation. However, the fact that most modernisation novels include an introduction that aims to defend their discourse, and that depicts the authors as leaders of change in their society, provides evidence that opposition to modernisation discourse was significant. Novelists declare their willingness to pay 'the price' for spearheading change in their society, which reflects the 'resistance' that they faced. In fact, Mahmud Kana'na, author of *Qalb fi Qarya*, sees his modernising mission in terms of sacrifice (*taḍḥiya*) and jihad, closing the introduction with the proverb *wa-mā al-ḥayātu illā jihādan*.

Other novels of this group have the same characteristics in this regard. For example, in *Hubb bila Ghad* (*Love without a Future*, 1962), by Mahmud Abbasi, the clash between modernisation and anti-modernisation discourse takes the form of intergenerational conflict. The introduction states that this novel:

> highlights the struggle (*ṣirāʿ*) between the old mentality (*al-ʿaqliyya al-qadīma*), and the negative sides of the obsolete traditions (*al-taqālīd al-bāliya*) under which our society toils (*yarzaḥ*), represented in the character of the father; and the progressive ideas (*al-afkār al-taqadumiyya*) depicted in the characters of the two brothers Hamdi and Karim. (Introduction)

Similar expressions of modernisation missions are expressed in the introduction of *Al-Layl wa-l-Hudud* (*The Night and the Borders*, 1964), by Fahd Abu Khadra.

The non-existence of 'anti-modernisation novels' – novels that voice opposition to modernisation discourse in this period – does not mean that such a discourse did not exist altogether. For example, Palestinian author and critic Ghassan Kanafani identified different discourses among Palestinians in Israel in his research on Palestinian poetry in Israel. It is possible it existed in other non-novelistic literary genres, such as short stories, journalistic essays and so forth. Further research encompassing these genres is required in order to expand our understanding of the modernisation of Palestinians in Israel during this period. Nonetheless, with regard to Palestinian identity transformation, we have seen in the above discussion the denationalisation of Palestinians as a result of their modernisation in Israel during the 1960s. Moreover, as we will see in the following section, as well as in Chapters 2 and 3 of this book, Palestinian novels published in Israel deal in depth with the 'price' that Palestinian society had to pay in return for its modernisation in Israel; namely, the loss or dismantling of its cohesive identity. The following section will focus on one novel that marks a turning point in Palestinian discourse in Israel, with regard to modernisation within the Zionist-Israeli framework.

Re-evaluation

In a New Light (1966), by Atallah Mansour, is the first Palestinian novel in Hebrew. The linguistic choice, as well as the reception among critics, of this novel has been at the centre of several academic works (e.g. see: Kayyal 2008). Writing in Hebrew raises important questions of representation ('do Palestinian authors who write in Hebrew represent Palestinian identity and discourse in Israel?') and assimilation/integration in Israel. Nevertheless, the importance of this novel to our discussion stems from its stance on questions of the modernisation of Palestinians in Israel within a Zionist framework. This outlook, as will become evident later, contributes to the existing debate, albeit from a different angle. The novel tells the story of Yusif Muhammad, a Palestinian orphan who was brought up in a Jewish family after the death of his father in the 1948 war. Yusif falls in love with Rivkah, a married Jewish woman from the kibbutz where he lives. The plot of the novel is about the failed attempts of Yusif to become part of the Jewish-Israeli society. Even marrying Rivkah did not avert his rejection from the kibbutz community, which resembles Israeli society.

There is a strong probability that *In a New Light* is based on a true story that took place in 1965. Palestinian journalist Fouzi El-Asmar tells in his autobiography *To Be an Arab in Israel* (1975a) the story of Rashid and Tzviah. Rashid, a Palestinian citizen in Israel, met Tzviah in a kibbutz, they fell in love and later married. The following excerpt from *To Be an Arab in Israel* summarises their story:

> Tzviah was a member of a kibbutz [...] and there she met Rashid, an Arab working in the kibbutz. They fell in love and were married. As the kibbutz on which she was born refused to accept an Arab as a member, the two turned to [another kibbutz] which was known for its favourable attitude towards Arabs. There they requested to be accepted, for a trial period, as candidates for membership. Their request was brought before a general meeting of the members of [the kibbutz]. After a prolonged argument their request was turned down. [...] The refusal [...] aroused a great deal of discussion [...]. At that stage [after their rejection], in order to prevent further embarrassment, the Political Committee of the Mapam Kibbutz Movement, decided to accept the two for a candidacy period at Kibbutz Ein Dor. The kibbutz agreed to this, but during the year that the two spent at the kibbutz, the attitude towards Rashid was so negative that they decided to leave. (El-Asmar 1975b: 112)

Since this story generated a wide public reaction, it is likely that Mansour, a journalist at the time, had full knowledge of the incident and found it important to retell it. *In a New Light* is important because it voices a 'post-modernisation' discourse. It addresses Zionist modernisation discourse and refutes it, by showing its internal weaknesses and contradictions, as I will show hereafter. Below I will present a number of excerpts from *In a New Light* manifesting several stages in the transformation in Palestinian identity in Israel during this period.[14]

At the beginning of the plot, Yusif aims to assimilate into the kibbutz community, reflecting the dual-layered modernisation discourse presented above: the need of Palestinians in Israel to modernise in order to be able to integrate into Israeli society, and the denationalisation of their discourse (in order to facilitate coexistence):

> A bulldozer rakes up and clears away the ruins of the abandoned Arab village. Such was my village, or rather my father's. My own is quite different. Its houses are built far apart, meticulously planned. My father's village did not even have a master plan [...] Why did I have to remember all this? I had no right to remember. My father's blood stood for war and destruction, whereas the bulldozer was a vehicle of peace and construction. (p. 40)

A number of points need to be addressed in this excerpt. First, note the modernisation juxtaposition between the Palestinian village and the kibbutz in terms of their organisation. The Palestinian village 'did not even have a master plan', while the kibbutz is 'meticulously planned'. This representation is similar to colonial juxtapositions regarding the attitude of the civilised man to the non-civilised man towards the land:

> A civilised man, it was believed, could cultivate the land because it meant something to him; on it accordingly he bred useful arts and crafts, he created, he accomplished, he built. For an uncivilised people land was either farmed badly (i.e., inefficiently by Western standards) or it was left to rot. From this string of ideas, by which whole native societies who lived on American, African, and Asian territories for centuries were suddenly denied their right to live on that land, came the great dispossessing movements of modem European colonialism, and with them all the schemes for redeeming the land, resettling the natives, civilising them, taming their savage customs, turning them into useful beings under European rule. (Said 1979: 27)

What modernisation discourse in *In a New Light* does not express is the connection that Said makes between being modern and the right to exist. Seen from this viewpoint, it is the backwardness of the Palestinian village – it not having a master plan – that is the reason for its demise. The 'abandoned' village did not deserve, or have the right, to continue to exist. Yusif, secondly, places himself on the modernised side of the juxtaposition, dissociating himself from his father and his village of origin. By doing so, by incorporating modernisation discourse, Yusif alienates himself from his space and past: 'this is rather my father's village'.

Related to this, thirdly, modernisation discourse expressed in *In a New Light* downplays political disparity between Palestinians and Jewish-Israelis, by depicting the Palestinian village as merely 'abandoned', with no reference to the political reasons that may have brought about the abandonment of the village. Moreover, the use of 'abandoned' places the responsibility of the eviction of the village on its inhabitants.

The attempt to dilute the political past in modernisation discourse is represented explicitly in the excerpt when Yusif thinks that he has no right to remember the blood of his father, shed during the 1948 war, because it is associated with war and destruction. Only by forgetting the blood of his father, by suppressing the political disparity between Palestinians and Jewish-Israelis, can he assimilate into Jewish-Israeli modern society. Such a modernist position regarding forgetting the past contrasts with, and highlights, Mu'ammar's struggle on the memory of the 1948 war and Palestine, as discussed earlier.

In addition to consciously trying to forget the conflictual past, in his attempts to assimilate, Yusif depicts the Israeli bulldozer as a tool of peace and construction. The Israeli bulldozer has a special place in Palestinian memory, since it is perceived by Palestinians to be a tool used to erase Palestinian existence. The destruction of hundreds of abandoned villages after 1948 aimed to erase not only the past but also future existence of Palestinians in Palestine.[15] The portrayal of the bulldozer as a symbol of peace and construction means going to extremes in order to belong, because holding such an idea reverses, and as a result erases, Palestinian historical narrative on the events of 1948. We have seen such a reversal of discourse in the preceding section. However, such a representation of Palestinian efforts to assimilate in Israel bear the function in *In a New Light* of highlighting the impossibility of such integration, as well as emphasising the price it requires from Palestinians, in terms of losing memory and identity.

In other words, the difference between *In a New Light* and modernisation novels is that the statement about forgetting the past is reversed at a later point. In the following excerpt, Yusif reacts to the kibbutz position regarding accepting him as a full member. When the members of the kibbutz council discovered that Yusif was a Palestinian, they did not approve his membership, explaining that discovering his true identity placed him in a new light:

> Year in, year out, they had stuffed me with fairy-tales, about love of humanity and soil and what-not, and all of a sudden they had discovered that they needed a new light. Some light! More like the darkness of the tomb! (p. 120)

In this excerpt, Yusif reverses the Zionist discourse altogether, as well as the discourse of modernisation novels. First, the 'enlightenment' that the Zionist project was said to have brought the backward Palestinians now resembles the darkness of the tomb. Secondly, in contrast to the receptive attitude Palestinians have to the Zionist narrative, the above excerpt expresses rejection of such deceptive discourse, depicted as 'fairy-tales' with which Palestinians have been 'stuffed'. Yusif aims to show the hollowness of the Zionist-Israeli discourse of coexistence in Israel. The members of the kibbutz could only speak theoretically in terms of humanity and coexistence, but they do not apply their talk in practice. Not only do they not apply theory in practice, it is impossible to do so, due to the racism inherent in Zionism leading them to view full membership in the kibbutz of a non-Jewish person as a threat. Although at the end of the novel the dream comes true, and Yusif is admitted to the kibbutz, he views this as a hollow victory:

> I had won my fight, but this kind of victory left a bitter taste in my mouth [...] I was pervaded by emptiness. *I saw everything in a new light.* (p. 176; italics in original)

The realisation that equality between Palestinians and Jewish-Israelis in Israel cannot take place in the context of Zionist ideology is expressed as seeing things in a new light. However, this is the second time that Palestinians in Israel view things in a new light in this period. Modernisation novels in the mid-1960s also expressed seeing the light of modernisation. What Mansour depicts in *In a New Light* is realising that modernisation of Palestinians results in loss of their identity. The emptiness that takes over Yusif is in fact 'identitylessness'. For most of his life, he has been trying to shed his Palestinian identity and become something new, but he never really succeeds in belonging and remains an alien to the people in the kibbutz. Not even after he was admitted as a full member of the kibbutz did he feel that he belonged. Yusif realises that true belonging is beyond mere 'administrative' admittance to a group.

Conclusion

In studying Palestinians in the period discussed in this chapter (1948–67), Israeli sociologists call the transformations in Palestinian identity 'Israelisation'. Surveys about self-identification of Palestinian citizens in Israel provide evidence for such shifts. For example, in 1966 Palestinian citizens in Israel identified themselves in this order: Israeli; Israeli-Arab; Arab; and finally Palestinian (Peres and Yuval-Davis quoted in Miari 2008: 45). However, such self-identification labels are 'crude' and do not expose the 'inner workings' and complexity of Israelisation. Palestinian novels, as we have seen in this chapter, provide fine details of the 'Israelisation' of Palestinians in Israel.

However, I will not adopt such a terminology in this book, primarily because the term 'Israelisation' is one-dimensional, since it ignores other (non-Israeli) dimensions of identity transformation. Moreover, there is no agreed-upon definition of what 'Israelisation' means. Does 'Israelisation' refer to political transformations, which could mean 'Zionisation' of Palestinians? In such a case, Israelisation cannot be used in reference to Palestinian citizens in Israel. Palestinian modernisation novels did not promote Zionist discourse. It is true that the modernisation promoted in these novels aimed to allow Palestinian integration into Israeli society, but it does not mean that Palestinians have become Zionists. Moreover, the use of 'Israelisation' in reference to cultural aspects is as difficult to define as it is hard to specify what 'Israeli culture' is. Above all, reading in Palestinian novels from this period shows, as we have seen above, that Palestinian discourse in Israel, both politically and culturally, is all but uniform.

An alternative depiction to Palestinian identification in Israel in this period is provided by Muhammad Amara and Izhak Schnell, who summarise Palestinian identity repertoires in Israel in this period:

> During the first period, 1948–67, most studies establish that there was a delicate balance in the identity of the Arabs in Israel; this period is called by Amara the 'quest for security and accommodation'. This found expression in the development of systems for adapting and a desire to become part of the life of the country. The Palestinian element in their individual and collective identity, it was reported, was extremely weak due to the defeat during the war of 1948, the lack of political and cultural leadership, and the disconnection of contact with the remnants of the Palestinian people. (Amara and Schnell 2004: 180)

The pattern that Amara and Schnell describe resembles the findings in this chapter. This chapter outlines the process in which Palestinian identification is transformed, providing further explanation as to the reasons why the 'Palestinian element' in the identity of Palestinians in Israel became 'weak'.

The first twenty years of Palestinian life under Israeli rule were tremendously eventful. The violent birth of Israel placed Palestinians under severe circumstances: the war; the ethnic cleansing of Palestine; the destruction of villages and cities; and later the imposition of an oppressive and discriminatory military rule. The narratives we have seen in the above three sections reflect Palestinian efforts to adjust to the new reality. During the early years, Palestinians in Israel maintained, as is evident in the writing of Mu'ammar, the Palestinian national discourse emphasising Palestinian indigenous rights for self-determination and independence from any foreign power. However, realising the balance of power between Palestinians and Israel, they seek to integrate into the Israeli state, based on their indigenous rights. Such a discourse highlighted both the conflictual relationship between Palestinians and Zionist Israel, and the racist-exclusive nature of Zionism, thus voicing the notion that a true democratic (non-racist) Israel is a place that Palestinians are willing to live in, and take part in building.

Modernisation discourse among Palestinians in Israel in this period aimed to downplay the two characteristics of Palestinian life in Israel (namely, the conflictual relationship and the exclusive nature of Zionism). Palestinian modernists, echoing Zionist modernists, saw that it is Palestinian backwardness that is to blame for lack of coexistence between the two nations. Thus, the path for Palestinian integration into Israel is tied to their modernisation.

Such a discourse, however, also required the erasure of Palestinian history and memory. Towards the end of the 1960s, Palestinian citizens in Israel realise that integration into Israel is not as easy a goal to achieve as they had hoped before. *In a New Light* foregrounds the inherent impossibility of Zionism, and Israel, to accept others – strangers – into their ranks.

Palestinian identity transformations have political and cultural aspects, both of which have Israeli and Palestinian components. In the words of Azmi Bishara, 'Israeli Arabs try to adapt to the hyphenated "Israeli-Arab" identity; that is, to imitate the role of the colonised and objectified Israeli Arab, which is a product of the Israeli media for the Israeli public' (quoted in Brenner 2001: 93). Bishara bases his observation on the balance of power between Jewish-Israelis and Palestinians. Applying similar logic hundreds of years earlier, the fourteenth-century Arab thinker and sociologist Ibn Khaldun presented the idea that the ruled people will try to imitate their rulers (Ibn Khaldun 1965: 399–401). Ibn Khaldun did not expand on the dynamics of imitation (*al-muḥākā*), a term that he used to explain this change, but suggested that as long as ruling powers change, social habits also change. Wanting to belong to the dominant society is not unique to the Palestinian case in Israel.

In a similar endeavour to understand discourse changes among subordinate communities, Frantz Fanon identified three stages in the development of the colonised intellectual:

> In the first phase, the native intellectual gives proof that he has assimilated the culture of the occupying power. His writings correspond point by point with those of his opposite numbers in the mother country. His inspiration is European and we can easily link up these works with definite trends in the literature of the mother country. This is the period of unqualified assimilation. [...] In the second phase we find the native is disturbed; he decides to remember what he is. [...] Finally in the third phase, which is called the fighting phase, the native, after having tried to lose himself in the people and with the people, will on the contrary shake the people. Instead of according the people's lethargy an honoured place in his esteem, he turns himself into an awakener of the people; hence comes a fighting literature, a revolutionary literature, and a national literature. (Fanon 2004: 222–3)

Table 1.1 Novels published between 1948 and 1967

Group	Novel	
I	Mu'ammar, Tawfīq (1958), *Mudhakkarāt Lāji' aw Ḥayfā fi-l-Ma'raka*, al-Nāṣira: Maṭba'at al-Ḥakīm.	1
I	Mu'ammar, Tawfīq (1959), *Bit-hūn*, al-Nāṣira: Maṭba'at al-Ḥakīm.	2
II	Kanā'ana, Maḥmūd 'Abd al-Qādir (1960), *Wa'yy fī wa-Waḥyy min Qurānā*, al-Nāṣira: Maṭba'at al-Ḥakīm.	3
II	Mansour, Atallah (1962), *Wa-Baqiyat Samīra*, Tel-Aviv: Dār al-Nashr al-'Arabi.	4
II	'Abbāsī, Maḥmūd (1962), *Ḥubb bilā Ghad*, al-Nāṣira: Maṭba'at al-Ḥakīm.	5
II	Kanā'ana, Maḥmūd 'Abd al-Qādir (1963), *Qalb fī Qarya*, al-Nāṣira: Maṭba'at al-Ḥakīm.	6
II	Abū Khaḍra, Fahd (1964), *Al-Layl wa-l-Ḥudūd*, al-Nāṣira: Maṭba'at al-Ḥakīm.	7
*	Fayyāḍ, Tawfīq (1964), *Al-Mushawwahūn*, Ḥayfā: Maṭba'at al-Ittiḥād al-Ta'āwuniyya.	8
III	Mansour, Atallah (1966), *Be-Or Ḥadāsh*, Tel-Aviv: Karni. Quoted version: Mansour, Atallah (1969), *In a New Light*, translated from the Hebrew by Abraham Birman, foreword by David Pryce-Jones, London: Vallentine-Mitchell.	9
*	Maṣālḥa, 'Abd al-'Azīz (1967), *Thawrat al-'Āshiqīn wa-ayna Karāmatī*, al-Nāṣira: Maṭba'at wa-Ūfsit al-Ḥakīm.	10
II	Khūrī, Salīm (1967), *Ajniḥat al-'Awāṭef*, al-Nāṣira: Maṭba'at wa-Ūfsit al-Ḥakīm.	11

Groups: I Caution and adaptation novels; II Modernisation novels; III Re-evaluation novels.
* Novels that do not belong to any of the groups.

It is possible to see that, generally speaking, Palestinian modernisation novels resemble the first phase described by Fanon. We have seen a number of examples where modernisation novels did 'correspond point by point' with those of Israeli modernisation discourse. Moreover, modernisation novels depict the 'unqualified assimilation' of Palestinians in Israel as a problem that needs to be solved: non-modern Palestinians need to modernise in order to be able to integrate into Israeli society.

In a New Light resembles Fanon's second phase. Postmodernisation discourse is one that re-examines the alienating consequences of modernisation. Mansour exposes the weaknesses and contradictions in Zionist–Israeli discourse, that which talks in terms of equality in theory, but fails to implement it in practice. The reason for the impossibility of attaining equality according to 'Zionist modernisation' is because of the 'Zionist' part of the term – being an exclusive ideology serving the interests of Jewish-Israelis.

However, despite realisation of their inability to integrate into a Zionist framework, Palestinians in Israel cannot return to their 'original' state. Modernisation discourse, as we have seen in this chapter, is a distorting one, resulting in the alienation of Palestinians in Israel and the erasure of their past.

There are no novels in this period that correspond to the third phase in the model presented by Fanon. In the following chapter, focusing on Palestinian novels published between 1967 and 1987, I will discuss other dimensions of Palestinian modernisation in Israel and its implications for Palestinian identity. In the following years, Palestinian citizens in Israel abandon their dream of integrating into Israel and start to deal with the implications of their modernisation in Israel.

Notes

1. 'Military rule', 'military government', 'military administration' and 'military regime' are different terms denoting the military rule imposed on the Palestinians inside Israel between 1948 and 1966.
2. *Al-Qaḍāʾ wa-l-Qadar* by Kāmil Niʿma was published in 1954, but this was a reprint of the same novel, originally published in 1940. This is the reason why it is not included in this survey.
3. <http://bit.ly/2KZJDV3> (last accessed 24 April 2019).
4. This is very close to the wording in the Israeli Declaration of Independence: 'We appeal – in the very midst of the onslaught launched against us now for months – to the Arab inhabitants of the State of Israel to preserve peace and participate in the upbuilding of the State on the basis of full and equal citizenship and due representation in all its provisional and permanent institutions.' However, note that Muʿammar omitted the appeal to the Palestinians to preserve peace, and chose to quote only the rest of the sentence. Source: <http://bit.ly/2KXwJqp> (last accessed 24 April 2019).
5. (*lā yarā sababan yamūtu min ajlihi fī ḥayfā*; pp. 88–9.)
6. 'Arab' in these novels refers in most cases to the Palestinian community in Israel. For the sake of standardisation and uniformity, these usages will be treated as 'Palestinian', unless indicated otherwise.

7. According to *Lisān al-ʿArab* dictionary, the word is historically related to 'riders' of camels or horses (ten or more) as they travel: *wa-l-rrakb aṣḥāb al-ibl fi-l-ssafar dūn-l-dawāb; wa-qāl al-Akhfash: huwa jamʿun wa hum al-ʿashra famā fawqa-hum, wa-urā anna al-rrakb qad yakūn lil-khayl wa-l-ibl.*
8. Ajami and Sours briefly outline the adoption of Israeli models in some African countries: 'Youth movements which are characteristic of Israeli society and of Eastern Europe and the Soviet Union were introduced to several African nations. Ghana's Young Pioneers was based on the Eastern European model. The use of Israeli Nahal (Fighting Pioneer Youth) and the Gadna (Youth Battalions) system which combines military service with agricultural pioneering has been adopted by Tanzania, the Ivory Coast [Côte d'Ivoire], Chad, Dahomey [today Republic of Benin], and the Cameroon' (Ajami and Sours 1970: 406).
9. A problem that has been highlighted by Bowes in an earlier study: 'There are almost no statistics available on the numbers of volunteers on kibbutzim' (Bowes 1980: 679, note 1).
10. The variety of erasure forms of the Palestinian history and existence from Israeli discourse is a vast topic that extends beyond the scope of this study. For more information on this topic (in addition to the works mentioned above), see: Benvenisti 2000; Piterberg 2001; Eyal 2006.
11. <http://bit.ly/2IOgidv> (last accessed 24 April 2019).
12. Taking place on 29 October 1956, hours before the launch of the Israeli, French and British war against Egypt. Forty-nine Palestinians were murdered by Israeli border police as they returned to their village, not knowing of new curfew hours that had been imposed by the military governor earlier in the day.
13. It appears that the commemoration of the massacre took mainly a ceremonial and performative dimension, rather than a textual one (Robinson 2003: 397–8).
14. Including Mansur's own stance on the question of modernisation, and the way it differs since his earlier novel, *Wa-Baqiyat Samira*, discussed above.
15. For more on this, see: Falah 1991; Home 2003.

2

POSTMODERNISATIONS, 1967–1987

In Chapter 1, I outlined the main characteristics of Palestinian modernisation discourse in Israel during the first two decades after 1948. The modernisation of Palestinian citizens in Israel encompassed interrelated social, technological, economic and political components. As manifested in novels, Palestinian proponents of modernisation aimed both to reform their society and to promote peaceful coexistence of Palestinians with Jewish-Israelis. To achieve this goal, Palestinian modernists downplayed the political context of animosity and the inherent incompatibility of Palestinians and Zionism. In other words, because Palestinian modernisation in Israel was promoted by, or at least derived from and operated within, Zionist discourse (which is both modernist and exclusivist nationalist), Palestinian denationalisation and erasure were inherent to Palestinian modernisation. Another point that was highlighted in the preceding chapter relates to suppressing voices of criticism of modernisation during the first period (1948–67). Only in *In a New Light* by Atallah Mansour is modernisation within a Zionist context criticised. In this chapter, analysing Palestinian novels published between 1967 and 1987, we will see that such a tendency will continue. Palestinian novels in this period can be described as 'postmodern', since they provide a response and reassessment of Palestinian modernisation in Israel.

My use of the term 'postmodernisation' in this chapter aims to outline the reaction, or the response, of Palestinian citizens in Israel towards their modernisation in Israel, as described in Chapter 1. Such a formulation suggests that there is a discursive reaction (postmodernisation discourse) to an earlier process (modernisation). This is true to a certain extent, especially if we take postmodernisation to be a stage in the evolution of modernisation. This relationship will become clearer in the following general discussion on these terms.

Academic literature on modernism and postmodernism depicts the relationship between these two in terms of 'continuity and change'. Andreas Huyssen summarises the debate over the nature of postmodernism:

> In much of the postmodernism debate, a very conventional thought pattern has asserted itself. Either it is said that postmodernism is continuous with modernism, in which case the whole debate opposing the two is specious; or, it is claimed that there is a radical rupture, a break with modernism, which is then evaluated in either positive or negative terms. But the question of historical continuity or discontinuity simply cannot be adequately discussed in terms of such an either-or dichotomy. [...] Modernism as that from which postmodernism is breaking away remains inscribed into the very word with which we describe our distance from modernism. (Huyssen 1984: 9–10)

This characterisation of postmodernism clarifies my use of postmodernism to describe Palestinian discourse in novels in this period: aiming to present reactions, or responses, to modernisation. Some Palestinian novels lead a more critical discourse, reflecting more of a 'rupture' rather than a 'continuation', as will be elaborated below. In addition to this, Palestinian postmodern discourse has two intertwined dimensions: the first relates to the response to modernisation, while the second relates to the response to Zionism. Responses to modernisation and Zionism vary between the nineteen novels studied for this chapter (see Table 2.1 at the end of this chapter for the complete list of novels). It is possible to identify two main groups of novels bearing similar responses to modernisation and Zionism. The division between the two groups relates to common characteristics in each group regarding their response to both modernisation and Zionism. With respect to the response to modernisation, the two groups divide along the thematic lines drawn by German sociologist Max Weber.

Weber identified rationalisation and differentiation to be the two major themes in Western modernisation. According to American sociologist Edward Tiryakian, these two Weberian themes are 'commonly accepted by scholars of different ideological leanings as being the master processes of [modernism]' (Tiryakian 1992a: 79–80). Rationalisation refers to the advancement of rational reasoning, science and technology over emotions or traditional beliefs (Tiryakian 1992b; Dallmayr 1992; Holub 2001). Differentiation refers to the process where

> [i]nstitutions gradually become more specialised. Familial control over social organisation decreases. Political processes become less directed by the obligations and rewards of patriarchy, and the division of labour is organised more according to economic criteria than by reference simply to age and sex. (Alexander 1992: 179)

Relatively speaking, the first group of novels reflects a greater focus on issues relating to differentiation (although responses are not 'uniform', reflecting a diversity of approaches), while the second group shows greater attention in response to Palestinian 'rationalisation'. As will become evident, responses to differentiation and rationalisation vary in both content and style.

With regard to responses to Zionism, a uniform response to Zionism constitutes the common denominator among novels in the first group. Here novels take the erasure of Palestinians to be the defining characteristic of Palestinian life in Israel, and their response to it is characterised by rejection and counter-erasure (which means, erasing the Other back). The second group, discussed in the latter section, presents Palestinian attempts to adjust to life in Israel, focusing on political aspects of the relationship between Palestinians, Jewish-Israelis and Israel as a state. In the second group, there is direct engagement with political issues and a portrayal of transformations in political orientations among Palestinians.

Counteraction Novels

This section deals with Palestinian responses to two aspects of life in Israel. The first response relates to the process of modernisation. The second response relates to Zionism and the erasure of Palestinians in Israel. I will address the two responses through analysing two illustrative novels: *Al-Juththa al-Majhula* (*The Anonymous Corpse*, 1973), by Kamal Salama, and *Hubb ʿAbir al-Qarrat* (*Intercontinental Love*, 1977), by Abd al-Rahman Hijazi.

Al-Juththa al-Majhula is the story of Muhammad, a young Palestinian citizen in Israel whose life is transformed as a result of modernisation. The life of Muhammad is portrayed in two parts. The first part, which I will call 'pre-modern', depicts Muhammad positively: he is loved and appreciated by his family and friends, because of the good manners and high moral and religious values that he represents (he is named after the Prophet after all). As a result of a dispute with his father, and in a bid to assert his individualism, Muhammad decides to leave the family home. He moves to Ramat-Gan, a Jewish-Israeli city near Tel-Aviv. The life of Muhammad in Ramat-Gan, constituting the second part of the plot, is portrayed to be the complete opposite of the first part. Here Muhammad rids himself of the social and religious values he used to be associated with. He becomes an alcoholic, a drug addict, a pimp and a gambler. At the end of the novel Muhammad dies lonely on a beach in Tel-Aviv.

This short synopsis lays the foundation for the discussion on the transformation in the life of Muhammad from two perspectives. First, it portrays the process of modernisation and its effects on Palestinian society in Israel: *Al-Juththa al-Majhula*, as well as other counteraction novels, adheres to a binary narrative structure, aiming to compare and contrast pre-modern and modern lifestyles. The structure of the narrative in counteraction novels contains the following characteristics:[1] (1) structure: the plot is built from two parts; (2) spaces: the two parts of the plot take place in different spaces; (3) identity of the spaces: one space would be Jewish-Israeli, the other non-Jewish-Israeli; (4) characterisation of the spaces: the non-Jewish-Israeli space is portrayed positively (or the plot tells a positive story), while the Jewish-Israeli space is portrayed negatively (or the plot tells a negative story).

The spatial association in this characterisation of the structure relates to the second dimension of novels in this period: the depiction of the relationship between Palestinians and Jewish-Israelis in the novels and the Palestinian response to erasure in Israel. I have chosen to start with discussing the Palestinian response to modernisation, more specifically differentiation, because the response to modernisation is part of the plot and part of the discourse of the novel, while the response to Zionism is implicit, as will become clear later in the section. The analysis of the Palestinian response to differentiation will be on three interrelated levels: individual differentiation (individualisation), social differentiation and religious differentiation.

The first part of the plot in *Al-Juththa al-Majhula* aims to draw a 'pure' image of the 'pre-modern' stage in the life of Muhammad. In the following excerpt, Muhammad approaches his father to tell him about a trip to Tiberias that he plans with his friends:

> Jalasa muḥammad baʿd an radd a-taḥiyya ʿalā abīhi, rafaʿa raʾsahu ḥaythu alqā nazra sarīʿa ʿalā abīhi, wa-ʿāda li-yuwaṭiʾ raʾsahu wa-kāna min ʿādatihi ʿindamā yawaddu shayʾan min abīhi an yataradd fī-l-bidāya, rafaʿa raʾsahu li-yatakallam fa-talaʿtham wa-rajiʿa li-yuhamliqa fī-l-arḍ ... Ammā abūhu fa-qad fahimahu ... Fahim annahu biḥāja ilā shayʾ mā ... Innahu yawaddu an yatakallam annahu biḥāja ilā nuqūd wa-ammā abūhu fa-nazara ilayhi wa-qāl:
>
> – Aturīdu shayʾan yā bunayy?
>
> – Lā, lā ... salāmatak yā abī
>
> – Atakhjal minnī yā muḥammad?
>
> – Lā wa-lākin aradtu an ukhbiraka ...
>
> Wa-baʿda an balaʿa rīqahu tābaʿa ḥadīthahu qāʾilan:
>
> – Laqad ittafaqtu maʿaṣdiqāʾī li-naqūm bi-riḥla ilā ṭabariyya atuwāfiqanīʿala dhalik?
>
> – Limā lā ... aturīdu nuqūdan?
>
> – Lā, ladayya kifāya min-l-nuqūd.
>
> – *Allāh maʿak yā bunayy*. (p. 17)
>
> Muhammad sat down after replying to his father's greeting, raised his head and sneaked a look at his father, then looked back down. He was used, whenever he needed something from his father, to hesitating at first. He raised his head to speak, but he stuttered and turned to look at the floor again ... but his father understood him ... he [the father] realised that he [Muhammad] needed something ... that he wanted to talk, that he needed money, so his father looked at him and said:

– Do you need anything, son?

– No, no … [I wish you] good health, father.

– Are you shy of me Muhammad?

– No, but I wanted to tell you …

and after gulping back he continued:

– I agreed with my friends to go on a trip to Tiberias, do you agree with me?

– Why not … do you need money?

– No, I have enough money.

– May God be with you, son. (p. 17)

The trip to Tiberias constitutes a reference point for comparison between the two parts of the plot. In the above excerpt, with the various events related to it, Muhammad is portrayed to be a humble son who respects his father. Respect for parents (father in this particular example) is considered a positive personality attribute in this novel. Presenting respect for parents in a positive light in this novel does not stem from Arab values and culture alone; it aims to emphasise the religious roots for the positive portrayal of the character of Muhammad. The relationship between the cultural and religious aspects of the behaviour of Muhammad are closely intertwined: respect for parents, or 'filial piety' (*birr al-wālidayn*), according to the British theologist John Chamberlayne,

> plays an important part in Muslim family relationships. In fact, it is closely linked with true worship. 'Thy Lord hath decreed that ye shall not serve any but Him. And with parents (exercise) kindness, whether one or both of them attain old age with thee' (XVII, 24). They should not be treated with impatience or reproof but 'bear thyself humbly towards them out of compassion, and say: "My Lord, have mercy upon them as they brought me up when young."'(Chamberlayne 1968: 136)

In light of this, the above excerpt from *Al-Juththa al-Majhula* aims to portray Muhammad as a humble and pious son. The religious dimension of Muhammad's behaviour is indicated by the narrator elsewhere, establishing that Muhammad believes that (*riḍā allāh min riḍā al-wālidayn*, p. 22) 'God's satisfaction derives from the satisfaction of the parents'. To use this well-known concept in Arab and Muslim culture, Muhammad 'performs' piety in a number of places in the excerpt: Muhammad sits down only after replying to the greetings of his father (*radda al-taḥiyya*); he does not have direct eye contact with his father (having a quick glance (*naẓra sarīʿa*) towards him), then continuing to stare at the floor (*yuḥamliq fī al-arḍ*); when the father asks Muhammad if he wants something, Muhammad replies by wishing his father good health (*salāmtak yā abī*). These 'performative acts' are cultural symbols of respect and subordination, aiming to express the piety of Muhammad. Cultural symbols are defined as 'objects, acts, concepts, or linguistic formations that stand *ambiguously* for a multiplicity of disparate meanings, evoke sentiments and emotions, and impel men to action' (Abner Cohen quoted in Turner 1975: 145; italics in original). The 'meaning' of sitting only after replying to greeting, not maintaining eye contact, or wishing 'good health' for somebody is inscribed in Arab culture. The 'acts', or code of conduct, of Muhammad stand for respect and subordination to his father.

Whereas the performance of filial piety by Muhammad is understood by his father (*fahimahu*), the ambiguity that Cohen refers to above relates to 'the manipulability of symbols in social action' (Turner 1975: 146), which, in turn, is directly related to the transformation in Palestinian values as a result of modernisation. The above excerpt from *Al-Juththa al-Majhula* reflects the patriarchal structure of the pre-modern Palestinian (Arab) family. Patriarchy, according to the Lebanese anthropologist Suad Joseph, is 'the prioritising of the rights of males and elders (including elder women) and the justification of those rights within kinship values which are usually supported by religion' (Joseph 1996: 14). We have seen already that the behaviour of Muhammad – his performance – with his father both relates to religious values and maintains a hierarchical system of authority and subordination – that of a patriarchal family. In a patriarchal family, according to Syrian sociologist Halim Barakat, 'a father-figure rules over others, monopolising authority, expecting strict obedience, and showing little tolerance of dissent' (H. I. Barakat 1993: 23). The above dialogue between Muhammad and his father has a number of examples that manifest the obedience that Muhammad bears out of respect and fear in his behaviour with his father: not maintaining direct eye contact; as well as hesitating (*taraddad*); stuttering (*talaʿtham*); and gulping back in fear (*bala ʿa rīqahu*, which literally means 'swallowed his saliva'). Whereas not maintaining eye contact could be interpreted both as 'performance' and as a sign of fear, the other bodily responses are not cultural symbols, but signs of fear or anxiety. On the face of it, there seems to be a contradiction between the performance of respect and 'actual' fear of the father. However, the performance of respect can be related to respect borne out of fear. Performance does not mean 'faking of behaviour'.

Despite the structure of the narrative in *Al-Juththa al-Majhula*, which aims to contrast two opposing world views, Palestinian postmodern novels derive from within the process of modernisation, registering transformations already taking place in Palestinian society. In an attempt to portray Muhammad in a positive light, some aspects of the modernisation process are concealed. Because of this, the above portrayal of the attitude of Muhammad when in the company of his father would seem to be misleading, primarily since it conceals the fact that Muhammad is the main breadwinner in his family. This fact is related to the proletarianisation of Palestinians in Israel.

As a result of massive land confiscation since 1948, agriculture ceased to be the main economy for Palestinians in Israel, leading to the proletarianisation of the Palestinian workforce in Israel (Rinnawi 2003: 21). Palestinian lawyer and sociologist Sabri Jiryis identifies a link between the economic and cultural transformations in Palestinian society. According to Jiryis, Palestinian individuals in Israel in the period under consideration were

> more economically independent and more self-reliant. Old values of the kind that usually predominate in agricultural village communities gradually disappeared and new values took their place, similar to those that prevail in working class and in industrial or industrialising societies. (Jiryis 1979: 50)

Like Jiryis, Palestinian thinker Hisham Sharabi holds the 'economic consideration' to be predominant in the 'erosion of traditional vertical relations' in Arab societies (Sharabi 1988: 31). Muhammad, being the main breadwinner in his family, reflects this erosion. Whereas the father in traditional society 'supports his power by control over land, resources, and income generation' (Joseph 1996: 14–15), financial independence wholly transforms the traditional 'balance of power' between Muhammad and his father.

The disturbance in the balance of power between father and son marks the beginnings of the transformation in Palestinian family structure, or the individual differentiation that took place in Palestinian society in Israel in this period. The gradual shifting in the 'balance of power' between father and son is evident in a number of places in the earlier dialogue. For example, Muhammad wants merely to inform (*aradtu an ukhbiraka*) his father about the trip to Tiberias, rather than asking for his permission to go, as the whole dialogue implies. Asking for permission is also implied in Muhammad asking whether his father 'agrees' (*atuwāfiqanī*). However, *atuwāfiqanī* does not, in fact, mean 'do you allow me?', but 'do you agree with me?'. Moreover, Muhammad had already decided to go with his friends (*ittafaqtu maʿ aṣdiqāʾī*). The fact that the trip was already decided leaves the father little choice but to say 'why not?' (*lima lā?*).

The interjections by Muhammad, or his expressions of independence, manifest the manipulability of social symbols, mentioned by Turner earlier, to mark a gradual shift in values reflected in the novel. Turner regards symbolic systems as 'the result of concrete interests and interacting wills rather than existing "out there" in a world of beliefs, norms, and values' (Turner 1975: 147). This dynamic depiction of symbolic systems elaborates the piecemeal transformation in the attitude of Muhammad. In the above excerpt, Muhammad aims to keep a balance between his interests and will to independence vis-à-vis the considerations, norms and values of the patriarchal authority of his father.

In light of this interplay of interests between Muhammad and his father, the latter asking whether the former has money for the trip could be interpreted in two ways: the first is that he wanted to make sure Muhammad has enough money for the trip, or that Muhammad should not be too shy to ask for money. The second interpretation relates to the father aiming to implicitly assert his authority, being the person in the family who possesses and controls the family finances. Muhammad keeping a portion of his salary for himself allows him financial independence from his father, taking away from him another aspect of his authority, and leaving him with little 'real' influence on the decision to go to Tiberias. The father is left only to 'give his blessing' (*allāh maʿak yā bunayy*). In other words, the financial independence of Muhammad from his father, his financial differentiation, marks his individualisation. Individualisation, according to Dutch sociologist Loek

Halman, 'denotes a process in which traditional meaning systems and values diminish in importance in favour of personal considerations and decisions concerning values, norms and behaviours' (Halman 1996: 198). In the following I will elaborate on the individualisation of Muhammad further, aiming to understand the implications of this process on Palestinian identity in Israel.

The above reading of the excerpt from *Al-Juththa al-Majhula* may seem arbitrary at first. However, it is important to remember that the first part of the plot aims to present a 'pure' narrative. Since the depiction of the pre-modern stems from the experience of modernisation, the above interpretation of the dialogue between Muhammad and his father makes (more) sense when seen from the 'comparative' binary narrative of the plot, as will be elaborated below.

One day, Muhammad is confronted by his father, who discovers that he smokes cigarettes. The father angrily reproaches Muhammad and warns him to quit this habit at once. The dispute with the father marks the turning point, or dividing line, between the first and second parts of the plot. In terms of understanding the Palestinian response to modernisation in Israel (the transformation in balance of power between father and son, as well as the transformation in values alluded to above), the crisis between Muhammad and his father over smoking – leading to the departure of the former from the family home – does not lie in the morality or immorality of the habit, but rather in the issues of patriarchal and social-communal authority. The following excerpt presents the turning point in the novel, as Muhammad decides to leave his family home:

> *Qarrara [muḥammad] an yakhruj, an yatruk baytahu, an yahjur qaryatahu, lam yastaṭiʿ intiẓāṛ al-kalima al-qāsiya min fam abīhi: kalimat ukhruj min hunā … Ukhruj min baytī … Arāda al-khurūj liwaḥdihi, an yaṭrud nafsahu bi-nafsihi, lam yastaṭiʿ jarḥ karāmatuh ḥattā wa-law kānat al-marra al-ūlā fī ḥayātih. Sa-yuḥawil raghm ḥubbih li-baladih, li-ahlih, li-ikhwatih wa-li-aṣdiqaʾih li-ʿamalih, wa-li-jamīʿ ahālī masqat raʾsih. Naʿam sa-yakhruj, qarra nihāʾiyyan an yatruk masqat raʾsih an yatruk baldatih li-abīh wa-li-abī ʿādil li-ummihi wa-li-umm sulaymān, li-fulān wa-ʿallān min al-wāshīn wa-l-ḥussād, wa li-dhawī al-wajhayn min al-nās.* (p. 33)

> He [Muhammad] decided to depart, to leave his home, to abandon his village; he could not wait for the harsh word from his father: get out of here … get out of my house …
>
> He wanted to leave by himself, to expel himself by himself; he could not bear being humiliated even if it was the first time in his life. He would try, despite his love for his village, his parents, his siblings and his friends at work, and everybody in his birthplace. Yes, he would get out; he decided to leave his birthplace and his village to his father, Abu Adil, his mother, Umm Sulayman, various snitchers and enviers, and those hypocritical people. (p. 33)

This excerpt marks the individualisation of Muhammad from a number of aspects. The first sign of his individualisation is evident in the opening word in the above excerpt: *qarrara* – he decided. Muhammad makes the decision to permanently leave home, which contrasts with him asking for permission from his father to go on a trip with his friends in the preceding excerpt. The turning point in the world view of Muhammad is evident in the fact that this is the first time (*al-marra al-ūlā*) that he perceives the patriarchy and authority of his father as insulting or humiliating (*jarḥ karāmatahu*).

Muhammad's experimentation (*sa-yuḥāwil*) with individualism marks the transformation in Palestinian society that this novel aims to critically address. Muhammad voices criticism of traditional, social and familial norms in a way that is reminiscent of modernisation novels we discussed in the preceding chapter. Such an orientation towards, or experimentation with, modernist values is invoked in this novel to be reassessed and rethought. For modernising Muhammad, to live on his own relates to his unwillingness to tolerate the humiliating authority of his father any longer. From a modernist point of view, the individualisation of Muhammad relates to breaking down the hierarchical structure of the traditional Palestinian family, aspiring to create, in the words of Hisham Sharabi, democratic relations inside the family. Sharabi explains that '[i]f the essential relation of patriarchy is subordination, that of the nuclear family is equality. Economic independence is the basis of the nuclear family's democracy, the condition for the overthrow of patriarchal tyranny' (Sharabi 1988: 31–2). Muhammad can no longer take the tyrannical humiliation of a patriarchal lifestyle, or traditional Palestinian norms. He associates this lifestyle with fear and intimidation, as portrayed in the preceding excerpt from the novel.

In contrast to fear of his father, in the above excerpt, Muhammad decides to expel himself (*yaṭrud nafsahu bi-nafsihi*). This decision marks his unwillingness to quit smoking, thereby asserting his own interests and will, and thus his individualism. In other words, by expelling himself, Muhammad not only recognises that his father will not tolerate such disobedience, but also appropriates for himself the authority of his father to expel.

The individualisation of Muhammad is evident in the above excerpt also in the choice of verbs to describe his departure from home. Muhammad decides to depart from home (*yakhruj*), used five times in the excerpt, and to leave (*yatruk*), used three times. The way these two words are employed in the text sheds light on the transformation that Muhammad undergoes. The root (*kh-r-j*) literally means 'exiting'. It conveys leaving from enclosure to openness, portraying the freeing of Muhammad from the confines of his family and village. *Yatruk*, like *yakhjur*, conveys desertion and abandonment – of leaving things behind. The final sentence starts with Muhammad affirming (*naʿam sa-yakhruj*) his decision to 'exit' (*qarrara nihāʾiyyan*) – conveying the fact that he is freeing himself. The rest of the sentence conveys what Muhammad is wilfully leaving behind him (*yatruk*) – the traditional patriarchal village lifestyle, embodied in his father and the rest of the people that share his beliefs, whom he lists. This leads to differentiation on the social level of Palestinian society as reflected in the above excerpt, and in the novel as a whole.

Differentiation overturns not only the relationship between Muhammad and his father, but also with his entire society. In modern societies,

> the individual has become free and independent upon the traditional, social and religious institutions. The prescriptions by these institutions are no longer accepted and taken for granted. [. . .] Instead, the individual wants to decide for himself what is good and bad, what is beautiful and ugly, what is right and wrong. (Halman 1996: 196)

Breaking away from traditional and social institutions is indicated already in the opening sentence in the above excerpt: Muhammad not only decides to leave home; he also decides to abandon (*yakhjur*) his village. The village here encompasses all the traditional institutions that can suppress individualism. In the closing sentence of the excerpt, listing all the people who interfere in his life, Muhammad wants to free himself from the social authority of his father, mother, Abu Adil, Umm Sulayman and the rest (*fulān wa-ʿallān*) of the hypocritical people (*dhawī al-wajhayn*) in the village. The only thing that we know about Abu Adil and Umm Sulayman is that they 'reported' seeing Muhammad smoking, to his father.

The social differentiation in this novel is evident in the portrayal of these individuals from the village, the 'agents' of traditional Palestinian lifestyle. Abu Adil, Umm Sulayman and the rest are depicted to be hypocritical (*dhawī al-wajhayn*). The reason that Muhammad thinks they are hypocritical stems from the transformation in his perception of society. Whereas in the traditional lifestyle, an intervention in the individual's personal affairs could be a sign of caring, in the modern world such an intervention means limiting of freedom of choice and action. For Muhammad, the people whom he knows from the village are 'two-faced' because even though they are friendly with him, they also harm him by informing about his behaviour to his parents.

Individualisation for Muhammad means that 'self-realisation, individual development and personal happiness have become the main wellsprings of individual actions. Individual autonomy and self-fulfilment are given priority, partly at the cost of duties and commitments traditionally connected to family, the church and community life' (Halman 1996: 197). Church in Western societies, about which Halman is writing, refers here to the religious institutions which individuals break away from. The reference to religious institutions and duties in the context of our discussion on *Al-Juththa al-Majhula* refers to the Muslim background of Muhammad. Muhammad rebels against the authority of all those who can interfere in the life of an individual. He no longer tolerates interference in his private matters. Despite his love (*raghma ḥubbihi*) for his village and society, Muhammad values his freedom more. He wants to decide for himself, 'what is right and wrong'.

In the discussion below, we will see the depiction of the results of the experimentation of Muhammad with individualism. In the following excerpt, the narrator summarises the lifestyle he leads in Ramat-Gan:

> *Asbaḥat layālihi kullahā ḥamrāʾ, layal anārathā shumūʿ al-farah wa-lākin ayy nawʿ min-l-faraḥ? Al-faraḥ al-iṣṭināʿī, dhālika al-faraḥ al-ladhī taṣnaʿahu al-khamra, al-faraḥ al-ladhī yakūn aḥyānan taraḥan. Al-layālī allatī qad ansathu qaryatah … nasiya abāhu … ummahu … ikhwatuhu. Nasiya jamīʿ asdiqāʾih, saʿīd, ʿali, wa-maḥmūd. Nasiya al-layālī al-barīʾa al-latī sahirahā maʿ asdiqāʾih, al-riḥlāt al-mumtiʿa allatī qāmū bihā. Nasiya ṭabariyyā, lam yaʿud yatadhakkar sāʾiqī al-sayyārāt: abū salīm. Taʿarrafa ʿalā ahlin ākharīn, ʿalā asdiqāʾ judud, ʿalā bayt ākhar, ʿalā bīʾa mukhtalifa, bīʾat al-kīf. Wa-hākadhā maḍat ʿiddat shuhūr ʿalā khurūjih min-l-bayt. Lan yadhkur aḥad, lan yashtāq li-aḥad min abnāʾ qaryatih. Asbaḥ insān ḥurr, qabaḍa ʿalā al-ḥurriyya bi-yadayhi, walakin, hal istaʿmalahā ʿalā ḥaqīqatahā? Hal al-ḥurriyya an tasnaʿ kull shayʾ tawwad? an takhmar? an-takhdar? Taṣnaʿ mā bi-bālik? rubbamā aḍarraka? rubbamā ḍarart ghayraka*. (pp. 52–3)
>
> His nights had become all red and were lit by the candles of happiness, but which kind of happiness?
>
> Artificial happiness, that happiness that is made by alcohol, happiness that can sometimes be grief. The nights that had made him forget his village … he forgot his father … mother … his siblings. He had forgotten all his friends, Saʿid, Ali and Mahmud. He forgot the innocent nights that he spent with his friends, the fun trips that he went on. He forgot Tiberias, he no longer remembered the car driver: Abu Salim. He met a new family, new friends, a new home, a different environment, the environment of fun.
>
> A few months had passed since his departure from home. He did not remember anybody, did not miss anybody from his village. He had become a free person. He clutched freedom in his hands, but did he use it correctly?
>
> Does freedom mean you can do what you like? Get drunk? Get drugged? Do what you like? Maybe it harmed you? Maybe you harmed others. (pp. 52–3)

In analysing this excerpt, we need to distinguish between the didactic tone of the narrator and what the excerpt reflects regarding Palestinian modernisation. I have made a similar distinction earlier, when referring to the 'intended' depiction of Muhammad in the first part of the plot as a pious person and the reflections of proletarianisation in Palestinian society. The didactic, and critical, tone of the narrator is evident in the final sentence in the excerpt, where he casts doubt on the way Muhammad interprets or uses individualism as being: 'the ideal of individual freedom to act as one desires, and the freedom to decide where one wants to live, to do as one likes, to believe what one wants, and so on' (Halman 1996: 198). The narrator in *Al-Juththa al-Majhula* questions whether the freedom (*al-ḥurriya*) of individualism should really mean 'to do as one likes' (*an taṣnaʿ kull shayʾ tawwad*), referring to the way Muhammad utilised his freedom (drinking (*an takhmar*), abuse of drugs (*an takhdar*)). The roots of this criticism lie in the collective consequences of individualism. Thus, although the final part of the excerpt is constructed from a series of questions that relate to individual freedoms, it ends with a suggestive statement about damaging others (*rubbamā ḍararta ghayraka*).

The reference to damaging others relates not only to differentiation of Palestinians in Israel on the social level, but more crucially it foregrounds the disintegration of Palestinian society as a result of this process. In other words, the above excerpt, *Al-Juththa al-Majhula*, as well as the other novels in this group, reflect a state of 'anomie' of Palestinian society in Israel as a result of its modernisation. First mooted by Emile Durkheim, anomie can be defined as:

> a society's decreasing capacity for individual integration [...] and regulations [...] because of macro-social change. This happens if traditional norms vanish in the course of social change but are not (fully) replaced by new ones. (Graeff and Mehlkop 2007: 522)

The 'macro-social change' that Graeff and Mehlkop refer to is the process of modernisation (Besnard 1988; Huschka and Mau 2006). The vanishing traditional norms are manifested in the excerpt in the multiple expressions of 'forgetting': firstly, on the individual level, Muhammad forgot (*nasiya*) his family. The implied consequence of forgetting his family is loss of identity. This is so because in traditional Arab society, 'kinship is the center of [...] society. It sustains a person's sense of self and identity, and shapes their position in society' (Joseph 1996: 15). Secondly, on the social level, in Ramat-Gan, Muhammad forgets not only his parents, but also his friends and the innocent nights (*al-layālī al-barīʾa*) they spent together. Muhammad no longer remembers (*lam ya'ud yatadhakkar*) the drivers of the cars (who drove him and his friends to Tiberias; more on this below); he will not remember (*lan yadhkur*) or miss (*lan yashtāq*) anybody in his village.

The loss of connection with friends, and forgetting the village, is very important to understanding Palestinian anomie in Israel. While discussing *Al-Qadiyya Raqam 13* (*Legal Case Number 13*, 1975), by Majid Hsaysi and Farhat Farhat, Palestinian critic Nabih al-Qasim points to the purpose of writing the novel:

> The authors aimed to portray a recurring reality (*wāqi' yatakarrar*), a reality which has our youth as its victims (*yarūḥ ḍaḥiyyatah al-kathīrūn min shabābanā*) who become prey to the many temptations of the city (*yaqa'ūn farīsa li-ighrā'āt al-madīna al-kathīra*). What happened to the protagonist [of *Al-Qadiyya Raqam 13*] is not strange (*gharīb*): how many young persons left their parents (*ahlahu*) and migrated to the city seeking education or work, but were crushed (*saḥaqathu*) by the city and its atmosphere (*ajwā'ihā*), losing their connections with their families and villages (*wa-faqada rawābiṭahu bi-ahlihi wa-baldatihi*). (al-Qasim 1979: 122–3)

This excerpt from al-Qasim is important from two points of view. First, the excerpt provides a brief synopsis of *Al-Qadiyya Raqam 13*, highlighting the main 'event', or phenomenon, in it: the protagonist, Ramzi, moves from his village to study in Haifa. As a result of a series of events, over which Ramzi is portrayed to have no control, he becomes a violent criminal, murdering three characters. The second point in the above excerpt refers to the language that al-Qasim employs to explain the purpose of publishing the novel: describing the deterioration of Ramzi to a state of anomie.

Al-Qasim depicts Palestinians such as Ramzi, and Muhammad from *Al-Juththa al-Majhula*, to be victims and prey, unable to cope with the temptations of the city. Al-Qasim points out that *Al-Qadiyya Raqam 13* reflects a recurring reality for Palestinians in Israel. Furthermore, the explanation that al-Qasim provides for Palestinian anomie in Israel relates to the fact that Palestinians not only lose connections with their families; they lose connections with their villages as well.

The social regulation of village life can be seen in the following excerpt from *Al-Juththa al-Majhula*. The narrator reminds us of an incident that took place during Muhammad's trip to Tiberias prior to his departure from home. While Muhammad and his friends are at Lake Tiberias, one of the friends volunteers to buy food and drinks for everybody. Replying to this offer, Muhammad asks his friend to buy him a bottle of beer:

> Fa-ḍaḥik al-jamīʿ ʿalā kalimat bīra, liʾanna muḥammad lan yashrab al-bīra, lā yaʿrifu li-l-khamra ṭaʿman, lam yadhuqhā fī ḥayātih, samiʿa bihā faqaṭ. (p. 26)
>
> Everybody laughed on [hearing] the word beer, because Muhammad would not drink beer, does not know the taste of alcohol, and has not tasted it in his life, only heard of it. (p. 26)

In addition to elaborating on social differentiation, this excerpt will lead to a discussion on the religious differentiation of Palestinians in Israel in this period. In line with the portrayal of Muhammad in the first part of the plot as a humble and pious person, in this instance being a good Muslim, Muhammad does not drink alcohol. This is indicated above by the use of three negative particles: Muhammad will not (*lan*) drink beer, he does not know (*lā*) the taste of alcohol and he never (*lam*) tasted it in his life. Muhammad has only heard of alcohol.

The relationship between the social and religious differentiation in this novel is very strong. For example, it is important to note that the narrator/author uses 'everybody' (*al-jamīʿ*) in every reference to the beer scene (in the two excerpts above and in the endnote).[2] The collective laughter at the request for beer implies conformity. In contrast, being by himself in Ramat-Gan (*liwaḥdahu*, see preceding excerpt), Muhammad is free from any collective social obligations – or, safety and security. 'From an individualistic perspective, anomie implies that people develop unlimited desires because their aspirations are no longer limited by groups or channelled by collective aims' (Graeff and Mehlkop 2007: 523). The happy life and the artificial happiness (*al-faraḥ al-iṣṭināʿī*) that the narrator associates with modernisation can lead to grief (*taraḥ*), or anomie; this is a clear indication of the fate that awaits Muhammad.

The time that Muhammad spent with his friends in Tiberias was an innocent time (*barīʾ*), contrasting with the sinful nights he spends in the new environment in Ramat-Gan. According to Mukherjee, anomie is 'a moral category characterised by impiety, sacrilege, irreligion and immorality. In short, it can be posed as one of the most powerful frames for violence, be it in the form of suicide or crime' (Mukherjee 2006: 10). I will deal with the reference to violence in this quotation later in the section. The turn that Muhammad took away from religion is further implied in the preceding excerpt in the use of *qabaḍa ʿalā al-ḥuriyya biyadayhi*. This formulation, in reference to Muhammad clinging to his freedom, reminds us of a hadith that says:

> Ya'tī ʿalā-l-nās zamānun al-ṣābir fīhim ʿalā dīnihi ka-l-qābiḍ ʿalā-l-jamr.
>
> A time will come on the people when the patient among them on his religion will be like one who holds live coal (in his hand).

This hadith contains a prophecy, according to which there will be times when evil will prevail over good, thus life for believers will be more difficult, and maintaining religious beliefs will be as hard as holding live ambers in the palm of one's hand. The narrator thus implies that Muhammad had failed to keep his faith in the face of the temptations of modernisation. The failure of Muhammad, from the point of view of the novel, to keep his religious beliefs, is related to the loosening of social bonds and values: Muhammad is no longer surrounded by the 'safety net' of his friends from the village and the rest of his community.

In light of its religious dimensions, *Al-Juththa al-Majhula* possibly marks the first signs or indications of an 'Islamisation' in Palestinian society in Israel. Although it is difficult to generalise regarding the religious dimension of one novel, this novel seems to provide an indication of one possible response to modernisation: one that resorts to religion (a Muslim response, in the case of this novel). In this regard, it is noteworthy that the Islamic Movement in Israel was established in 1972, one year prior to publishing *Al-Juththa al-Majhula*. The reason for such a deduction is related to the history of the rise of Islamic movements in the Arab world. The Islamic awakening (*ṣaḥwa*) is primarily associated with the Arab defeat in the 1967 war. Historian Yvonne Haddad outlines the various ideological reactions and explanations to the Arab defeat. According to Haddad,

> The Islamists [...] argued that the war was punishment for misplaced trust in the promise of alien ideologies that had been fostered as a means of mobilising for development. The defeat was devastating because the margin of deviance from the faith was great. (Haddad 1992: 267)

In other words, Islamists in the Arab world associated the defeat in the war with the modernisation of Arab societies.

Modernisation being a factor in an Islamic revival in the Middle East may lead to similar deductions on the rise of Islamic discourse in Israel in the early 1970s. However, this point requires further investigation. It is interesting to note that this is so because in the academic literature on the rise of the Islamic Movement in Israel there is little attention, as far as I am aware, to the issues of modernisation, and its implications on the rise of Islamic thought and movements. Generally speaking, the 'historical background' of the establishment of the movement in Israel is usually described as follows:

> Many developments contributed to the emergence of the Islamic Movement in Israel. The more significant among them included the June 1967 war and Israel's occupation of the West Bank and Gaza Strip. This development reconnected the Palestinians in Israel with their people in the newly Occupied Territories, and had two main implications. First, teachers and preachers from the West Bank began not only to visit Palestinian villages and cities in Israel, but also to spread their religious ideology. Second, young Palestinians from Israel began to study at the religious institutions in the West Bank. (Aburaiya 2004: 442)

Aburaiya points to the importance of the 1967 war. The emphasis is put on the occupation of the West Bank and Gaza Strip as leading to a renewed contact of Palestinians in Israel with Palestinians in those territories, allowing, thus, the opportunity for Islamic education there. Aburaiya, however, does not explain why the war led Palestinians to become more interested in Islam.

Not all novels in this group express a religious response to modernisation. In the following, I will discuss a novel that presents an alternative, secular response. *Hubb ʿAbir al-Qarrat* tells the story of Samya, who is a law student at university. She meets Shadi at a birthday party and they soon fall in love. Her father is a religious, conservative and traditional man, and he wants her to marry her cousin. Samya secretly continues her relationship with Shadi and does all she can to maintain it. After she finishes her university degree, Samya manages to persuade her father to allow her to travel abroad (to Miami) to continue her studies. She lives there happily with Shadi and soon they marry and have very successful careers. As a result of her marriage to Shadi, Samya loses connection with her parents, but she maintains a secret line of communication with her younger brother, Yusif. At one point, she rejects an offer of promotion at work and decides to leave everything and return home to deal with family disputes. After her return, she starts to practise law. One day, a woman (her mother) comes to see Samya in her office for a consultation. The mother does not recognise Samya, and wants her help in solving a family dispute. Samya uses the court as a stage to criticise her family and to explain her position. When Samya finally reveals her identity to everybody in the courtroom, her father cannot take the shock: he collapses and dies.

The structure of the narrative in *Hubb ʿAbir al-Qarrat* is similar to the model presented earlier: the plot is built around two parts. The two parts take place in two different spaces. The first part is about life in Israel (which is implied); the second part is about life in the USA (which is described in detail). The section of the plot that takes place in Israel tells a negative story (the struggle Samya carries against her father, who wants to force her to marry her cousin; her secret relationship with Shadi), while the section of the plot that takes place in the USA is the opposite (Samya is free from the authority of her father; she marries Shadi; their relationship is not secret anymore; and they both become very successful).

Hubb ʿAbir al-Qarrat compares with *Al-Juththa al-Majhula* in two respects: the portrayal of the patriarchal family is similar, while attitude towards religion differs. Samya is a rebellious individual from the start of the novel. She opposes the tyrannical authority of her father and mocks his religious beliefs. In this sense, *Hubb ʿAbir al-Qarrat* does not start with a depiction of 'pre-modern' society, but with the struggle for individualisation. In line with the modernist starting point, the attitude towards religion is 'negative'. In the following dialogue between Samya and her father, Samya voices her criticism regarding the religious attitudes of her father:

– [The father:] Allāh yi'fina min hādhā al-jīl … Jīl bi-ḥāja li-l-akhlāq akthar mimmā huwa bi-hāja li-l-akl wa-l-shurb … Jīl bidūn dīn.

– [Samya:] Wa-hal ta'taqid anna al-tadayyun huwa al-sabīl al-waḥid li-l-akhlāq? Qult al-tadayyun lā al-dīn liwujūd fāriq kabīr baynahumā. (p. 38)

– [The father:] May God help us with this generation … a generation that needs moral values more than it needs food and drink … a generation without religion.

– [Samya:] Do you think that religiosity is the only way to promote morality? I said religiosity, not religion, for there is a great difference between them. (p. 38)

The stance voiced by the father reminds one of the discourse expressed by the narrator in *Al-Juththa al-Majhula*: seeing the young generation as immoral. There is a duality of meaning in the use of the phrase 'immoral generation' (*jīl bidūn dīn*) by the father. A standard translation of the phrase would be 'irreligious generation'. However, the phrase is traditionally used to mean 'immoral generation', also mentioned explicitly (*jīl bi-ḥāja li-l-akhlāq*) by the father. In her reply to her father, Samya addresses both aspects of his comment. She distinguishes between religiosity and religion, saying that religiosity (*al-tadayyun*) is not the only way for morality. The distinction between religiosity and religion is similar to the distinction drawn by Egyptian reformer Khalid Muhammad Khalid between clergy and religion in his earlier works, the most famous of which is *Min Huna Nabda'* (*From Here We Start*, 1950). Samya refers to Muhammad Khalid directly elsewhere in the novel.

Khalid promoted a discourse according to which, 'the whole religious system, as interpreted and practiced by Muslims today [modern times], is shown to be incompatible with modern life' (Khadduri 1953: 520). According to Khalid, 'the clergy were selfish, tyrannical, and ignorant, aiming to control the minds of the people; religion was an altruistic, democratic and rational revelation, which held up the attainment of earthly happiness and love as the highest goal' (Hatina 2000: 44). It is this view of religion that Samya aims to voice. Seen from this angle, the modernist discourse promoted by Samya focuses on differentiation from religious institutions, in contrast with *Al-Juththa al-Majhula*, which warns that such differentiation would lead to the complete disintegration of society. The postmodern discourse in *Hubb ʿAbir al-Qarrat* voices continuity with modernisation, rather than a break with it.

Although this novel takes a clear modernist-secular stance with regard to religious differentiation, the main focus in it is directed towards a reassessment of modern individualism (which leads to the disintegration of society) while presenting an alternative, postmodern individualism, which is more 'socially responsible'. The individualism of Samya is expressed in the novel through her accumulation of wealth and professional success. From a material point of view, Samya resented the house of her parents: 'our house was a ruin, and when I say a ruin I am not insulting the house, but the ruin' (p. 13). In contrast with the 'ruin' in which she lived with her parents, in the USA she lived in a 'luxurious palace' ('I wanted to tell you that our new house was a luxurious palace, but you will not believe me so I will just call it an elegant house. I feel impelled to describe the house [...]' (p. 87)). In addition to material wealth, which will be discussed below, Samya makes clear the link between her individualism and the social responsibilities that are associated with it:

> ʿArift anna ḥubbanā kān madsūsan min nawāḥī ukhrā [...] fa-huwa lam yajurranā anā wa-shādī ilā mayāmī faqat kay natazawwaj wa-nasʿad, wa-lākin kay ashghila manāsib kathīra ... kay akūn masʾūla ʾan al-ālāf, kay usāʿid al-kathīrīn. Fa-l-jarīda wa-mansib sikritīrat taḥrīr, thumma muhāmiya thumma qāḍiya, kull hādhihi al-umūr bidūn shakk tusāʿid ʿalā khidmat al-jumhūr ... wa-taʿnī masʾūliyya kabīra. Wa-hākadhā badaʾt ashʿur anna lī qīma, wa-anna lī ahamiyya mā ... aqūlu ahamiyya bi-ʿazama wa-anā ushaddid ʿalā al-ḥurūf: al-alif, wa-l-hāʾ wa-l-mīm wa-l-yāʾ wa-l-hāʾ. (p. 89)

> I knew that our love meant other things [...] since it did not drag us, me and Shadi, to Miami just to get married and be happy, but for me to occupy many positions ... So I became responsible for thousands, in order to help many. The newspaper and the positions of editorial secretary, then lawyer, then judge, all these things without doubt help serve the public ... and they mean a huge responsibility. This way I started to feel that I have value, and that I am important, and I say importance along with greatness while I stress its letters I, M, P, O, R, T, A, N, C, E. (p. 89)

It is important to address a number of points in this excerpt in relation to the individualism of Samya. First, as indicated above, Samya associates individualism with material success. Halman distinguishes between different types of individualism in modern and postmodern contexts. The type of individualism that Samya expresses is similar to a certain degree to what Halman calls 'utilitarian individualism'. Utilitarian individualism

> stresses personal interest, material success, personal responsibility, accomplishment, property, work, earning and saving money. Furthermore, this individualism advocates the Darwinistic stance that only the best and the strongest can survive. Solidarity is thus not encouraged by this form of individualism, for everybody should take care of himself, and each individual is personally responsible for his acts. (Halman 1996: 198–9)

This definition both affirms and denies the representation of individualism by Samya. On the one hand, Samya is very interested in material success (luxurious palace), great personal responsibility (*mas'ūliyya kabīra*), accomplishment (the various professional positions she achieves), and so forth. Note, for example, that Samya perceives her individualism in terms of great personal responsibility, echoing similar terminology used in modernisation novels.

On the other hand, Samya feels that her responsibilities are towards serving the public (*khidmat al-jumhūr*). This stance contradicts the definition of utilitarian individualism provided by Halman, which does not encourage solidarity, and according to which only the strongest can survive. In other words, serving the public prevents the creation of a state of individual alienation from society, or anomie. Samya sees her individual fulfilment through helping others; an activity that allows her to feel she is valuable (*lī qīma, lī ahhamiyya*). In a Palestinian critique of modernisation in Israel, Samya expresses the idea that 'Individualism or the duty of one towards oneself [...] can only be rendered moral if it converges with duty and obligation towards the social body' (Mukherjee 2006: 12).

The above excerpt, and *Hubb 'Abir al-Qarrat* as a whole, suggest that individualism for Samya does not lead to selfishness and disregard of society. Individuals, where they are allowed to integrate into their societies, such as the way in which Samya integrated into the surrounding social environment of the USA (*insajamtu ma' al-bī'a al-muḥīṭa*), will then be able to contribute to the benefit of the general public.[3] In other words, in contrast to the discourse voiced in *Al-Juththa al-Majhula*, where the process of individualism means alienation and is therefore associated with harm to others (*ḍararta ghayraka*), individualism in *Hubb ʿAbir al-Qarrat* is associated with benefit to all: individuals as well as others.

Another point to address with regard to the individualism of Samya relates to the depiction of family values, or the importance of family for the individual. Firstly, the fulfilment of the love between Samya and Shadi, according to the above excerpt, is the ultimate goal in achieving her individualism, leading to the creation of a new and happy family with Shadi, the person she loves. The other (*nawāḥī ukhrā*) aspects of her individualism (material success and social standing) were second to this.

Secondly, it is possible to say, on the one hand, that the departure of Samya to the USA marks the disintegration of her patriarchal family (here referring to the family of her parents), in the same way that the departure of Muhammad in *Al-Juththa al-Majhula* marks the disintegration of his patriarchal family. However, on the other hand, Samya never wants to completely break away from her parents. Although she despises the tyrannical authority of her father, in several instances in the novel Samya expresses her love for her father. Moreover, when her parents refuse to respond to her letters from the USA, Samya maintains a 'line' of communication with them through Shadya, Shadi's sister, who passed to Samya information and news about her family. Samya also kept in contact with her brother Yusif secretly. The following excerpt shows the dilemma Samya has between achieving individualism and the consequences of individualism on her relationship with her parents:

> Anā hunā [mayāmī] aʿīsh fī baḥbūḥa, fī naʿīm sābigh lā yanqusunī shayʾ. Saʿīda jiddan, walākin ahlī ʿalā khilāf minnī, wa-hum akthar min dhālik qaliqūn yatanāzaʿūn li-atfah al-asbāb wa-kull dhālik li-annī anā … anā al-sabab … saʿādatī ʿalā ḥisāb shaqāʾ al-ākharīn. Wa-lākinnī barīʾa … mutaʾakidda annī barīʾa. (p. 85)

> I am here [in Miami] and I live in luxury, in great wealth, I lack nothing and I am very happy, but my parents are different. They, more than that, are worried, quarrel for the simplest of reasons, and all that because of me … I

> am the reason ... My happiness comes at the price of others' misery. But I am innocent ... I am sure I am innocent. (p. 85)

In the excerpt, Samya contrasts her happiness (*sa ʿīda jiddan*), which is directly linked to her prosperity (*baḥbūḥa, na ʿīm, lā yanquṣunī shay ʾan*), to the misery of her family. They are unlike her (*ʿalā khilāf minnī*), which means they are poor; moreover (*akthar min dhālik*), they are unhappy and in constant dispute. Contrary to Halman, Samya does not think in Darwinistic terms, because she does not lay the responsibility for the misery of her parents on them, but on herself. Samya acknowledges that other people have paid the price of her happiness (*sa ʿādati ʿalā ḥisāb shaqā ʾ al-ākharīn*), but she also thinks she is innocent (*barī ʾa*). At the end of the novel, Samya decides to return from the USA in order to deal with the problems within her family. However, her return does not mean she gives up her individualism, but rather the eradication of patriarchalism of her family, which is symbolised by the death of her father.

Samya wants to be a responsible individual who wishes to free herself from the tyranny of her father, but without losing all social bonds and values she thinks are important, such as family values, having social responsibilities and serving the public. Such a discourse in this novel aims to negotiate modernist values, rather than reject them altogether. It remains secular (as modern discourse), in comparison to the 'Islamic' religious discourse expressed in *Al-Juththa al-Majhula*.

One additional difference between *Al-Juththa al-Majhula* and *Hubb ʿAbir al-Qarrat* lies in their representation of the consequences of modernisation. As mentioned earlier, in *Hubb ʿAbir al-Qarrat*, modernisation is depicted positively (Samya creates a family with Shadi, and they are both successful). The success of Samya is directly linked to her integration with American society. In *Al-Juththa al-Majhula*, Muhammad does not integrate into Israeli society in Ramat-Gan. The state of anomie and alienation of Muhammad is expressed in his deterioration into alcoholism, drug abuse and so forth. The contrast between the two novels in this regard relates to the binary structure and spatial differentiation between Israeli and non-Israeli spaces in counter-action novels. In other words, alienation and integration are linked to spatial categories in this group of novels. This point leads us to the second response in Palestinian novels in this group: the erasure of Palestinians in Israel.

Counter-erasure

As briefly indicated above, violence in counteraction novels is related to the state of anomie of Palestinians in Israel. Anomie is the state of alienation of the individual from society (Seeman 1959). The anomie in Israel of Muhammad from *Al-Juththa al-Majhula* relates to the point I raised earlier, quoting Mukherjee, regarding the relationship between anomie, crime and violence. For Mukherjee:

> Individualism or the duty of one towards oneself [. . .] can only be rendered moral if it converges with duty and obligation towards the social body. The slightest deviation from such a concurrence opens the floodgates to anomie and the negation of the social – violence in its many forms. (Mukherjee 2006: 12)

The most evident manifestation of anomie in counteraction novels is seen in the violence 'in its many forms' that they convey. All novels in the group include violence and crime.[4] For example, *Al-Qadiyya Raqam 13* highlights criminality right from its title, and includes many violent incidents, the most obvious being the murder of three characters. Similarly, *Darih al-Hasna'* (*The Beauty's Tomb*, 1982), by Yusif Nasir, includes rape and a graphic suicide scene. This novel delivers the idea of unnatural death already in the title: the tomb (*ḍarīḥ*), death, contrasts with the beautiful woman (*ḥasnāʾ*), which conveys youth, vitality and life. This contrast between vitality and death suggests that the death was probably unnatural. *Al-Juththa al-Majhula* also conveys unnatural death in its title about an anonymous corpse. Anomie is exemplified in the anonymity of the corpse, depicting the alienation and loneliness of the dead person. *Al-Juththa al-Majhula* includes a number of violent incidents as well. Counteraction novels are distinctively more violent than both earlier novels (modernisation novels), as well as other novels in this period.

According to Stedman Jones, Durkheim 'has a wider conceptualisation of violence than the concept of intentional injury, or verbal and emotional abuse towards others and extends towards characterising a society that denies freedom as violent' (Stedman Jones 2006: 64). This broad view of violence highlights the collective dimension of Palestinian anomie, or alienation, in Israel and its manifestation in counteraction novels. The erasure of Palestinians in Israel could be considered a form of 'epistemic violence' (Simatei 2005: 86), by virtue of denying their history and rights in Palestine. In the words of American social workers, Dorothy Van Soest and Shirley Bryant, 'violence by alienation deprives people of higher rights, such as the right to emotional, cultural, or intellectual growth' (Van Soest and Bryant 1995: 555). The erasure of Palestinians in Israel could be considered, according to the Norwegian sociologist Johan Galtung, 'cultural violence', which refers to 'those aspects of culture, the symbolic sphere of our existence – exemplified by religion and ideology, language and art, empirical science (logic, mathematics) – that can be used to justify or legitimise direct or structural violence' (Galtung 1990).[5] Both Zionism, the encompassing ideology in Israel, as well as science in Israel (as we have seen in Chapter 1 regarding the ideological origins of Israeli sociology) are used to justify direct violence (expulsion, land confiscation) and structural violence (state laws, discrimination in allocation of wealth and so forth) against Palestinians in Israel. Similarly, Van Soest and Bryant would consider erasure of Palestinians in Israel to be structural-cultural violence (Van Soest and Bryant 1995).

Counteraction novels respond to the epistemic and cultural violence of erasure in Israel by violent plots and counter-erasure. The difference between erasure and counter-erasure lies in the direction in which it is applied: Palestinian erasure of Israelis is similar to Israeli erasure of Palestinians. The use of the prefix 'counter' comes only to identify the phenomenon of Palestinians' literary erasure of Israelis and to indicate that it is a response to Israeli erasure of Palestinians. Counter-erasure signifies the fact that most of the plots in this group of novels take place in an Israeli-Jewish space but with near complete absence of any Jewish characters or any significant interaction with Jewish-Israeli culture. When Jewish characters appear in a novel in this group they 'are not portrayed as real, multifaceted human beings, and no attempt is made to explore them in depth' (Ghanayim 2008: 136). Names of cities and streets may appear along with other distinctive Israeli characteristics (currency, proverbs and so on), but they are used to set a 'physical' backdrop of a plot that is completely Palestinian. In other words, Israel appears through objects, not subjects, in this group of novels.

Counter-erasure is a constant feature in counteraction novels, not adhering to the binary structure of the plots. In the first part of the plot in *Al-Juththa al-Majhula*, for example, we are told that Muhammad works in a factory on an industrial estate close to his village. It is implied that the industrial estate is in a Jewish-Israeli town,[6] but the name of the town, or of the owner of the factory, are not mentioned. It is further implied that the owner is Jewish because towards the end of the week he wishes Muhammad and his fellow colleagues a 'happy Saturday', which is a Jewish-Israeli greeting equivalent to 'happy weekend'. In contrast to erasing Jewish-Israeli characters, the friends with whom Muhammad socialises are Palestinians and their names and activities are described in detail.

In the second part of the novel, names of Jewish-Israeli locations are mentioned (Muhammad moves to Ramat-Gan). However, erasure of Jewish characters continues in this part of the novel too. Muhammad's prostitute-partner, who is implied to be Jewish since she is blonde, remains nameless throughout. There are a number of characters in the novel who, it is suggested, are Jewish, but this is never clearly stated in the plot. The only supposedly Jewish characters whose names are mentioned are Umm Dahud,[7] the landlady who owns the house where Muhammad lives, and the fishermen who find his corpse at the end of the novel (Ibrahim, Musa and Yusif) – all are names that could be Arab or Jewish[8] – but there is nothing else to indicate their identity. None of the Jewish characters are central to the plot of the life of Muhammad.

Counter-erasure in *Hubb ʿAbir al-Qarrat* is very clear – not even the names of Palestinian locations in Israel are mentioned in this novel. There are a few hints in the novel that indicate that the plot was situated in Israel: namely, the use of Israeli currency in the 1970s (the Lira – Pound) (p. 21), as well as the use of proverbs.[9] The first time Samya and Shadi meet, he asks her about where she lives, and she replies, 'my address is (…)' (p. 11). The author omitted her address (and also Shadi's afterwards) and did not even invent an imaginary name for her (or for his) village or city. At the end of the novel, after they return from Miami they live 'in a city … not coastal … and not like Miami' (p. 93). She does not mention the name of the city, but only that it is unlike Miami. There are no Israeli-Jewish characters at all – not even at the university, where Israeli-Jews dominate numerically and in every other way. There are no Palestinian universities in Israel, so Samya cannot possibly be studying in an Arab university.

In contrast to this 'secrecy', in the second part of the novel Samya and Shadi decide to live in 'Miami in the United States' (p. 42). She flies through London (p. 66), lands in Florida (p. 66), and visits New York, Washington and Boston (p. 78). Her law office is on '1 Garden City Street and 21 Miami Beach' (p. 80) and the editorial office of the magazine, where she used to work, is on 'Blue-Sky Street' (p. 86). In contrast to her life in Israel, she gains, in the USA, integration on both personal and public levels: 'One month has passed since I entered university […] I integrated with the surrounding [social] environment [*insajamtu maʿ al-bīʾa al-muḥīṭa*] … and became like the rest of the students' (p. 71). Later, Samya becomes a successful lawyer (one of the best ten in the state), a magazine editor and is offered the post of judge.

In order to understand the meaning of counter-erasure in Palestinian discourse, it is useful to examine the 'type' of discourse of counter-erasure. Mikhail Bakhtin distinguishes between two forms of discourse: monologic and dialogic. Monologic discourse 'recognises only direct unmediated orientation of discourse toward its referential object, without taking into account anyone else's discourse or any second context' (Bakhtin 1984: 186). A dialogic discourse includes within itself two social languages in a single utterance. Many labels have been attached to dialogic discourse, and it refers to 'double-talk', 'heteroglossia' or 'the conversation with many voices' (de Man 1983: 100). This group of Palestinian novels, I will show, are neither dialogic nor monologic, they are rather un-dialogic because they erase the other 'voice'.

If dialogism, in the words of Paul de Man, is 'an *assertion* of otherness of the other, preliminary to even the possibility of a *recognition* of his otherness' (de Man 1983: 102; italics in original), the assertion of otherness in un-dialogic discourse is in the act of erasure itself, while, like dialogic discourse, un-dialogic discourse functions in a heteroglossic space. Un-dialogic discourse is an attempt to 'withdraw' back to monologism, but since this is impossible, un-dialogic discourse is therefore violent. In other words, Palestinian counteraction novels use counter-erasure in an attempt to remove or cancel the heteroglossic nature of Palestinian life in Israel.

If we consider *Al-Juththa al-Majhula* again, the request of Muhammad for a bottle of beer while with his friends on Lake Tiberias is absurd in the eyes of his friends. Palestinians and Israelis on the beach of Lake Tiberias seem to have been in two different spaces, and these spaces differ in their values and world views. There are two acknowledged world views in the 'beer scene', but there is only one voice, one discourse that emerges from it, that which depicts Muhammad and his friends as pious Muslims. The implication that one would emulate the lifestyle of the Other, which stands in complete opposition to such a depiction, seems absurd because of its impossibility. The request for a bottle of beer thus constitutes a funny joke, so all of the friends laugh. The beer scene shows that counter-erasure acknowledges the presence of the Other (for it is impossible to erase something that does not exist) but chooses to ignore and marginalise it, while un-dialogism acknowledges two voices but utters only one.

Muhammad and his friends spend their time on the beach of Lake Tiberias, which was 'full of all kinds of people' (p. 26), implying the presence of Jewish-Israelis. Erasure of Jewish-Israelis from this scene does not mean not mentioning them at all, but rather marginalising them so they become a little more than part of the landscape. In other words, had the author completely erased the Israeli-Jews from this scene, the laughter at the request for a bottle of beer would have been incomprehensible, since the absurdity of the situation requires a reference to a viewpoint completely opposed to what the protagonist believes.

To sum up, the narrative emanating from counteraction novels shows the failure of the Zionist modernist utopia promoted in modernisation novels (Chapter 1). It is important to remember that both modernisation and integration of Palestinians in Israel go hand in hand in the utopia that modernisation novels aim to achieve. The narrative in counteraction novels continues with the same equation but shows the impossibility of achieving Zionist modernisation-integration in Israel. Counteraction novels reflect a Palestinian distinction between modernisation and Zionism. This is evident in the narrative of the novels. On the one hand, counteraction novels depict various responses to modernisation, ranging from a religious rejection (*Al-Juththa al-Majhula*), to a secular reformist (*Hubb ʿAbir al-Qarrat*), only to mention the examples used in this chapter. By that, they reflect that Palestinians in Israel are grappling with issues posed to them by their modernisation. On the other hand, counteraction novels present a uniform rejection of Zionist erasure, or alienation, of Palestinians in Israel.

In other words, counteraction novels reflect a discourse among Palestinians in Israel according to which issues of modernisation are open for discussion and debate, coupled with the realisation such a debate should be independent and separate from the Israeli context. For example, Samya from *Hubb ʿAbir al-Qarrat* could achieve the utopia of modernisation and integration only in a space that is not Israeli. In contrast, due to inherent Palestinian alienation in Israeli society, Muhammad from *Al-Juththa al-Majhula* could not achieve his individualism, leading him to a state of anomie and death.

However, with regard to understanding Palestinian identity in Israel, counteraction novels do not articulate what Palestinian identity *is*. As a matter of fact, counteraction novels maintain the erasure of Palestinian identity in Israel, even if they intend to oppose it. In other words, by counter-erasing the Jewish-Israeli, counteraction novels assert the erasure of Palestinian citizens in Israel. This is so because by counter-erasing Jewish-Israelis they lose the 'space' for any meaningful political discussion on Palestinian life in Israel. As a result, counteraction novels do not address the political reality of Palestinians in Israel. Novels in the group I will discuss in the following section reverse this tendency. They do not counter-erase the Jewish-Israeli, or the political context of the relationship between the two societies. On the contrary, these are central themes, taking most of the focus of most of the novels in the group.

Re-enchantment Novels

In terms of the Weberian characterisation of modernism as consisting of two main themes, differentiation and rationalisation, which were introduced in the preceding section, we have seen so far that counteraction novels focus on differentiation and its immediate consequences on Palestinian family structures and social values. Novels under consideration in this section reflect a greater focus on rationalisation.[10] The focus of novels in this group on response to rationalisation is evident in their stylistic features. From this point of view, being postmodern, they do not 'belong to a unitary frame of reference, not to a project, or a Utopia' (Kvale 1995: 23). In light of this, some of the postmodern features of novels in this group include: temporal disorder; fragmentation of narrative; pastiche (the combination of different literary styles together); and so forth.[11] One common postmodern characteristic of

Palestinian novels in this group relates to incorporating fantastical elements into the plots. Two novels have resurrecting characters (*Darih al-Hasna'*, *Ila al-Jahim Ayyuha al-Laylak*); two novels include encounters with aliens from outer space (*Al-Waqa'i' al-Ghariba fi Ikhtifa' Sa'id Abi-l-Nahs al-Mutashā'il*, *Ikhtayya*); and *Arabesques* by Anton Shammas includes fantastical and magical animals, spaces and events.

The fantastical elements in novels in this group can be associated with one aspect of rationalisation: disenchantment. Disenchantment is a process that 'involves emptying the world of magic (*Entzauberung*) [...] *and* the replacement of magic rationalisation by rational calculation' (Tiryakian 1992a: 79–80; italics in original). The response to modernist disenchantment is a postmodernist re-enchantment: 'All in all, postmodernity can be seen as restoring to the world what modernity, presumptuously, had taken away; as a *reenchantment* of the world that modernity had tried hard to disenchant' (Zygmunt Bauman quoted in Bertens 2003: 222; italics in original). In addition to the fantastical and magical elements, spiritual and religious discourse in other novels represents a possible variation of de-rationalisation and re-enchantment. The religious discourse in *Al-Juththa al-Majhula* could be considered a response to rationalisation and secularisation of society as a result of modernisation; *Ruh fi-l-Butaqa* (*Soul in the Crucible*, 1986), by Salim Khuri, includes long 'theological discussions' on the Palestinians, Jewish-Israelis and possibilities for peace in the Middle East.

Apart from being stylistic characteristics of novels in this group, de-rationalisation and re-enchantment 'can forcefully highlight the contradictions and paradoxes of discrimination and disenfranchisement and foreground the constructed and shifting nature and ethnic distinctions' (Heise 2011: 975). Accordingly, the discussion below will not focus on the Palestinian postmodern style as such but will concentrate on dimensions in the narrative that contribute to our understanding of Palestinian identity transformation in Israel in this period (1967–87). As will become evident later, the fantastical elements in novels in this group represent a response to the rational, denationalising, modernist Zionism by re-enchanting Palestinian national discourse.

With this approach in mind, I will analyse a number of novels that reflect various transformations in Palestinian identity over this period. The 're-enchantment' that the title of this section refers to relates to the disillusionment of Palestinians in Israel regarding the utopia of life in Israel, to use the words of Kvale above; a life of prosperity and coexistence between Palestinians and Jewish-Israelis, as it is presented in modernisation novels. In contrast with the utopian harmony of modernisation novels, Palestinian novels discussed in this section reflect a doubly contradictory identity, according to which Palestinian citizens in Israel are neither 'really' Palestinian, nor Israeli. Depicting Palestinians as living in a doubly contradictory reality problematises their existence in Israel, expressing, in light of the initial utopia, a sense of a 'missed opportunity' to achieve peace and coexistence in Israel and in the Middle East.

Missed Opportunity

The 'missed opportunity' expressed in novels in this group refers to the failure of Jewish-Israelis and Palestinians to achieve reconciliation and peace. As will be elaborated in the following two examples, there are different manifestations of 'missed opportunity'. The common denominator between the different expressions of missed opportunity is the holding of Israel or Jewish-Israelis responsible for missing the opportunity.

Al-Sura al-Akhira fi-l-Album (*The Last Photo in the Album*, 1980), by Samih al-Qasim, tells the story of Amir, a Palestinian citizen in Israel. The first two paragraphs of the novel introduce the reader to Amir and establish the central theme of the novel. Amir, who has just received his Master's degree in Political Science from the Hebrew University of Jerusalem, is now looking for a job. The second paragraph says:

> Sa-taftaḥ dukkānan yā walad, wa-tabīʿ ṭaḥīnan wa-shafrāt ḥilāqa. Mājistirak fī-l-ʿulūm al-siyāsiyya lan yajʿalak mulḥaqan fī ayyat safāra isrāʾīliyya. Iʿtarif bi-annaka lan taqbal aṣlan bi-l-ʿamal fī-l-safārāt al-isrāʾīliyya. Innahā laysat safāratuk. Qulhā bi-ṣawt ʿāli wa-lā takhjal. Anta ʿalā ḥaqq. Innahā laysat safāratuk wa-lā safārat al-marḥūm abīk. Wa-lākin mādhā tafʿal bi-shihādat al-mājistīr allatī ḥaṣalta ʿalayhā min al-jāmiʿa al-ʿibriyya fī "yirūshalāyim"? Lā tatasarraʿ. Lan taqdhif bihā ilā-l-mirḥaḍ fa-hiya laysat ṣāliḥa ḥattā ka-waraqat twālīt! ʿUlūm siyāsiyya yā ibn-l-kalb? Min ajl mādhā al-ʿulūm al-siyāsiyya? Li-l-ʿamal al-diblūmāsī? Lā baʾs ʿalayk – hā ant safīr mutajawwil

ladā al-baṭāla. Safīr mutajawwil ladā al-ya's wa-l-marāra wa-l-qaraf wa-l-ḥiqd al-jamīl ka-tuffāḥa nāḍija fī arḍ muṣādara. Ḥiqduka tuffāḥa ladhīdha wa-huwa warda mutafattiḥa tamāman amām buldūzurāt al-kīrin kayyīmit. Uqṭuf ḥiqdika bi-riqqa akādimiyya wa-shummahu bi-ḥaraka muhadhabba masraḥiyya thumma 'alliqhu fī yāqat badlatik al-waḥīda li-yatafarraj al-nās wa-liyumatti'ū anẓārahum bi-warda falasṭīniyya lam tabraḥ arḍahā. (pp. 7–8)

You will open a grocery shop, boy, and will sell flour and shaving blades. A Master's degree in Political Science will not make you an attaché in any Israeli embassy. Admit that you will not even accept to work in the Israeli embassies. It is not your embassy. Say it aloud and don't be embarrassed. You are right. It is not your embassy, nor your late father's. But what would you do in the Master's degree that you have obtained from the Hebrew University in "Yirushalayim"? Don't be reckless. You will not throw it down the toilet because it is not even good as toilet paper! Political Science, you son of a bitch [*yā ibn al-kalb*]? Political Science, what for? For diplomatic work? No worries – here you are a travelling ambassador for the unemployment. A travelling ambassador at the despair, bitterness, disgust and the beautiful resentment, like a ripe apple in a confiscated land. Your resentment is a delicious apple and is a blooming flower against the Keren Kayemet bulldozers. Pick your resentment in an academic gentleness and sniff it in a theatrically mannered move then hang it on the collar of your only suit so that everyone can see it and enjoy a Palestinian flower that has not left its land. (pp. 7–8)

Al-Sura al-Akhira fi-l-Album, as well as other novels in this group, is characterised by the direct engagement of its narrative with the political reality of Palestinian life in Israel. So far, the political relationship between Palestinians and Jewish-Israelis or Israel as a system has been either downplayed, as is the case in modernisation novels, or implicit, as it is the case with counteraction novels. Moreover, the engagement with the political is not only direct; it is critical, marking a transformation in Palestinian discourse in comparison to modernisation novels.

The sense of missed opportunity in the above excerpt relates to the transformation in Palestinian discourse in Israel during this period. The transformation is evident in a number of places in the above excerpt. Firstly, it is evident in Amir's realisation that his initial choice to study political science would not lead to employment in the Israeli diplomatic service (*al-ʿamal al-diblūmāsī*). Choosing to study political science marks Palestinian hopes to integrate into Israel. Aiming to serve in its diplomatic service, representing Israel and what it stands for, would be the ultimate expression of integration. The reversal in such a Palestinian attitude is evident in calling for refusing to serve as an Israeli diplomat. According to the excerpt, Amir cannot work in the Israeli diplomatic service because it is not 'his', meaning that it does represent him. The reversal in Palestinian orientation is a violent 'event'. This is evident in the formulation (*ʿulūm siyāsiyya yā ibn al-kalb?*). If we take the above excerpt to be Amir's stream of consciousness,[12] *ʿulūm siyāsiyya yā ibn al-kalb* marks his regret at choosing to study political science. He regrets this choice because even with obtaining an academic degree, he is unable to find a job.

The incapability of Amir to find a job is linked to the nature of the relationship between Israel and its Palestinian citizens – that of animosity and incompatibility. This is expressed in contrasting the Palestinian flower with the might of the bulldozers of the Keren Kayemet, Israel's land authority. The Keren Kayemet is responsible for the confiscation of Palestinian land and is a symbol of the Israeli destruction of Palestinian life. In light of this, the slapstick, or dark humorous, question *ʿulūm siyāsiyya yā ibn al-kalb?* (which translates as: 'political science, you son of a bitch?'), aims to highlight and expose the absurdity of the situation of Palestinians in Israel. In other words, the initial intention of Palestinians to integrate into Israel seems to Amir/the author so absurd and naive. Dark humour uses 'cruelty, bitterness, and sometimes despair' to underlie the absurdity of the world (O'Neill 1983: 146). Indeed, the despair (*yaʾs*) and bitterness (*marāra*) are evident in the fact that the only criterion for employment in the Israeli diplomatic service is not citizenship or professional qualification, but rather nationality or ethnicity. Jewish holders of equivalent degrees will be employed by the Israeli diplomatic service.

The dark humour in the above excerpt aims to 'encourage sympathy [towards the Palestinians] as well as to expose [the] evil [nature of Israel]' (Donald J. Greiner quoted in Sharma 1988: 62). In order to achieve this objective:

> A Black Humorist in a bid to save the 'self' from forces of dehumanisation and fragmentation brings his readers face to face with equally threatening or horrifying human conditions and then employs tricks to undercut 'its fear by some witty or comic turn. This position is seen as a liberating one, as an assertion of human independence, because it acknowledges the pains and fears of life and transcends them'. (Sharma 1988: 70)

In the above excerpt, al-Qasim attempts to save Amir from the forces of Israeli 'dehumanisation and fragmentation', which at this stage in the novel are expressed in the incapability of Amir to find a job, despite the advanced academic degree that he holds. The Master's degree that Amir holds in Political Science does not save him from unemployment. The reason for his unemployment is only because Amir is Palestinian. Thus, al-Qasim rejects the idea of working for an employer of this kind and urges Amir to express his rejection loudly.

The sense of missed opportunity is expressed in another dark humour instance in the above excerpt. By throwing away the university degree into the toilet (*taqdhif bihā ilā al-mirḥāḍ*), Amir expresses the shift in his orientation towards life in Israel. If he initially acquired the academic degree in order to integrate into Israel, now he no longer wants to do that, rendering the degree useless. Moreover, throwing away the university degree into the toilet is an act of empowerment and superiority, rejecting Israeli racist standards. Hence, the refusal to serve in the Israeli diplomatic service, or expressing rejection of becoming Israeli, becomes a liberating act because it inverts Israeli superiority into a weakness, represented by its inherent racism.

The final scene in the excerpt also demonstrates a liberating and empowering act, as with throwing the university degree into the toilet. Al-Qasim calls Amir to 'pick his hatred in an academically gentle way, smell it in a theatrical move and then hang it on the only suit he owns so that all people can witness a Palestinian flower that did not leave its land'.[13] The call for such an action marks a refusal to 'treat what one might regard as tragic materials tragically' (O'Neill 1983: 148). The tragedy of Palestinian life inside Israel should not be treated tragically, but Amir is encouraged to invert his tragic situation into a message of moral superiority and a symbolic act of perseverance.

The message of perseverance that emanates from the above excerpt is that Palestinian citizens in Israel should persevere despite the difficult circumstances in which they live: Palestinian academics in Israel are depicted as 'ripe apples' (*tuffāḥa nāḍija*) and they are unable to achieve their potential because they live in a confiscated land. The apple metaphor consists of the apple fruit (symbolising Palestinian intellectuals in Israel), the apple tree (the Palestinian nation) and the confiscated land/soil (Palestine). The apple tree, leaves, branches, trunk and roots are alive and capable of producing healthy and ripe fruits. The apple tree, however, cannot function without its connection to the soil, and this soil is confiscated and ruled by an external power: Israel. The Palestinian academic should not leave his land, since such an act would spell his doom. This message is exemplified by the story of Amir's younger brother. Ali dreams of becoming a doctor (a 'ripe apple') but is not allowed to enrol at the university (confiscated land), and is, instead, shot dead at the border while trying to escape the country to try to achieve his dream elsewhere.

Instead of calling for integration through development and modernisation, perseverance conveys the idea of missed opportunity, depicting a conflictual relationship between Palestinians and Israel. Moreover, the expression of missed opportunity puts the blame on Israel. This is evident in the portrayal of Israel as a racist country in the above excerpt. The following novel, *Ruh fi-l-Butaqa*, blames Israel for actively working to prevent peace in the Middle East. In addition to conveying a sense of missed opportunity, this novel is an example of postmodern de-rationalisation and re-enchantment.

Ruh fi-l-Butaqa (*Soul in the Crucible*, 1986), by Salim Khuri, tells the story of a number of characters who live in an apartment building.[14] Ibrahim, the main character, has been married to Samira for four years, and they have many problems and quarrels. Abu al-Ni'm is a seventy-year-old man who lives in the same apartment building as Ibrahim and Samira. Abu al-Ni'm is usually drunk, and likes to talk about politics, religion and philosophy with whoever is willing to listen to him. According to Ghanayim, the role of Abu al-Ni'm, as an 'explicit propagandist', is to analyse the political situation in Israel and the Middle East (Ghanayim 2008: 100). The other characters often listen, sometimes responding and challenging him. The following quotation from Abu al-Ni'm summarises the political message of the novel, explaining its title:

> U'akkid lak yā ustādh ibrāhīm anna hādhihi al-rūḥ ta'mal wa-bi-intiẓām … akthar min thalāthīn sana maḍā 'alā qiyām isrā'īl wa-ṭard al-'arab … wa-lākin al-manṭiqa lam tahda' … al-qāda al-isrā'īliyyūn yurīdūn taghyīr al-wāqi' … Lam yaqtani' aḥad bi-buṭūlātihim wa-a'mālahim … Fa-baqaw yuḥissūna bi-l-wiḥda … yuḥissūn bi-l-in'izāl … wa-mā hādhihi al-ḥurūb wa-hādhihi al-ṭā'irāt illā ta'bīr 'an fashalihim amām hādhihi al-rūḥ allatī tas'ā li-ḍammihim ilā būtaqat al-shu'ub fī hādhihi al-manṭiqa. (p. 123)

> I assure you, Mister Ibrahim, that this soul is working, and continuously at that … More than thirty years have passed since Israel was established and the expulsion of the Arabs … but the region has not subsided … the Israeli leaders want to change reality … no one was impressed by their heroics and actions … so they continued to feel lonely … they feel isolated … and these wars and airplanes are only an expression of their failure against this soul that aims to bring them into the crucible of the nations in this region. (p. 123)

Ruh fi-l-Butaqa is an example of de-rationalisation and re-enchantment, utilised to express the political narrative of the novel. Abu al-Ni'm talks throughout the novel about a spirit (*rūḥ*), which dominates the actions of the people. The spirit transforms and takes different shapes in the long history of the Middle East. The re-enchanted discourse here refers not to religious beliefs, but to providing an explanation of a long political history of the Middle East as being controlled by a spirit. In other words, the spiritual discourse of Abu al-Ni'm, although derived from religious scripts (Jewish, Christian and Islamic), does not see religion as a practice, as is the case in *Al-Juththa al-Majhula*, for example. The spirit helped the inhabitants of the region to stand in the face of the many invading forces and occupations. The spirit is one of, it is possible to say, adaptability, of the melting pot of the Middle East nations (*būtaqat al-shu'ūb*). The sense of missed opportunity in *Ruh fi-l-Butaqa* is cast at Israel for not integrating into the Middle East, rather than talking about Palestinian integration into Israel.

Abu al-Ni'm blames Israel for resisting the spirit, which since the establishment of Israel (*qiyām isrā'īl*) and the expulsion of the Arabs (*ṭard al-'arab*) is continuously (*bi-intiẓām*) calling for its integration with the nations of the Middle East. The use of *ṭard al-'arab* instead of 'the expulsion of the

Palestinians' reflects the adaptability of the people of the Middle East, voicing acceptance of the new reality and an intention to move forward. This is evident when Abu al-Ni'm says, 'However, the region has not calmed down' (*wa-lākinna al-minṭaqa lam tahdaʾ*). This sentence means that, despite the establishment of Israel, the Middle East has not calmed down, implying that the establishment of Israel should be the end point of the conflict. This is so because the Zionist movement has achieved its goal to establish the country, although at the price of the expulsion of the Palestinians (*ṭard al-ʿarab*). Abu al-Ni'm voices by this a willingness to live with this price, if it marks a starting point for Israeli integration into the region. However, Israel since 1948 refuses to become part of the Middle East, making this point clear by its wars (*ḥurūb*) and, sarcastically, acts of bravery (*buṭūlāt*).

The Israeli wars in the Middle East, according to Abu al-Ni'm, reflect an Israeli failure (*fashal*) to change the reality (*taghyīr al-wāqiʿ*); that of its inevitable integration into the region. In other words, Israeli wars in the Middle East are not against nations or countries, but against a spirit of peace and coexistence. Missed opportunity in *Ruh fi-l-Butaqa* refers to the continuous Israeli action against an opportunity for peace and integration into the Middle East. Israeli actions against integration keep Israel, as a result, lonely (*wiḥda*) and isolated (*inʿizāl*).

The sense of missed opportunity in novels in this group conveys a transformation in, or reassessment of, the political orientation of Palestinians in Israel. As can be seen in the two examples above, missed opportunity is expressed in direct engagement in political discourse. In the following discussion, I will analyse the implications of this transformation on Palestinian identity in Israel, focusing on the reflection of a doubly contradictory identity in novels in this group.

Doubly Contradictory Identity

As indicated on its front cover, *Ila al-Jahim Ayyuha al-Laylak* (*To Hell with You Lilac*, 1977), by Samih al-Qasim, is an autobiographical novel (*ḥikāya aūtūbayughrāfiyya*). In the following discussion, I will present the doubly contradictory identity as expressed in this novel.

The postmodern narrative in *Ila al-Jahim Ayyuha al-Laylak* consists of six chapters, which alternate between past and present periods in the life of the author. The first chapter, titled *al-inshiṭār* ('The Rupture'), describes the childhood of the author and his love for Dunya – a little girl from his Galilean village, Al-Rama. Dunya becomes a refugee in Lebanon as a result of the 1948 war. From these childhood memories, the narrative then turns to describe the daily routine of adult Samih a few years later. The second chapter is titled *al-hāwiya* ('The Abyss'). Here, the narration turns back to the past and the experience of Samih in his village when he was a child during the years after the 1948 war. The most vivid memory of these years for Samih is the torture and cruelty that he and his friends inflicted on a paralysed refugee, Hasan. Hasan comes from a nearby village and was left in Al-Rama in 1948. The inhabitants of Al-Rama abandon Hasan to suffer hunger and the cruelty of the children of the village. As a result of such treatment, Hasan eventually dies. The third chapter, titled *al-muwājaha* ('The Confrontation'), is set in the present and depicts the encounters and political debates Samih holds with Jewish-Israeli artists and intellectuals in a coffee shop in Tel-Aviv (Cafe Kasit). Here, Samih describes Uri and Ilana, two Jewish-Israeli young people, who serve in the novel as parallels to himself and Dunya.

In the fourth chapter, *al-mustaḥīl* ('The Impossible'), Samih relates his experience in Moscow and introduces Samir, a Palestinian refugee from the West Bank, and Tania. Samir and Tania serve as a parallel couple to Uri and Ilana, and Samih and Dunya. Samir returns to the West Bank and dies in clashes with the Israeli army. The fifth chapter is titled *al-qatl* ('The Killing'), and here the author talks about Samir and the Palestinian refugees. In the sixth chapter, titled *al-qiyāma* ('The Resurrection'), Samih meets with Hasan, the paralysed refugee who died in the village in 1948. The resurrection of Hasan symbolises the 'resurrection' of Palestinian national identity in Israel, and the reunion of Palestinian citizens in Israel with Palestinians in the West Bank and Gaza Strip as a result of Israeli occupation.

As a postmodern novel, in addition to the fragmented narrative of the plot, alternating between past and present, the 'freezing' of time is another temporal characteristic in *Ila al-Jahim Ayyuha al-Laylak*. In the following instance, time stops while Samih sits in a coffee shop waiting to meet Ilana, a Jewish-Israeli character who frequents the same coffee shop: 'A few hours ago it (the watch) indicated that it was seven o'clock, and here it is indicating seven o'clock' (p. 70).[15] The freezing of time prevents Samih from meeting with Ilana after 1967. Another postmodern characteristic in this novel relates to the obsession the author has with the colour lilac, the colour of the dress that Dunya wears when she becomes a refugee in 1948. The colour lilac 'haunts' the author, and in many instances it appears in the form of a flood (*ṭūfān*) that submerges him and the space around him ('A wave of lilac blocks the room's exits and submerges me until suffocation' (p. 38)).[16] Similar to the resurrection of Hasan, the lilac flooding and the appearance of Dunya at the end of the novel, wearing her lilac dress of 1948, symbolise the memory of the Nakba and the Palestinian refugees (for more on the postmodern aspects of this novel, see: al-Qasim 1979).

The idea of doubly contradictory identity can be best defined by presenting the excerpt from which the title of this section is taken. In the following excerpt, taken from the first chapter of the novel, Samih describes an incident during a trip he makes from Haifa to Tel-Aviv with a Jewish lady, Rut. Samih and Rut are driving for a workshop on peace and coexistence between Palestinians and Jewish-Israelis that Rut has organised in Tel-Aviv. The two are stopped at a police roadblock, which was set up 'after one of the Palestinian guerrilla waves' (*ʿaqiba iḥdā mawjāt al-fidāʾyīn al-falasṭiniyīn*):

> Alʾān, fī hādhihi al-laḥẓa, fī muwājahat hādhihi al-ḥaqīqa al-muzdawaja al-mutanāqiḍa, ḥaqīqat ḥājiz al-shurṭa wa-ḥaqīqatī anā. Bal al-ḥaqīqa allatī hiya naḥnu al-thalātha: al-shurṭa – al-ʿarabiyy alladhī yushakkilu khaṭaran ʿalā al-amn – wa-anti. Sayyidat isrāʾīl al-marmūqa. (pp. 13–14)

> Now, at this moment, confronting this doubly contradictory truth, the truth of the police roadblock and my truth. But the truth that is the three of us: the police – the Arab man who poses a threat to security – and you. The distinguished lady of Israel. (pp. 13–14)

The doubly contradictory reality (*al-ḥaqīqa al-muzdawaja al-mutanāqiḍa*) is represented through three characters in this scene: a Palestinian man; a Jewish-Israeli woman; and a representation of Israel as a state – the police roadblock. First, Samih and Rut symbolise the Palestinian and Israeli individuals who are trying to foster understanding through dialogue. Israel, symbolised by the police roadblock, is obstructing the way to dialogue by, quite literally, blocking the road. The contradiction lies in the fact that a Palestinian citizen in Israel is seen as a security threat by the Israeli establishment (police) on the one hand, while being considered a partner in an enterprise for peace and coexistence by a Jewish-Israeli, on the other. In other words, the contradiction is between the police and Rut, who does not see Samih as a security threat.

The doubly contradictory reality means, in terms of Palestinian identity in Israel, that the Palestinians in Israel are neither 'really' Palestinian, nor 'really' Israelis. On the one hand, contradiction in Palestinian identity is evident in the change from the first person, 'me' (*anā*) in the above quotation to the third person, 'the Arab who poses a threat to security' (*al-ʿarabī al-ladhī yushakkil khaṭaran ʿalā al-amn*). The shift from first person to third person implies that Samih dissociates himself from Arabs who pose a threat to Israeli security. The doubly contradictory reality, in this sense, refers to the paradoxical situation, in the eyes of Samih, where somebody who is not involved in resistance against Israel, but is rather taking an active part in dialogues aiming to achieve reconciliation, is being treated as a threat. On the other hand, Palestinian citizens in Israel belong to the Palestinian nation – Samih is going to the workshop to talk as a Palestinian; the police roadblock and the need to obtain a travel permit relate only to the Palestinian citizens in Israel. In other words, despite efforts to achieve coexistence with the Jewish-Israelis, Palestinian citizens in Israel are inherently conceived to be aliens or even a threat to the country.

The participation of Samih in dialogue workshops with Jewish-Israeli artists and intellectuals relates to an activity that took place during the military rule years (1948–67), and which disintegrated after the 1967 war. Dialogue workshops were intended to promote understanding between Palestinians and Jewish-Israelis. The termination of such an activity marks a transformation in both Palestinian and Jewish-Israeli attitudes. Dialogue workshop meetings are mentioned in a number of novels. In addition to *Ila al-Jahim Ayyuha al-Laylak*, Palestinian journalist Fouzi El-Asmar mentions such groups in his autobiography, *To Be an Arab in Israel* (1975b). Also, Atallah Mansour refers to similar groups in his autobiography, *Waiting for the Dawn* (1975). However, since there seems to be no historical research on these workshops, our knowledge of them remains limited. The autobiographical, retrospective insights into this activity, which took place during the military rule period

(1948–67), provide an additional layer of understanding of Palestinian political discourse during these years.

In Chapter 1 of this book, dealing with Palestinian identity during the military rule years, I outlined a discourse of attenuation, voiced by Tawfiq Mu'ammar. This discourse aimed at integrating Palestinians into the Israeli state on equal grounds, preserving and acknowledging Palestinian national rights in the country. Modernisation novels presented a radical approach for integrating Palestinians into Israeli society, promoting a discourse that meant the denationalisation of Palestinians, accepting the exclusivist approach of Zionism. Dialogue groups mentioned in autobiographies constitute a middle ground between the two diametrical ends of the other two. Here, Palestinians do not promote a discourse of Palestinian national self-determination, nor do they rid themselves completely of their Palestinian identity. Dialogue between parties is in itself an acknowledgement of their differences, with the aim of achieving a coexistence in spite of their differences.

After the 1967 war, dialogue groups between Palestinian and Jewish-Israeli intellectuals ceased to take place. From the few sources referring to such activity, only Fouzi El-Asmar proposed an explanation as to the reason for the termination of these groups. El-Asmar says:

> Nina [Jewish-Israeli host of a dialogue group] was carried away with the exuberance of victory which hit many Jews immediately after the war, and many of the people who frequented her house concluded that the root of the problem of the bad relationship between Jews and Arabs could not be understood or removed by means of friendly talk between Jews and Arabs who meet once a week for a cup of tea together. (El-Asmar 1975b: 77)

It is difficult to assess whether the interpretation of El-Asmar applies to other groups, or to all members of his group. Moreover, El-Asmar provides little insight into the Palestinian 'perspective' on this issue, laying the blame initially on Jewish-Israelis who got carried away with the excitement of their victory. The following example elaborates the transformation in Palestinian discourse and the termination of the dialogue groups as expressed in *Ila al-Jahim Ayyuha al-Laylak*:

> Kull yawm taqrīban naltaqī (kunnā naltaqī) fī 'kasīt'. Mundhu sā'āt al-ghurūb al-ūlā nataḥawar wa-natanāḥar, fī-l-siyāsati ghāliban in lam yakun dā'iman. (p. 306)

> Every day almost we meet (used to meet) in [Cafe] Kasit. Beginning with the early hours of the sunset, we converse and battle, in politics usually, if not always. (p. 306)

This excerpt highlights two points. First, it indicates the intensity of the political debates that the members of the group used to have. This is expressed in the contrast between *nataḥāwar* (to have a dialogue or a conversation, implying tolerance to the opinion of the Other) and *natanāḥar* (to kill each other, having no tolerance towards the Other). Secondly, and more importantly, there is the contrast between the past and present tense in reference to the meetings. Starting with the present tense, 'we meet almost daily' (*naltaqī*), and then correcting to 'we used to meet' (*kunnā naltaqī*), not only indicates the termination of the dialogue group, but also the transformation in the attitude of the author towards the practice. The fact that the author has kept the 'correction' in his narration emphasises the transformation. In other words, had the author written this sentence in the past tense only, the focus of the sentence would have been on the heated debates, not on the fact that the debates had ceased to take place.

The transformation in the political orientation of Samih, expressed in the novel by the termination of the dialogue group, coincides in the novel with the resurrection of Hasan, the paralysed boy who was abandoned and tortured to death in 1948. In the final chapter of *Ila al-Jahim Ayyuha al-Laylak*, Samih is on his way back from Jerusalem to Haifa. In the taxi, he meets Hasan. In the following excerpt Hasan talks about his paralysis and his return to Samih:

> Lam akun kasīḥan fī yawm min-l-ayyām. Kāna al-kusāḥu fī 'uqūlinā wa-qulūbinā.
> […]
> Kullu dhālik kāna mu'aqatan. Al-kusāḥu kana mu'aqqatan. Wa-l-mawtu kana mu'aqqatan. (p. 96)

> I have never been paralysed. Paralysis was in our heads and hearts.

> [...]
> All that was temporary. Paralysis was temporary. And death was temporary. (p. 96)

The postmodern aspect of the resurrection of Hasan consists of 'incompatible' features: death and life; paralysis and good health; powerlessness and powerfulness. The contrast between these features allows Hasan to symbolise Palestinian national awareness. Resurrected Hasan, symbolising Palestinian national awareness, is now a healthy and strong guerrilla fighter. This contrasts with the paralysed Hasan, who was tortured to death in 1948 by the inhabitants of Al-Rama. Hasan inverts the weakness (paralysis and death) of 1948 by denying it altogether (*lam akun kasīḥan fī yawm min-l-ayyām*), because the paralysis is only perceived (*kāna al-kusāḥu fī ʿuqūlinā wa-qulūbinā*). The portrayal of the paralysis to have been in the minds and hearts of Palestinians in 1948 implies criticism, and regret, for not fully acknowledging the severity of the 1948 events. Such a collective implication is evident in the fact that Hasan depicts the paralysis to be collective, rather than individual, by switching from first-person singular to first-person plural. The perceived death and paralysis of 'Hasan', or Palestinian national awareness, were only temporary (*muʾaqqatan*).

The resurrection of Hasan, now a guerrilla fighter (*fidāʾī*), marks the end of this temporary state and the fact that Palestinians will take political initiative to preserve their national identity. By the end of the 1960s, according to Dina Matar, 'the [*fidāʾī*] had come to dominate Palestinian national narrative of steadfastness, struggle and resistance. Armed struggle became the central element of the "imagined community" of the Palestinians' (Matar 2011: 94). In other words, whereas at the beginning of the novel Samih dissociates himself from Palestinian guerrilla fighters, while on his way to a dialogue workshop in Tel-Aviv, the end of the novel includes Samih's reunion with resurrected Hasan, a symbol of Palestinian resistance.

However, the following excerpt shows that Palestinian doubly contradictory identity in Israel continues despite the transformation in their discourse. This is evident in the following excerpt from the final chapter of the novel. Here, Samih talks about a workshop meeting he attended in Jerusalem:

> Kāna liqā'ī bi-jumhūr al-quds al-muḥtalla liqā'an 'ā'iliyyan ḥamīman.
>
> Saṭa'at 'uyūnuhum al-jamīla al-ḥazīna bi-barīq 'ajīb ḥīna ikhtatamtu al-nadwa bi-'ibāra anqadhatnī min al-ikhtināq:
>
> 'Sa-naltaqī ayyuhā al-ikhwa marra ukhrā. Sanaltaqī hunā fī-l-quds wa-satakūn al-quds 'āṣimat falasṭīn al-ḥurra!'
>
> *Hā anadhā fī ṭarīq 'awdatī min al-quds al-muḥtalla ilā* hayfā, *ḥaythu tabda' min jadīd ḥālat al-intiẓār al-qātil.* (p. 91)
>
> My meeting with the audience in occupied Jerusalem was intimate.
>
> Their beautiful eyes shone with a strange flicker when I concluded the seminar with a statement that saved me from choking:
>
> 'We will meet, brothers, again. We will meet here in Jerusalem and it will be the capital city of the free Palestine!'
>
> Here I am, on my way back from occupied Jerusalem to Haifa, where a new state of a deadly wait starts. (p. 91)

The above excerpt includes several clues regarding the transformation in Palestinian discourse in Israel in the 1970s. First, the workshop (*nadwa*) that Samih attends at the end of *Ila al-Jahim Ayyuha al-Laylak* takes place in Jerusalem with Palestinian participants, in contrast with dialogue workshops that he attended in Tel-Aviv with Jewish-Israeli participants. Secondly, the workshop in Jerusalem takes place after the dialogue groups in Tel-Aviv were terminated, which suggests that the former replaced the latter. This is further evident in the fact that in the preceding excerpt the encounters with Jewish-Israelis are expressed in the past tense, while in the above excerpt, Samih assures the Palestinian audience that he will meet with them again in the future, using *sa-naltaqī* ('we will meet') twice for emphasis.

Thirdly, the contrast between the two workshops is evident in the depiction of the relationship between their participants. The encounter with Palestinian participants in the above excerpt is portrayed to be 'warm familial' (*'ā'iliyyan ḥamīman*), which contrasts with the fierce encounters with Jewish-Israeli participants (*natanāḥar*) mentioned earlier. Another example is to be found in the first excerpt used from this novel. In the first excerpt, there is a relationship that is based on power between Rut and Samih. Rut, depicted as 'the eminent lady of Israel' (*sayyidat isrāʾīl al-marmūqa*), is the organiser of the workshop, while Samih is merely a participant. Rut is driving the car, her car, while Samih is the passenger. The car driver can be perceived to be the leader, the one who is in control, while the passenger is 'subordinate'. In comparison, Samih addresses the participants in Jerusalem as 'brothers' (*ikhwa*), putting them on equal grounds.

However, the doubly contradictory identity of Palestinians in Israel continues despite the transformation in their discourse (the resurrection of Hasan). First, in the same way that dialogue workshops between Palestinians and Jewish-Israelis reflected their differences (which they attempted to bridge), the setting of the workshop in Jerusalem also reflects the distinct status of the two Palestinian sides. Samih speaks as a Palestinian citizen in Israel, to an audience of Palestinians who are not citizens in Israel. Moreover, Samih in both cases goes from, and to, Haifa. He is a guest at both workshops. He does not belong in Tel-Aviv or in occupied Jerusalem. Secondly, the use of *sa-naltaqī* in the above excerpt also stresses the doubly contradictory identity of Palestinian citizens in Israel, because the two Palestinian 'parties' (inside and outside of Israel) will continue to be distinctive. 'Meeting again' means a momentary meeting, followed by another separation.

Thirdly, the doubly contradictory identity in this excerpt is also evident in the contrast between, on the one hand, considering the audience/population of occupied Jerusalem (*al-quds al-muḥtalla*) familial; thus Samih associates himself with the Palestinians outside Israel, and, on the other hand, indicating that he is on his way back from occupied Jerusalem to Haifa. Using the adjective 'occupied' only with reference to Jerusalem (*al-quds al-muḥtalla*), and not with Haifa, draws a distinction between the two parts of the 'Palestinian family', focusing only on the 1967 occupation, and ignoring the Nakba in this context. According to Palestinian sociologist Honaida Ghanim, the renewed contact of Palestinian citizens in Israel with Palestinians from the West Bank and Gaza Strip after the 1967 war may have strengthened Palestinian identity in Israel, but it also highlighted the cultural differences between the two Palestinian groups (Ghanim 2009: 97).

Moreover, the return to Haifa means for Samih the continuation of the 'killing anticipation' (*al-intiẓār al-qātil*) for Dunya, which implies that they have not reunited as of yet. Returning from Jerusalem to Haifa (*ṭarīq ʿawdatī*) reminds us of the opening scene of *ʿAʾid ila Hayfa* (*Returning to Haifa*, 1969), a novel by the Palestinian writer and journalist Ghassan Kanafani. In this novel, a Palestinian refugee couple return to the city after the 1967 war to look for their son, Khaldun, whom they left behind during the 1948 war. In the final scene of *Ila al-Jahim Ayyuha al-Laylak*, Dunya 'appears' to Samih on the beach near Tel-Aviv. This 'meeting' between the two indicates their imminent reunion. It is only imminent because the novel ends with Dunya and Samih running towards each other, not reaching each other yet. The reunion of Palestinian citizens in Israel with Palestinians outside Israel is thus incomplete, or not yet achieved. In the following discussion, I will present other manifestations of the Palestinian doubly contradictory identity in Israel.

Identity, Space and Time

Al-Waqaʾiʿ al-Ghariba fi Ikhtifaʾ Saʿid Abi-l-Nahs al-Mutashaʾil (*The Secret Life of Saʿid, the Ill-Fated Pessoptimist,* 1974), by Emile Habiby, is the story of Saʿid, a Palestinian citizen in Israel, and his experience in Israel since its establishment.

The complex, postmodern writing style in *al-Mutashaʾil* has attracted the attention of many scholars, who have made detailed analyses of the numerous techniques and narrative devices utilised by Habiby (al-Qasim 1979; Mahraz 1984; Khater 1993; Heath 2000; Muhawi 2006; Shhada 2007). I do not intend to do the same because, first of all, this would contribute little to already established knowledge. Secondly, what is of interest here is not a micro analysis of the writing of Habiby, but rather the portrayal of Palestinian life in Israel and what we can learn from it about Palestinian identity in Israel in the years 1967–87. Therefore, the discussion on *al-Mutashaʾil* will highlight the manifestation of the 'doubly contradictory identity' of Palestinian citizens in Israel. The contradiction is to be found in the political stance vis-à-vis the spatial narrative of the plot.

The story of Saʿid is told in three parts, each part called *kitāb*, a letter from the protagonist Saʿid to his friend. In the first *kitāb*, titled *Yuʿad*, Saʿid explains to his friend how he ended up being with aliens from outer space. He also talks about his family (*al-Mutashaʾil*) and the meaning of their special name; how he survived *'al-naḥs al-awwal'*, the first misfortune of 1948 (the Palestinian Nakba); and he remembers how he met his first love, Yu'ad, on a train between Acre and Haifa when they were students. Sa'id remembers how, after the establishment of Israel, he became a member of *ittiḥād 'ummāl falasṭīn* (Palestine's Workers' Union) and a collaborator with Israel. Sa'id recalls the time that Yu'ad visited him in Haifa after she became a refugee, and how she was expelled by the police.

In the second *kitāb*, titled *Baqiya*, Sa'id meets and marries Baqiya al-Tanturiyya. Baqiya tells him about her secret undersea cave, where her refugee parents hid some treasure. The son of Sa'id and Baqiya, Wala', forms a secret cell with his friends and they dig up the treasure box, which is full of gold and weapons. Baqiya tries to persuade Wala' to leave his hiding place when he is surrounded by Israeli police, but later she joins him and they both disappear into the sea. The third *kitāb*, titled *Yu'ad al-Thaniya* ('The Second Yu'ad'), tells how Sa'id is sent to jail and meets another man named Sa'id who is the brother of the second Yu'ad – and both are sons of the first Yu'ad (from the first letter). Sa'id al-Mutasha'il quits his service as an informer for Israel and ends the letter by saying that he has found himself seated on top of a high impalement stake.

The doubly contradictory identity in *al-Mutasha'il* is evident in the contrast between the 'political' and the 'spatial' discourses in the novel. The spatial representation in the novel is very 'political', as will become clear later. By 'political' discourse I mean the depiction of the political participation, or activity, of Palestinian citizens in Israel. I will begin by outlining this political world view according to Habiby as expressed in this novel.

The second book (*kitāb*) of *al-Mutasha'il* tells the story of Wala' (the son of Sa'id and Baqiya), who establishes a cell with his friends to fight Israel. Wala' and his friends are exposed by the Israeli police and are surrounded in their hiding-place on the beach of Tantura (a Palestinian village destroyed in 1948) along with their ammunition. Baqiya and Sa'id are brought to the site by the police to try to persuade their son to surrender. There is evidence that the story of Wala' and his resistance cell may be based on a true story of a group of Palestinian citizens in Israel. 'Group 778' was a code name for a Fatah-affiliated cell, which was established in Acre in the 1970s by a group of Palestinian citizens in Israel. Group 778 carried out several attacks in Israel, the most famous of which was the attack on the oil refinery plant in Haifa. The story of this group was documented by Tawfiq Fayyad (1978) in a documentary-novel titled *Majmuʿat Akka 778* (*The Acre Group 778*). There are a number of similarities between the documented events and those in *al-Mutashaʾil* in several incidents in the second book (*Baqiya*) of *al-Mutashaʾil*. In the following excerpt, Saʿid talks about a group of Palestinian fishermen, arrested on the beach of Nahariya (a Jewish city north of Acre):

> Fa-lammā takātharat layālī ḥuzayrān ʿalā al-ʿarab, takāthara ṣayyādū al-samak al-huwātu minhum. Fa-qīl: yahrubūn min humūm azwājihim.
>
> Wa-kānū bi-l-ḥaqq, yabḥathūn fī-l-baḥr ʿammā yuqniʿahum bi-anna thammat mā huwa aqwā min dawlatinā.
>
> Wa-rubba laylatin dahamathum al-shurṭa fīhā, wa-hum qiyām ʿalā ṣukhūr al-shāṭiʾ fī nahāriyya, ḥaythu yablaʿu al-baḥru bāluʿatiha, fa-yakhṣab bi-ashtāt al-samak, wa-qad istakhaffahum iṭmiʾnān al-baḥr, fa-istakhaffū bi-asʾilat al-ʿasas, fa-bātū baqiyyat laylatahum fī sijn. (p. 98)
>
> During those terrible nights of the June War, Arab men flocked there to fish. They were avoiding, it was said, the nagging of their wives. But in reality they were searching in the sea for reassurance that there was something stronger than our state.
>
> Many a night as they stood there on the rocks of Nahariyya, where the sea swallows the town's sewage to fertilise the fish, the police would make a sudden appearance. The calm security of the sea made the fishermen feel bold. Taking the questions from the police too lightly, they would end up spending the rest of the night in jail. (p. 70 in the English version; modified spelling and transliteration for uniformity)

A number of similarities between the novels of Habiby and Fayyad are evident in the above excerpt. First, the establishment of Group 778 was a direct result of the 1967 war. The defeat in the war was a major setback (*naksa*) for Arabs and Palestinians alike, including Palestinian citizens in Israel. The occupation of the West Bank and Gaza Strip in the war allowed renewed contact with Palestinians in these territories. For the members of Group 778, access to the West Bank meant an opportunity to join the Palestinian resistance movement. They were especially motivated in light of the defeat in 1967. In the above excerpt, Habiby makes a direct link, through the use of 'and when' (*fa-lammā*), between the recurrence of the 'evenings of June' (*layālī ḥuzayrān*), alluding to the recurring defeats of the Arab countries against Israel, the last of which was in June 1967, and the fishermen seeking 'reassurance that there was something stronger than our state' (*dawlatinā*), Israel. More specifically, the similarity lies in the fact that most members of Group 778 were fishermen, and that they used to 'fish' boxes of ammunition and explosives sent to them by sea from Fatah members in Lebanon.

The 'reassurance that there was something stronger than our state' is an ironic way to refer to the hope that members of Group 778 had in Fatah and the Palestinian resistance movement. It is ironic because 'irony is the intentional transmission of both information and evaluative attitude other than what is explicitly presented' (Hutcheon 1994: 11). In the example from *al-Mutasha'il*, this is evident in the contrast between depicting Palestinian belonging to Israel as 'our state' (*dawlatunā*) and the fact that some of them search for something more powerful than it in order to defeat it, defying by that their 'explicitly' stated belonging to the state.

Secondly, similarity is to be found in the specific reference to the beach of Nahariya. Fayyad refers in his documentary-novel to a small island called '*jazīrat al-simsim*' (The Sesame Island) off the coast of Nahariya that was the collection-point for boxes of explosives, delivered by Fatah members from Lebanon by sea (Fayyad 1978: 22). The third similarity is implied in the depiction of the fishermen as amateurs (*huwāt*) in the excerpt from *al-Mutasha'il*. The use of the term 'amateur' here refers to the 'military' capabilities of the members of Group 778, rather than their fishing skills. This is evident in their underestimation (*istikhfāf*) of the Israeli security forces (*al-'asas*). As a result of that, they ended up 'spending their night in a jail'. In other words, it is only through this reading of the above excerpt that jailing of 'amateur fishermen' can make sense.

The second *kitāb* in *al-Mutasha'il* provides further evidence that Habiby may have been alluding to Group 778 in his novel. The following scene takes place on the ruins of Tantura:

> Innahu [walā'] ansh'a, ma' ithnayn min zumalā' al-dirāsa, khaliyya sirriyya. Fa-intashalū min kahf, fī ghawr ṣakhriyy fī baḥr al-ṭanṭūra al-mahjūra, ṣunḍuq muḥkam al-ṣinā'a wa-l-aqfāl […] fīhi silāḥ wa-fīhi dhahab kathīr.
> […]
> Fa-ishtarū silāḥan wa-dhakhīra wa-mutafajjirāt. Wa-aqāmū makhzanan wa-maw'ilan sirriyyan fī qabw mahdūm wa-mahjūr fī kharā'ib al-ṭanṭūra. Fa-arsalū aḥadahum ilā lubnān ḥattā yuqīm al-ṣila bi-l-fidā'iyyīn. (p. 146)
>
> He [Wala'], along with two of his schoolmates, had founded a secret cell. Then he had retrieved, from a cave in a deep hollow in the rocks off the deserted beach of Tantura, a well-made strongbox, shut tight so that no moisture could penetrate it. It was filled with weapons and gold.
> […]
> The story went on that the boys had bought weapons, ammunition, and explosives with the gold and had established a hideout and storage depot in the basement of one of the uninhabited ruins of Tantura. They had then sent one of their cell to Lebanon to contact the guerrillas there. (p. 106 in the English version; modified spelling and transliteration for uniformity)

This excerpt explicitly mentions that Wala' and his friends established contacts with Palestinian guerrilla fighters (*fidā'iyyīn*) in Lebanon. The fourth similarity between the novels of Habiby and Fayyad is the planting of a box of explosives on the beach of Tantura (Fayyad 1978: 74), and the fishing of boxes of explosives from the sea of Tantura, the Mediterranean.

The most important similarity between the story of Wala' and his friends and Group 778 lies in the discourse that they hold, one which Habiby opposes. Wala' and his friends represent a Palestinian revolutionary attitude in Israel. They, as a result, seek to join the Palestinian resistance movement. For Wala' and his friends, as well as the members of Group 778, 'Israeli occupation' means not just the occupation of the West Bank and Gaza Strip but also Tantura, which is part of Israel.

Like the fishermen from the earlier excerpt from *al-Mutasha'il*, who 'spent their night in a jail', the members of Group 778 were eventually arrested, tried and jailed. They had a few successful operations but could not liberate Palestine in this way. The message that Emile Habiby tries to deliver in the novel is that violent resistance is futile. In an interview, he said:

> In *al-Mutasha'il* I intended to be faithful to the nation that I am writing about and for … I intended to expose the negative extremist positions which appeared in some groups in our nation and what grievances it had caused … and next to it I exposed the positive positions that opposed extremism … and I believed in the rational way which is remote of emotions and reactions. (Habiby quoted in al-Qasim 1979: 27)

Instead of armed resistance, Habiby proposes a non-violent attitude. In terms of the postmodern style of *al-Mutasha'il*, and the way it serves the political discourse Habiby wishes to deliver, Peter Heath shows how the intertextuality, pastiche (the borrowing from different literary and cultural traditions) and irony aim to express a passive political attitude:

> Habiby's ironic attitude toward [literary Arab] canonical knowledge serves to subvert it. He continually contrasts lofty historical and cultural references from the school canon, which are intended to teach Arab schoolchildren about the greatness and nobility of their past, to the pathetic realities of Sa'id's predicament, in which heroism or idealism are unrealistic expectations, since what is at issue in Sa'id's life is less boldness and heroism than simple survival. In effect, Habiby uses the juxtaposition of intertextual references and Sa'id's thoughts and actions to emphasise that although Palestinians are taught about kings, heroes, and great thinkers from the past, the daily realities they actually face are quite different. The gap between cultural rhetoric and current fact is great. Hence, expecting someone like Sa'id, who is less a hero than an anti-hero, the negation of heroic virtues, to emulate his glorious forebearers is ridiculously unrealistic. (Heath 2000: 167)

The conclusion that Heath presents complements the argument presented above. The passive political orientation is expressed in the final scene in *al-Mutasha'il*. In the third book (*kitāb*) in the novel, titled *Yu'ad al-Thaniya* ('The Second Yu'ad'), Sa'id ends the letter by saying that he found himself seated on a high impalement stake. To remain seated on top of a stake expresses passivity and reluctance to resist; however, it also conveys the message of perseverance – holding on, despite the pain and difficulties. The irony in the title of the penultimate section of the letter, *misk al-khitām, al-imsāk bil-khāzūq* ('The Conclusion, Clutching the Impalement Stake'), lies in the contradiction between the positive connotation of *misk al-khitām*, which is used for positive endings to Arabic stories and tales,[17] and the clutching of the stake, symbolising the source of the pain and suffering of Palestinians in Israel. This irony is made more humorous due to the play with the sounds of the two words: *misk* and *imsāk*. The contrast between *misk* and *imsāk*, conveying 'positive' and 'negative' connotations, mirrors the contrast between the political and spatial discourse in this novel.

In contrast to the passive political stance that Habiby espouses, the spatial portrayal in *al-Mutasha'il* delivers an active attitude. As we have seen in the preceding section, one response to Israeli erasure of the Palestinian was counter-erasure. In *al-Mutasha'il*, Habiby resorts to an approach, which I will call 'un-erasure'. If counter-erasure means 'erasing the Other back', un-erasure means the undoing of erasure, or its cancellation. To achieve this, Habiby not only resorts to the simple 'reversal' of erasure (Muhawi 2006: 35), but also to active exposure. In her doctoral thesis, 'Documenting Palestinian Presence: A Study of the Novels of Emile Habibi and the Films of Elia Suleiman', Abu-Remaileh called this 'direct documenting techniques' (Abu-Remaileh 2010). Exposure, or direct documentation, comes to stress the 'Palestinianness' of the space, its old Arab history, the human personal memories and lives that filled the space, along with the flourishing life that had been ruined. If Suleiman (2004) talks about the 'cartographic cleansing' of Palestinian locations in Israel, then the work of Habiby can be regarded as 'toponymic resistance', since the whole work is filled with Palestinian Arab names. Stressing the Palestinianness of the space takes two complementary forms in *al-Mutasha'il*, namely, repetition and indigenousness (using indigenous Palestinian toponyms).

The repetition technique that Habiby utilises in *al-Mutasha'il* is evident on a number of levels. First, Habiby mentions Palestinian names and toponyms in a greater number and frequency than Hebrew names. As a result, even though the space in which the plot takes place is Israel, it becomes Palestinian in its identity. To achieve this, in the entire novel, Habiby mentions only six Jewish-Israeli cities: Tel-Aviv, Nahariya, Natanya, Zichron Yaa'kov, Nahlal and Affula. In comparison, he mentions the names of more than 100 Palestinian villages, cities, neighbourhoods and sites. Not only are more Palestinian locations mentioned, they also appear with greater frequency than their Jewish-Israeli counterparts. For example, Tel-Aviv is mentioned seven times (the most frequent among the Jewish-Israeli locations), Zichron Yaa'kov and Affula are mentioned three times each, and the rest of the Jewish-Israeli cities are mentioned only once each.

In comparison, Haifa is mentioned more than sixty times, Acre more than forty times and Tantura thirty-seven times. Wadi al-Nisnas, a neighbourhood in Haifa, is mentioned as many times as the biggest Jewish city in Israel, Tel-Aviv. To show the magnitude of the naming strategy in *al-Mutasha'il*, I will list the names of Palestinian sites that appear in this novel. This list reflects other aspects of this strategy, such as the use of local names for places (indigenousness) – an issue that will be addressed later. In the list below, villages marked with an asterisk are villages that have been destroyed by Israel and the numbers in brackets (in selected places) refer to the number of times the location is mentioned in the novel:

> *ʿAkkā* (Acre) (42),[18] *Ḥayfā* (Haifa) (67), *al-Nāṣira* (Nazareth) (13), *Bīr al-Sabʿ** (Be'er Sheva), *Tarshīḥā*, *Miʿilyā*, *Abū Snān*, *Kufr Yāsīf*, *Sabīl al-Ṭāsāt*[19] (in Acre), *al-Birwi** (7), *al-Kwīkāt** (3), *al-Manshiyya**, *ʿAmqa**, *al-Rwīs**, *al-Ḥadathi**, *al-Dāmūn**, *al-Mazrʿa*, *Shaʿab*, *Mīʿār**, *Waʿrat al-Sarrīs**, *al-Zīb**, *al-Baṣṣa**, *al-Kābri**, *Iqrith**, *Rās al-Nāqūra*, *Ḥārat al-Kharāba*[20] (in Acre), *al-Muṣrāra* (in Jerusalem), *al-Qasṭal*,[21] *Wādi al-Ṣalīb* (in Haifa), *Wādi al-Nisnās* (in Haifa) (7), *Shāriʿ al-Jabal* (in Haifa), *Furn al-Armanī*,[22] *Shāriʿ al-Mulūk* (in Haifa), *al-Khalīl* (Hebron), *al-Ṭīra*, *al-Ṭanṭūra** (37), *ʿAyn-Ghazāl**, *Ijzim**, *ʿAyn Ḥūḍ**, *Umm al-Zīnāt**, *Shāriʿ ʿAbbās* (in Haifa) (5), *Qaṭamūn* (in Jerusalem), *al-Quds* (Jerusalem), *Ramallah*, *Nablus* (5), *Wādi al-Jmāl* (in Haifa) (3), *Shafa-ʿAmr*, *Ibṭin*, *al-Ḥāra al-Sharqiyya*[23] (in Nazareth), *Jinīn*, *al-Mqībla**, *Ṣandala*, *al-Ḥallīṣa* (in Haifa), *al-Mjīdil**, *Yāfā** (Jaffa),[24] *Maʿlūl*, *ʿBillīn*, *Ṭamra*, *al-Ṭayba*, *al-Lidd**[25] (Lydda), *Barṭaʿa*, *Jisr al-Zarqāʾ* (12), *al-Frīdīs* (5), *Ghazza* (Gaza), *Jabālya*, *Bayt Lāhyā*, *Bayt Ḥānūn*, *Dīr al-Balaḥ*, *Khān Yūnis*, *Rafaḥ*, *Qalqīlya*, *Ṭūl Karm*, *Ṭūbās*, *al-Sīla*, *al-Lubbūn*, *Ḥayfā al-Taḥtā*,[26] *Bāqa al-Gharbiyya*, *Bīsān*,[27] *al-Laṭrūn*, *ʿImwās**, *Yālū**, *Bayt Nūbā**[28], *al-Silka* (8).

The second level of the repetition technique in *al-Mutashaʾil* serves historical or memorial goals: the mention of so many destroyed villages exposes

Israeli atrocities and crimes against the Palestinians by showing the magnitude of the destruction of Palestinian villages.[29] Moreover, the mention of the names of destroyed Palestinian villages reminds the reader of them and aims at 'asserting its claims of ownership over them' (Suleiman 2006a: 8). Naming these villages un-erases them. Remembering and un-erasure are complementary actions, since they address two different 'audiences'. Remembering is directed towards the Palestinian nation and aims to keep the existing memory of these places in the Palestinian national memory. Un-erasure is directed against the Israeli erasure of Palestinian space and history.

In the words of Ali Al-Khalili, the repetition technique by Habiby aims to shows his insistence on 'refusing to forget' (*rafḍ al-nisyān*) (Al-Khalili 2001: 28). Refusing to forget combines both components of remembering and un-erasure. If we consider refusal to be a simple negation, refusing to forget means simply 'remembering'. However, refusal here is not a simple negation: it is an active and conscious intention to resist forgetting. In this sense, it means 'active remembering', which corresponds to the active intention of un-erasure. It is in this context that the Chinese philosopher and geographer Yi-Fu Tuan deals with issues of space and identity. He recognises the importance of active 'maintenance' of naming:

> To continue to exist, places must be kept in good repair [...] Much the same is true of places created by language, oral and written. 'Mount Misery' will fade from consciousness if it is not kept alive by social support – if the name is not passed on by word of mouth or written on a map that is periodically consulted. (Tuan 1991: 689)

By writing so many Palestinian names, Habiby wants to keep the original Palestinian names alive by resisting their physical erasure by Israel. In addition, Habiby employs a third form of repetition: in many instances when he mentions a destroyed village, he mentions its name twice in the same sentence. On many occasions, he adds information about the destruction of the village. For example:

> Naḥnu min al-kwīkāt, allatī haddamūhā wa-sharradū ahlahā, fa-hal iltaqayta aḥadan min al-kwīkāt?. (p. 31)

> We're from al-Kwikat. They demolished it and evicted everyone. Did you meet anyone from al-Kwikat?. (p. 21 in the English version; modified spelling and transliteration for uniformity)

The excerpt begins with the speaker or speakers stating the name of their village of origin (*naḥnu min-l-kwīkāt*). The mentioning of the name of the village usually includes information about its fate during the 1948 war. The example above indicates that al-Kwikat village was destroyed and its population was driven away (*al-latī haddamūhā wa-sharradū ahlahā*). This interjection of 'documentary information within the narrative text' is one of Habiby's 'direct documenting techniques' (Abu-Remaileh 2010: 54). The excerpt ends with the name of the village, in the form of a question: 'did you meet anybody from al-Kwikat?' Repetition acts as a reminder of the village, and an emphasis of its history. In many instances, the question will be asked in the plural ('we are from …') to express collective experience and ownership.

I mentioned above indigenousness to be a complementary technique to repetition in *al-Mutasha'il*. Indigenousness relates to the fact that Habiby mentions variations of names of Palestinian sites. Haifa and Acre appear in the text many times (sixty-seven and forty-two times respectively). This is not surprising since both cities are central to the plot, but apart from the numerous appearances in the text, Habiby often includes different variations of the names of the cities. For example, in the case of Haifa: *ḥifāwiyya* (Haifan woman); *al-ḥayāfina* (the Haifans – the people of Haifa); *ḥayfā'ayn* (two Haifas). In addition, Sa'id referred to Haifa as *madīnatī, ḥayfā* (my city, Haifa) (p. 60) or *madīnatī al-ḥabība, ḥayfā* (my beloved city, Haifa) (p. 60). In the case of Acre: *'akkiyya* (Acrian woman or Acrian characteristic); *'akkā'* (old version of the name);[30] *'akkāwī* (Acrian man); *'akkiyūn* (Acrians); *'akka* (old version of the name). For the Norwegian architect and architecture historian Christian Norberg-Schulz, both the individual and the space participate in the evolution of both identities:

> we identify with the indication of our place of origin, as when we say: 'I'm Roman,' or 'I'm Viennese' […]. Man's identity, in other words, is a function of his participation in the identity of a place. […] Identity means living in a world that comprehends both the place and the community in which one lives. (Norberg-Schulz 2000: 33–4)

Space 'imprints' itself on its inhabitants (and vice versa), so that they become Viennese, Haifans or Acrians. Being a Haifan means to have something in common with other Haifans. To stress the Palestinian sense of belonging to Palestine, the references in this novel are only used in relation to Palestinian spaces and people.

A fourth example of the interest in spatial identity that Habiby shows is the use of local naming when he describes and orientates Sa'id around the streets of Haifa (on the 'urban level'). What Norberg-Schulz called 'the urban level' can be associated with any 'dense' social space such as a city, a neighbourhood or a village. This social interaction contributes to the social cohesion of the space where the neighbourhood stops being an alien place:

> The neighbourhood can thus be grasped as this area of public space in general (anonymous, for everyone) in which little by little a *private, particularised space* insinuates itself as a result of the practical, everyday use of this space. The fact that dwellers have their homes here, the reciprocal habituation resulting from being neighbours, the processes of recognition-of identification-that are created thanks to proximity, to concrete coexistence in the same urban territory: all these 'practical' elements offer themselves for use as vast fields of exploration with a view to understanding a little better the great unknown that is everyday life. (de Certeau, Giard and Mayol 1998: 9; italics in original)

The best expression of the social cohesion of Palestinian society in the writing of Habiby, providing a further example to the indigenousness technique, comes in the form of the use of local names to orientate Sa'id around the streets of Haifa. On one occasion, Sa'id is walking next to *furn al-armanī* (the Armenian's bakery). Local names associate a place with its owners – in this case, its Armenian owner. '*Furn al-armanī*' is not the name of the shop, but it is the way Haifans always refer to it. To describe the bakery in Haifa as the 'Armenian's bakery', one needs to know that the shop-owner is of Armenian origin, and to know this, one needs to be familiar with the shop-owner.

Haifa was a crucible (*būtaqa*), to borrow the metaphor from *Ruh fi-l-Butaqa*, a melting pot, which over time melted all the various cultures that lived in the city into one identity that unified them. Haifa and Acre 'built' their identities through a long history of social evolution. The other side of this argument is that the Zionist-Jewish enterprise did not 'participate' (to use Norberg-Schulz's term) in the evolution of the identity of the city of Haifa (or Palestine). Rather, Zionism destroyed it altogether and sought to replace it with a new identity.

Al-Mutasha'il expresses a doubly contradictory identity, one that associates and dissociates Palestinian citizens in Israel from both Jewish-Israelis and Palestinians outside Israel. On the one hand, the political discourse that it promotes opposes violent actions against Israel, meaning that Palestinian citizens in Israel should not take part in the struggle for liberation that Palestinians outside Israel are participating in. On the other hand, the spatial discourse in *al-Mutasha'il* aims to place Palestinian citizens in Israel within Palestinian history, by un-erasing the history of the Nakba of 1948. Habiby, then, sees that Palestinian citizens in Israel are in a particular situation, and that they should seek to find solutions to their problems within the Israeli system. This discourse reflects the political orientation of Palestinians of Israel in the 1970s. According to Palestinian political scientist Nadim Rouhana, up until the first Palestinian Intifada in 1987, Palestinians in Israel subscribed to a tripartite consensus:

> (1) unequivocal support for the establishment of a Palestinian state in the West Bank and Gaza Strip under the leadership of the PLO; (2) a demand for full equality as citizens of Israel; and (3) agreement that all forms of political activity be conducted within the limits allowed by Israeli law. (Rouhana 1990: 59)

The three components in Palestinian consensus that Rouhana mentions correspond to the doubly contradictory identity expressed in *al-Mutasha'il*, as indicated above. The multiplicity of components in both the 'tripartite consensus' or 'the doubly contradictory identity' mean, for Azmi Bishara, that Palestinians in Israel between the years 1967 and 1987 did not form a coherent political or ideological movement (see: Bishara 1993).

However, although the conclusions of Rouhana may be correct regarding the Palestinian political stance, they do not reflect the sense of 'missed opportunity' that Palestinian novels express in this period. Missed opportunity is a marker of change and transformation in orientation towards the Other, because it means failing to achieve an opportunity of peace. The discourse in *al-Mutasha'il* does not convey a sense of missed opportunity. The political stance in the novel, the call for perseverance and clutching to the stake, reflect a hope that things will improve in the future for Palestinians in Israel. However, Habiby expresses a sense of missed opportunity in a later novel, which will be discussed below.

Passage of Time

Ikhtayya (1985), the second novel by Emile Habiby, is about *'āmil murūr al-zaman* – passage of time factor. Passage of time in this novel refers to the narrator understanding events occurring during his childhood in Haifa. The narrator is a resident of Haifa who works for *Al-Ittiḥād* newspaper, which is affiliated to the communist party in Israel.[31] The plot consists of three chapters, each of which is called 'Notebook' (*daftar*). The plot revolves around the memories of the narrator regarding an unexplained gridlock, which paralysed the traffic in Haifa ten years prior to the time of writing his memoirs. His memories of the gridlock lead him to his childhood memories of an event that took place in Haifa during the 1940s – almost four decades prior to the time of narration (1984). These childhood memories are of central interest to the narrator, since only with the passage of time can he now (at the time of writing) understand some of the formative events of his childhood. In the plot of *Ikhtayya*, the passing of time represents the realisation and understanding of the consequences of Palestinian existence in Israel. I will analyse the manifestation of the passage of time in the spatial narrative of *Ikhtayya* in comparison to the spatial discourse in *al-Mutasha'il*, aiming to understand the implications of passage of time in terms on Palestinian identity in Israel in this period.

Whereas in *al-Mutasha'il*, Habiby advocates a passive political approach, according to which Palestinian citizens in Israel need to cling to their impalement stake and wait until things improve, in *Ikhtayya*, by contrast, Habiby realises the effects of the passage of time and the message he wants to deliver here is that Palestinian citizens in Israel cannot be passive about their existence in Israel, because this has implications for their identity, which is already becoming fragmented. In the following excerpt from *Ikhtayya*, the narrator follows one of the characters in the plot as he walks through the streets of Haifa:

> Thumma nushāhiduhu yanzil, fī sāʿa thābita min sāʿāt al-ʿaṣr, ilā wādī al-nisnās marra ukhrā. Yahbiṭ fī shāriʿ al-jabal thumma yaʿruj, yamīnan, ʿalā zaqāq al-ḥarīriī fa-l-wādī yaṣʿad fīhi ḥattā maṭābiʿ 'al-ittiḥād' wa-dukkān al-jammāl wa-malḥamat al-shafāʿamrī, thumma yaltaff, yasāran, ʿalā shāriʿ qīsārya wa-yamḍī fīhi ḥattā yaʿbur bayt abī ilyās fa-yataḥawwal, yamīnan, mukhtariqan al-zaqāq al-mufḍī ilā 'shāriʿ al-mukhalliṣ' yasīru fīhi ḥattā ākhirihi, muʿrijan ʿalā saāriʿ 'shabtay līfī' ʿāʾidan, ṣaʿdan, ilā shāriʿ ʿabbās fa-ilā baytihi. (p. 131)

> Then we see him descend, in a regular hour in the afternoon, to Wadi al-Nisnas again. Lands in al-Jabal Street, then turns right to Ziqaq al-Hariri, then the wadi, which he climbs upwards until he reaches *al-Ittihad* [newspaper] printers and al-Jammal's shop and the Shafa-Amri's butchery, then turns left, to Qisarya Street, which he walks through until he passes Abu Ilyas's house, where he turns right, through the alley that leads to al-Mukhallis Street, which he walks until its end, where he turns to Shabtay Levy Street, returning upwards to Abbas Street, then to his home. (p. 131)

As we saw in the discussion of un-erasure in *al-Mutashaʾil*, Habiby aims to portray Haifa (and Israel) as a Palestinian space. He does so by showing the intimate and organic relationship between human life and participation in the evolution of the identity of the place. In the above excerpt from *Ikhtayya*, the narrator follows the character as he walks through the streets of Haifa. There are examples of local naming similar to that of *furn al-armanī*: *maṭābiʿ al-ittiḥād* (*al-Ittiḥād* newspaper's printing house), *dukkān al-jammāl* (al-Jammal's shop), *malḥamat al-shafāʿamrī* (the Shafa-Amri butchery), *bayt abī Ilyās* (Abu Ilyas's house, or Ilyas's father's house). All of these are local identification markers that have evolved with the daily social interaction of the inhabitants of Haifa.

However, what 'disrupts' this near-pure Palestinian space is the use of Shabtay Levi Street[32] to orientate the character in Haifa. In the discussion on *al-Mutashaʾil* we took the example of *furn al-armanī* to show how 'the identity of a place is derived from the fact of the permanence of existence of the place and the time that passes' (Norberg-Schulz 2000: 54). The passage of time in *al-Mutashaʾil* relates to the construction of the identity of Haifa until 1948. The portrayal of the identity of this city in *al-Mutashaʾil* does not take into consideration the evolution of the spatial identity of the city after 1948. The passage of time in *Ikhtayya* refers to the transformations in the spatial identity of the city after 1948. The passage of time since the occupation of the city means that Palestinian spatial identification has started to use Jewish-Israeli names, and hence the city has taken on a Jewish-Israeli identity. In the same way that the Armenian has become part of the local identity of Haifa through the slow process of identity evolution, so has the Jewish-Israeli.

Passage of time factor is evident in *Ikhtayya* on two levels, relating to the repetition and indigenousness techniques that Habiby utilises in the earlier novel, *al-Mutasha'il*. First, with regards to repetition, in *Ikhtayya* Habiby uses Hebrew names in a considerably greater number and frequency in comparison to *al-Mutasha'il*: the gridlock around which most of the novel revolves takes place in HaHalutz Street in Haifa. Not only do Hebrew names of locations appear in *Ikhtayya* (Tel-Aviv, Dimona, Paz Bridge in Haifa, HaGiborim Street in Haifa, Yisrael Bar-Yehuda Street in Haifa), this novel is full of names of Hebrew daily terms: *Hul*, acronym of 'abroad'; *Ramzor*, 'traffic light'; *Ashaf* (PLO); *Sfaradim*, Sephardic or oriental Jews; *Hel Raglim*, 'infantry'; *Mapai*, acronym of *Mefleget Poale yisrael* (Mapai – Israel Labour Party); *Mafdal*, acronym of *Miflaga Datit Liomit* (Mafdal – National Religious Party); *Hadash*, acronym of *Hazit Demokratit LaShalom* (Hadash – The Democratic Front for Peace); *Nahal*, acronym of *Noar Halutzi Lohem* (Fighting Pioneer Youth); *Zahal*, acronym of *Zava Hagana LeYisrael* (Israel Defence Army); *Zadal*, acronym of *Zva Drom Levanon* (South Lebanon Army); *Shabak*, acronym of *Shirute Betahon Klali* (General Security Services); *Mankal*, acronym for CEO. Moreover, Habiby mentions names of Zionist and Jewish-Israeli leaders and politicians (Hertzl, Ben Gurion, Dayan, Begin, Shamir, Ariel Sharon, Bar-Yehuda and Pinhas Sapir).

Secondly, with regards to indigenousness and passage of time, in *Ikhtayya* Habiby outlines the transformation in toponyms of a number of streets and other locations in Haifa, highlighting the transitory nature of the identity of space: the main hospital in Haifa, Rambam, named after Rabi Musa Bin Maymon, used to be called *Mustashfa al-Doktur Hamza* before 1948 (p. 24); Paz Bridge in Haifa used to be called Shell Bridge (both named after petroleum companies, p. 32); Al-Nasira Road in Haifa, which became Yisra'el Bar-Yehuda (p. 34); *Maydan al-Malik Faysal* (King Faysal Square) became

Hativat Golani Street (p. 34); Al-Jabal Road, which was renamed after the United Nations (p. 36); *Sahat al-Hanatir* ('Carriages Square'), which became *Sahat al-Khamra* ('Wine Square') during the British Mandate, became Paris Square after 1948 (p. 37); and Al-Muluk Street, which became HaAzmaut Street ('Independence', p. 40).

As a result of the passage of time, Haifa in *Ikhtayya* is no longer a 'pure' Palestinian space, as it is portrayed in *al-Mutasha'il.* Instead, after the disruption of this space in 1948, a new process of spatial evolution begins to take place. The realisation that the identity of Haifa is in constant evolution, due to the passage of time, initiates nostalgic emotions for the lost culture of the city. In the following excerpt, the narrator talks about the life that was lost with the occupation of Haifa in 1948:

> Kānat al-dunyā ḥalālan, wa-kāna al-ʿayshu fīhā ḥalālan. Wa-lam nakun naʿrifu min al-ḥarām mā natajannabahu siwā al-namīma. Wa-kunnā natajannabuhā mahma ghalā al-thaman.
>
> Fa-bi-ayyi maḍi yuhaddidūnak bi-l-kashf ʿanhu, yā ʿabd al-karīm? Bimā yusammunahu, taʿassufan, bi-l-ḥubb? hal yaʿrifunahu?
>
> Law kānū yaʿrifūnahu laʾabqū daghlan bikran nalʿabu fīhi al-ghummīḍa. Aw ghayḍa ṣanawbariyya nastariqu al-ḥubb ilayhā, aw saṭḥ bayt, khuluwwan min-l-sawārī wa-l-ṣahārīj, kunnā natabādal fīhi naqsh asmāʾina al-mukhtāra, zawjayn, dhakaran wa-unthā, kamā khalaqahumā rabbuhumā al-khāliq.
> [...]
> *Kānat al-jīra ḥalālan, wa-l-jār min ahl al-bayt. Wa-kan al-jār yantasib ilā jārihi [...]. Wa-qad maḍā wa-inqaḍā wa-dhahab mundhu an 'dhahab al-ʿarab'*. (pp. 119–20)
>
> Our world was legitimate and living in it was legitimate. And we knew no sin, apart from gossip. And we used to avoid it at all cost.
>
> So about what past are they threatening to expose, Abd al-Karim? What they call, tyrannically, love? Do they know it?
>
> If they knew it they would have left an untouched bush where we can play hide and seek. Or a pine forest where we hide our love, or a rooftop, empty

> from antennae and water tanks, where we used to carve our names, in couples, male and female, as God created them.
> [...]
> Neighbouring was legitimate, and neighbours were are like family members. And a neighbour was related to his neighbour [...] and this time has passed since the 'Arabs left'. (pp. 119–20)

Abd al-Karim is a Palestinian refugee who returns to Haifa after thirty years in search of his childhood love, Ikhtayya. Abd al-Karim is accused by the Israeli investigation committee of causing the gridlock that paralysed the traffic in Haifa and was so severe that it reached the outskirts of Tel-Aviv, some 100 kilometres to the south, and Acre to the north. The narrator wonders how the love of Abd al-Karim for Ikhtayya could be considered an offence. Abd al-Karim talking to Ikhtayya about his love for her takes the narrator back to their childhood, which occurred prior to 1948.

In the above excerpt, the narrator distinguishes between two periods in the life of Palestinians in Haifa, a legitimate (*ḥalāl*) period and an illegitimate period, having the 1948 war as the dividing point between the two. This distinction is made clear in the above excerpt, starting with mentioning the legitimate life (*kānat al-dunyā ḥalālan, kāna al-ʿayshu ḥalālan, kānat al-jīra ḥalālan*). Palestinian legitimate, or harmonious, life in the city was terminated when the Arabs left (*mundhu dhahaba al-ʿarab*), alluding to the establishment of Israel in 1948 and the expulsion of the Palestinians from Haifa. With regard to understanding Palestinian identity in this discourse, according to Norberg-Schulz,

> [i]dentity means living in a world that comprehends both the place and the community in which one lives. And when that world is thwarted and rendered fruitless [...] the alienation persists, inasmuch as there is no longer anything that has either proximity or significance. (Norberg-Schulz 2000: 33–4)

In *Ikhtayya*, Habiby portrays the destruction of Palestinian life in Haifa as a result of the destruction of the space in which community life can take place. Such a depiction of life in Haifa is nostalgic, focusing on what is lost and is no longer there. Nostalgia, in other words, is another expression of the passage of time. In fact, *Ikhtayya* is not the only Palestinian novel that presents a nostalgic narrative. From the late 1980s, nostalgia becomes a dominant theme in Palestinian novels in Israel. Chapter 3 of this book will deal with Palestinian nostalgia in Israel in greater detail.

The nostalgic narrative in *Ikhtayya* constitutes not only a direct accusation of Zionist destruction of Palestinian life, it also marks a new form of Palestinian response to modernisation. This response, it seems, is not unique to Palestinian citizens in Israel. According to Linda Hutcheon,

> it was postmodernism that brought the conjunction of irony and nostalgia quite literally into the public eye through the forms of its architecture [...] This return was in reaction to modern architecture's ostentatious rejection of the past, including the past of the city's historical fabric. (Hutcheon 2000: 191)

In the case of Palestinian novels, the nostalgic discourse responds to modernisation novels' 'ostentatious rejection of the past' and aims, in the case of *Ikhtayya*, to revive the 'past of the city's historical fabric'.

In the above excerpt from *Ikhtayya* – on childhood, youth and maturity – the space of the city has accommodated almost a complete cycle of life. Not mentioning death as part of the life cycle prior to 1948 also reflects the narrator's/author's memory of this period – a memory that is associated with life and love. The *ḥalāl* life in pre-1948 Haifa is linked to the space in which it took place. The couples who met in the hiding places of the neighbourhood, in the gardens, bushes (*daghl*), forests (*ghayḍa*), rooftops (*saṭḥ bayt*) and streets of the city, are depicted as being innocent, 'the way their God created them' (*kamā khalaqhumā rabbuhumā al-khāliq*). The young children of the neighbourhood grow and love each other and end up forming families with each other. '*Al-jār min ahl al-bayt*' has two meanings here. In Arabic, '*bayt*' means 'home' or 'house', but also has the meaning of 'family'. The first meaning suggests that people spend such a long time in the homes of their neighbours that they are considered inhabitants of the house. *Bayt* as family is shown by the use of '*yantasibu*', meaning 'to become a relative' by marrying each other.

If we compare *al-Mutashaʾil* with *Ikhtayya*, we notice that in the latter, Habiby recognises the temporal dimension of spatial identification and that this is a continuous and unstoppable process. *Ikhtayya* reflects both the changes in the spatial identification and social cohesion of Palestinian society after 1948. The sense of missed opportunity is evident in the nostalgic tone of the novel, which sees no hope in the present and seeks solace in the past. In addition, the nostalgic tone of this novel reflects the fact that there is no clear political line in *Ikhtayya* in comparison to *al-Mutasha'il*, and Habiby offers no 'solution' to the Palestinian identity problem in Israel – not even that of clutching to an impalement stake. The end result is a sad and nostalgic work on a fragmented society whose social and physical space has been disrupted.

Conclusion

The modernisation process that Palestinians in Israel have undergone since 1948 has had notable effects on various aspects of life of this society. Fundamentally, modernisation is manifest in the differentiation process in Palestinian society, beginning with individualisation, through, as a result, the weakening of Palestinian family structure, through to fragmentation in social institutions, social cohesion and religion. Palestinian counteraction novels symbolise a 'public debate', inscribed on the pages of the novels, contemplating the ongoing modernisation of this society. The perspective manifest in *Al-Juththa al-Majhula* represents an orientation that warns of the complete destruction of society, pointing to the state of anomie of some of the Palestinians in Israel. Conversely, *Hubb 'Abir al-Qarrat* outlines an adaptive approach, according to which modernisation of Palestinians in Israel is a necessary process. However, according to this novel, Palestinians need to be 'selective' in choosing the value of modernisation that they want to incorporate. Samya represents this approach. She sought to fulfil her individualism and personal freedom with preserving values regarding the preservation of family solidarity. Although the individualism of Samya meant the destruction of traditional patriarchal family structure, such destruction did not leave her Palestinian family in a void. A modern Palestinian family, according to *Hubb 'Abir al-Qarrat*, is a non-patriarchal, but a democratic family, to reuse the terminology of Hisham Sharabi.

Nonetheless, by no means do these two novels represent the entirety of perspectives in the Palestinian literary debate on modernisation. Palestinian counteraction novels reflect a wide range of orientations in this regard. My choice to bring these two illustrative novels was intended for showing that

Palestinians in this period were grappling with questions relating to the social transformations they underwent. The debate on social issues proves to be paramount to understanding Palestinian identity in Israel in these years (1967–87). The binary structure of counteraction novels is a clear indication for this: the distinction between 'pre-modern' and 'modern', notwithstanding any approach in particular novels, is depicted in spatial (Israeli–non-Israeli) terms. This distinction both associates Palestinian modernisation to being related to Israel, and, more importantly, to the question of Palestinian belonging or alienation there.

The binary structure of the plots, as well as counter-erasure, reflect Palestinian alienation and dissociation from Israel. In comparison to modernisation novels from the earlier period (1948–67), which made a clear connection between integrating into Israel and Palestinian modernisation, counteraction novels reflect a different position. *Al-Juththa al-Majhula*, for example, associates modernisation in Israel with alienation in it, thus completely reversing the earlier approach. *Hubb ʿAbir al-Qarrat* voices the notion that modernisation (here with a focus on individualisation) can be fulfilled in a place where the individual is integrated into society. The fact that Samya achieved this in a space that is not Israeli implies, thus, Palestinian alienation in Israel. Moreover, the fact that Samya comes back to her family, resulting in the death of the father, means that Palestinian modernisation in Israel can be isolated from the political context. However, not all counteraction novels portray such an approach.

Palestinian alienation in Israel is evident in counter-erasing Jewish-Israeli characters in counteraction novels. With regards to Palestinian identity in Israel, counter-erasure not only reflects Palestinian lack of integration there, but, above all, conveys lack of Palestinian identity. In other words, counter-erasure only expresses the fact that Palestinians in Israel are not Israelis. Moreover, counter-erasure does not convey what Palestinians in Israel are. Because counter-erasure is a mirror reflection of Israeli erasure of Palestinians, by employing it, Palestinians maintain their own erasure.

To sum up, counteraction novels reflect the disintegration of Palestinian identity in Israel. From the response to modernisation, this group attempts to address social fragmentation in Palestinian society. The response to Zionism reflects, and maintains, Palestinian alienation and erasure in Israel.

In comparison to the self-erasing narrative in counteraction novels, disenchantment novels directly address issues relating to Palestinian presence and life in Israel, focusing on the political dimensions of these. In other words, whereas counter-erasure discourse prevents, by default, addressing political questions explicitly (because that would necessitate dealing with Jewish-Palestinian relations), disenchantment novels bring these relations to the fore. As a result, issues of modernisation and its effects on Palestinian society are relatively marginalised in favour of the political discourse.

With regards to the 'continuity and change' with which Andreas Huyssen characterised the relationship between modernism and postmodernism, outlined at the beginning of this chapter, the theme of missed opportunity relates to the initial Palestinians modernist hopes to integrate into Israel. Missed opportunity reflects a transformation in this regard, but not a complete reversal. Palestinian narrative attributes the failure to achieve coexistence in Israel to the exclusivist nature of Zionism. Disenchantment novels reflect a Palestinian doubly contradictory identity in Israel. Doubly contradictory identity means that Palestinians in Israel acknowledge that they are neither completely Israeli, nor fully Palestinian: on the one hand, the sense of missed opportunity that appears in novels after 1967 is coupled with the 'resurrection' and reappearance of Palestinian national awareness in Israel. This is further evident by the efforts to un-erase Palestinian history and memory, as well as asserting Palestinian indigenousness. On the other hand, Palestinians in Israel, according to novels in this period, should restrict their political activity to fall within the boundaries of Israeli law, thus opposing joining the (also violent) Palestinian struggle for self-determination outside Israel.

However, doubly contradictory identity could sustain itself only as long as the balance between the two sides of the contradiction is maintained. However, in *Ikhtayya*, Habiby shows that the temporal dimension of Palestinian existence in Israel disturbs such a balance. The Palestinian component in the doubly contradictory identity is based on the memory of Palestine, the past traditions and the lifestyle that were altered with the creation of Israel. Moreover, Israeli inherent erasure of Palestinian existence, history and memory poses a severe threat to Palestinian identity. As a result, Palestinian discourse towards the late 1980s becomes nostalgic, in an attempt to revive the diminishing Palestinian identity. The nostalgic discourse strengthens the

Palestinian component at the expense of the Israeli. Nostalgic narratives in Palestinian novels become more dominant after 1987, as a result of the first Palestinian Intifada. In the following chapter, I will analyse Palestinian novels published in Israel after 1987, examining in greater detail the nostalgic aspect, as well as other common characteristics, that appear in these novels.

Table 2.1 Novels published between 1967 and 1987

Group	Novel	
I	Ḥāṭūm, Muʿīn (1973), *Wa-Dhawat Basmat Allāh*, al-Nāṣira: al-Maṭbaʿa al-ʿAṣriyya.	1
I	Dhyāb, Fāṭma (1973), *Riḥla fī Qiṭār al-Māḍī*, ʿAkkā: Dār al-Qabs al-ʿArabiyy.	2
I	Salāma, Kamāl (1973), *Al-Juththa al-Majhūla*, al-Nāṣira: al-Maṭbaʿa al-ʿAṣriyya.	3
II	Habiby, Emile (1974 [2006]), *Al-Waqāʾiʿ al-Gharība fī Ikhtifāʾ Saʿīd Abī-l-Naḥs al-Mutashāʾil*, Ḥayfā: Dār ʿArābesk. Quoted translations from this English version: Habiby, Emile (1974 [2003]), *The Secret Life of Saeed, the Pessoptimist*, translated by S. K. Jayyusi and T. LeGassick, Northampton: Interlink Books.	4
I	Ḥsaysī, Majīd, and Farḥāt Farḥāt (1975), *Al-Qaḍiyya Raqam 13*, al-Quds: Maṭbaʿat al-Sharq al-Taʿāwuniyya.	5
II	Nāṭūr, Salmān (1976), *Anta al-Qātil Yā Shaykh*, Dalyat al-Karmil: Maṭbaʿat al-Sharq al-Taʿāwuniyya.	6
II	Al-Qāsim, Samīḥ (1977), *Ilā al-Jaḥīm Ayyuhā al-Laylak*, al-Quds: Manshūrāt Ṣalāḥ a-Dīn.	7
I	Ḥijāzī, ʿAbd al-Raḥmān (1977), *Ḥubb ʿĀbir al-Qārrāt* Kufr Qāsim: Maktabat al-Shaʿb.	8
II	Al-Qāsim, Samīḥ (1977), *Al-Ṣūra al-Akhīra fī-l-Albūm*, al-Quds: Dār al-Nawras al-Falasṭīniyya.	9
I	Ẓāhir, Nājī (1981), *Al-Shams Fawq al-Madīna al-Kabīra*, ʿAkkā: Dār al-Aswār.	10
I	Nāṣir, Yusif (1982), *Ḍarīḥ al-Ḥasnāʾ*, ʿAkkā: Maktabat wa-Maṭbaʿat Abū Raḥmūn.	11
I	Jubrān, Kamāl (1984), *Masāriḥ al-Dhiʾāb*, Ḥayfā: Maṭbaʿat al-Ittiḥād al-Taʿāwuniyya.	12
I	Habīballah, ʿAzmī (1984), *Wa-Jāʾ al-Ghurūb*, ʿAyn Māhil: n.p.	13
II	Habiby, Emile (1985 [2006]), *Ikhṭayya*, Ḥayfā: Dār ʿArābesk.	14
I	Fāʿūr, ʿAdnān (1985), *Gharīb*, al-Quds: Manshūrāt al-Bayādir.	15
II	Shammas, Anton (1986), *Arabeskot*, Tel-Aviv: Am Oved. [Hebrew]	16
II	Khūrī, Salīm (1986), *Rūḥ fī-l-Būtaqa*, ʿAkkā: Dār al-Aswār.	17
I	Dhyāb, Fāṭma (1987), *Qaḍiyya Nisāʾiyya wa-Alwān Dākina*, Shafā-ʿAmr: Dār al-Mashriq.	18
*	Ḥalabī, Muṣbāḥ (1987), *Druzim*, Dalyat al-Karmel: n.p. [Hebrew]	19

Groups: I Counteraction novels; II Re-enchantment novels.
* Novels that do not belong to any of the groups.

Notes

1. The best examples are: *Hubb 'Abir al-Qarrat* (1977), by Abd al-Rahman Hijazi, and *al-Qadiyya Raqam 13* (1975), by Majid Hsaysi and Farhat Farhat. Other works from this period (1967–87) share similar characteristics as well, although less clearly than in these three.
2. Elsewhere in the novel, the narrator directly reminds us of everybody's laughter at the request for beer: '*Aṣbaḥat kalimat bīra ʿādiyya bi-l-nisba lahu. Tudhakkirahu ʿindamā kān fī ṭabariyyā wa-qāl: aḥḍir lī bīrā. ʿIndamā ḍaḥika jamīʿ aṣdiqāʾihi*'. 'The word beer has become normal for him. It reminds him of the visit to Tiberias when he asked his friend: bring me beer. When all his friends laughed at the request' (p. 58).
3. Note that Samya could have such an important social role because she was able to integrate into society in the USA. This point is related to the second characteristic of novels in this period – namely, the erasure of Palestinians in Israel, which means their lack of integration into Israeli society.
4. Other violent novels (according to date of publication) include: *Wa-Dhawat Basmat Allah* (*And God's Smile Faded*, 1973), by Mu'in Hatum; *Hubb ʿAbir al-Qarrat* (*Intercontinental Love*, 1977), by Abd al-Rahman Hjazi; *Masarih al-Dhi'ab* (*The Wolves' Stages*, 1984), by Kamal Jubran.
5. For Galtung, 'Direct violence is an *event*; structural violence is a *process* with ups and downs; cultural violence is an *invariant*, a "permanence"' (Galtung 1990: 294; italics in original).
6. At the time of publishing this novel in the early 1970s (only a few years after lifting the military rule in 1966), Palestinian villages in Israel did not enjoy basic public utilities, let alone industrialisation programmes. For example: 'As late as 1971, about half of Arab villages [in Israel] were still unconnected to the national electricity grid and by 1976, only one of the 104 Arab villages had a sewer system' (R. Khalidi 1984: 69).
7. The only indication that Umm Dahud, the landlady, was Jewish is that she asked Muhammad: 'Do you think I don't know the names of the villages?' (p. 42). To show her knowledge of Palestinian villages she mentioned some of them (using their correct Arabic name): *Majd al-Krum, Al-Taybe, Kafr-Yasif, Al-Mghar, Shafa-Amr, Tamra.* Her attempt to show her knowledge of Palestinian villages shows that she was not expected to know them. Many Israeli-Jews do not know where Palestinian villages are nor do they have a personal relationship with people from these villages.

8. Jews of Arab origin, which in the case of Ramat-Gan, would most probably have been of Iraqi descent.
9. The fact that proverbs are used gives the strong impression that this is a Palestinian context. However, it is difficult to make such an assertion as there are no Palestinian-specific proverbs, and geographical categorisation can only be limited to relatively large areas. For example, proverbs that were used in this novel can be considered as *Amthāl Shāmiyya* – an area that includes Syria, Lebanon, Palestine and Jordan. On the other hand, there has never been an extensive study on proverbs and their geographic variations; therefore, it is difficult to assess this matter in either direction (personal communication with Shukri Arraf).
10. It is important to note that categorisation of novels in this book aims to highlight the main patterns and themes in Palestinian literature in order to promote our understanding of transformations in Palestinian identity. Categorisation does not aim to suggest complete distinctiveness.
11. For more detailed discussion on postmodern literary styles, see: Lewis 2001.
12. For Palestinian literary critic Adil al-Usta it is unclear in this passage whether the 'speaker' is the narrator or if Amir is talking to himself. The sentence that preceded the excerpt was narrated in the past tense third person: 'Amir opened his eyes suddenly' (p. 7), but in the quotation the narrative switches to the present tense second person (for a detailed discussion on the narration in this novel, see: al-Usta 2002: 152–8).
13. *Uqṭuf ḥiqdika biriqqa akādīmiyya wa-shummahu biḥaraka muhadhdhaba masraḥiyya thumma ʿalliqhu fī yāqat badlatuka al-waḥīda li-yatafarraj al-nās wa liyumattiʿū anẓārahum biwarda falasṭīniyya lam tabraḥ arḍahā* (pp. 7–8).
14. The name of the city in which the plot takes place is not mentioned, but there are many signs to support the impression that it is Haifa: it is a mixed city; it has a hospital that has a helicopter pad; in the novel, the hospital receives wounded soldiers that come from Lebanon.
15. *Qabl sāʿāt ʿadīda ashārat ilā al-sābiʿa, wa-hā hiya al-ān tushīr ilā al-sābiʿa* (p. 70).
16. *Ṭūfān min al-laylak yasuddu manāfidha al-ghurfa wa-yaghmirunī ḥattā al-khināq* (p. 38).
17. The Arabic *misk* means in English '[a] substance which imitates or resembles musk; any of various synthetic compounds having the characteristic persistent odour of musk and often used in perfumery' (OED). Musk is mentioned in Quran 83:26. *Al-Abrār* (the pious believers of Islamic monotheism): (*Khitāmuhu*

miskun wa-fī dhālika fa-liyatanāfasa al-mutanāfisūn) 'The seal thereof will be Musk: and for this let those aspire, who have aspirations'.

18. Akko in Hebrew. The city still exists, but most of its population was expelled in 1948.
19. Local naming. Literally, 'Path of Bowls'.
20. Local naming. Literally, 'The Ruin Neighbourhood'.
21. An area near Jerusalem where a historic battle took place in the 1948 war during which Palestinian leader Abd al-Qadir al-Husayni was killed.
22. Local naming. Literally, 'The Armenian's Bakery'.
23. Local naming. Literally, 'The Eastern Neighbourhood'.
24. Yafo in Hebrew. The city still exists, but most of its population was expelled in 1948.
25. Lod in Hebrew. The city still exists, but most of its population was expelled in 1948.
26. Local naming. Literally, 'lower Haifa'.
27. Bet-She'ān in Hebrew. The city still exists and is populated by Jews. Its Palestinian population was expelled in 1948.
28. These three villages were occupied and destroyed by the Israeli army during the 1967 war.
29. Elsewhere in the novel, Habiby goes on to recount other atrocities that Israel inflicted on the Palestinians: transforming a school into a military compound and its blackboards into ping-pong tables (p. 19); the military governor expels a Palestinian woman and her infant child at gunpoint (p. 24); the looting of the deserted Haifa homes (p. 64); and the imprisoning of the parents whose children wanted to swim in the sea (p. 104).
30. Other examples include *al-farādisa* (the people of *al-frīdīs*) – a village near Haifa.
31. Emile Habiby, too, was a resident of Haifa and the editor of *Al-Ittiḥad* newspaper. He was, also, a leader of the communist party.
32. Shabtay Levi Street was named after the first Jewish mayor of Haifa.

3

PALESTINIAN NOVELS IN ISRAEL, 1987–2010: UNITED BY ALIENATION

This chapter discusses the evolution of Palestinian identity in Israel after 1987, a period marked by sharp political transformations. The first Palestinian Intifada in 1987 swept through the West Bank and Gaza Strip in a popular uprising against twenty years of Israeli military occupation. The Intifada, the collapse of the Soviet Union and the Gulf War in 1991 led to the Madrid peace talks in 1992, followed by secret talks in Oslo. This peace process proceeded until its collapse in 2000, with the outbreak of the second Intifada. The first Intifada and its associated developments moved Palestinians in Israel to reconsider their political stance and identity in light of a peace process that excluded them from the solution to the Palestinian problem. The outbreak of the second Intifada in 2000 marked a transformation in Palestinian political participation in Israel, evidenced in the local demonstrations held in solidarity with Palestinians in the Occupied Territories.

These events had a marked influence on Palestinian identity in Israel. The publication of four 'vision documents' in the years following the second Intifada highlights this political activity, aiming to define the relationship between the Palestinians and Israel, as well as to form a political discourse that begins to address key questions in the Zionist–Palestinian conflict. The four 'vision documents' were proposed by Palestinian academics and politicians (both individually and institutionally[1]) inside Israel. The four documents address different aspects of Palestinian life in Israel (legal rights, education and so forth) but above all they mark the emergence of a collective Palestinian discourse inside Israel.

In a study of Palestinian political identification in Israel after the outbreak of the first Intifada, Nadim Rouhana concluded that it did not affect the aforementioned tripartite consensus, and that the solidarity of Palestinian citizens in Israel with the Palestinians in the Occupied Territories during the uprising remained symbolic, consisting *only of verbal or artistic* expressions of 'sentimental identification' (Rouhana 1990: 61). The conclusion that Rouhana presents may be correct with regard to Palestinian political *activity*, but his dismissal of the verbal and artistic sentimental identification fails to acknowledge the valuable political and national identification components that Palestinians in Israel carry, as I will show in this chapter.

Transformations in identity are not always reflected in political activity. Rouhana's reference to the sentimental identification emphasises, in fact, the 'doubly contradictory' identity of Palestinians in Israel. Palestinians in Israel 'identify' (express solidarity) with the Palestinian struggle outside Israel, but they do not take an active part in that struggle in terms of political participation. Moreover, political activity is related to structural and pragmatic considerations of balance of power and political interests. This is reflected in the third component of the tripartite consensus among Palestinians in Israel, regarding their desire to remain law-abiding citizens.

A study conducted by Palestinian political scientist As'ad Ghanem (2002) shows transformations in Palestinian identification in Israel. By comparing two surveys, carried out in 1995 and 2001, relating to Palestinian political orientations in Israel, Ghanem concludes that 'there has been a decline in the number of Arabs who see themselves as Israeli without a Palestinian component as well as an increase in the percentage of those who emphasise the Palestinian component of their personal identity' (Ghanem 2002: 137). Moreover, the surveys show a decline in those who 'recognised the existence of the state without reservations', percentages plummeting from 93.3 per cent in 1995 to 50.7 per cent in 2001 (Ghanem 2002: 137). Novels in the period under consideration in this chapter reveal tangible Palestinian identity transformations in Israel after 1987, along the lines reflected in the analysis presented by Ghanem, and contrary to the conclusion of Rouhana.

The first Palestinian Intifada in 1987 marks a turning point in the identification and association of Palestinians with 'time' and 'space'. Forty-five Palestinian novels were published in the third period (1987–2010; see Table 3.1 at the end of this chapter for the complete list of novels). This corpus reveals Palestinian novelists in Israel grappling with the relationship between 'present'[2] and 'past', or 'here' and 'there'. The analysis of Palestinian identity in these years can be divided into three groups.[3] The first group may be categorised as nostalgic-folkloric. Novels in this group focus on the Palestinian past in great detail. They also stand in opposition to most of the novels from the first period (1948–67). Instead of rejecting Palestinian past altogether, novels after 1987 seek to revive and reaffirm Palestinian history and culture: these novels no longer ignore the events of the 1948 war; they instead folklorise the Nakba. Folklorification of the Nakba means enfolding the Nakba into Palestinian folklore by infusing the Nakba with a folkloric narrative.

Another important characteristic of novels in this folkloric group is that their narratives are nostalgic. As we have seen in the discussion on *Ikhtayya* in the preceding chapter, nostalgia refers to a yearning for the past, experienced in the present, rendering the 'present' an inseparable part of nostalgia. In fact, nostalgia exists wherever there is a 'troubled' present. This relationship between past and present characterises novels in this period, forming, moreover, the relationship between here and there. This latter description refers to the relationship between Palestinian citizens in Israel and Palestinians outside Israel, forming a link with the novels of the second group.

In contrast to nostalgic-folkloric novels, the plots in the second group are located in the present. They focus on Palestinian life outside Israel since the outbreak of the Intifada in 1987. Plots in this group, which I will call 'Intifada novels', are situated in Palestinian villages and refugee camps outside Israel, especially in the West Bank and Gaza Strip. Intifada novels reflect commonalities with the nostalgic-folkloric group, conveying a sense of shared history and purpose, and reflecting the distress of Palestinians in Israel at having been 'left out' of the Palestinian national struggle.

Novels in the third group deal directly with contemporary Palestinian life in Israel and reflect on its 'perplexity'. These novels are situated in the present and inside Israel. Thus, they contrast both spatially and temporally with the two preceding groups: while in the first two groups the plots are situated 'there' (outside Israel) and 'then' (in the past), the plots in the third group are placed in the here and now. At the close of this chapter I will discuss the importance of this contrast as a means to our understanding of Palestinian identity in Israel.

Nostalgic-folkloric Novels

Nostalgia is an aspect of memory that is difficult to define. It is usually understood as a sense of longing for a bygone era that will not return (F. Davis 1979; Lowenthal 1985; Dickinson and Erben 2006; Walder 2011). Mikhail Bakhtin saw nostalgia as a 'historical inversion': 'the ideal that is *not* being lived now is projected into the past' (Hutcheon 2000: 195; italics in original). Eric Hobsbawm placed nostalgia in the twilight zone between history and memory, 'between the past as a generalised record open to relatively dispassionate inspection and the past as a remembered part of, or background to, one's own life' (quoted in Walder 2011: 2).

In the study of nostalgia, several components tend to be foregrounded. Nostalgia is concerned, first of all, with a lost past: but its longing is born out of an experience in the present. Secondly, nostalgia is said to occur when the present is 'troubled', causing the need to look for comfort in the past. Thirdly, nostalgia as memory is related to a lived past (F. Davis 1979: 47), thus evidence of that past must be apparent in the present (Hutcheon 2000: 196). Finally, nostalgia relates, on the whole, to other people (Dickinson and Erben 2006: 239). This is an important aspect, explaining, as it does, the connection between personal and collective nostalgia. Moreover, nostalgia is very much related to matters of identity: 'Not only is nostalgia deeply implicated in the political life of people, it is a part of their historical sense of themselves' (Walder 2011: 3), while also remaining 'deeply intertwined with nationalistic and patriotic sentiments' (F. Davis 1979: 98).

Since the novels in this section compare past and present, they yield important clues relating to the evolution of Palestinian identity in Israel in the past two decades. The connection between nostalgia and Palestinian identity in Israel is very strong, which is why I will present in this section some aspects of Palestinian nostalgia discussing one of the most primary aspects of Palestinian collective nostalgia: Palestinian folklore prior to 1948.

Memory and the Folklorification of the Nakba

In the 1980s, Palestinians in Israel and elsewhere began to publish village memorial books collecting information about their villages (many of which no longer exist), with the primary aim of preserving the history and memory of these villages (Slyomovics 1998; R. Davis 2007).[4] According to Palestinian historian Nur Masalha, the accounts in village memorial books

> reflect the beauty of the landscape, richness of the land and of village and city lives. These narratives about the land testify to the intimate and intense experience of everyday life on the land—the names of the valleys and wadis, hills, shrines, streets, springs and water wells, cultivated fields and vineyards; the importance of all kinds of trees (olive, almond, grape) and other natural elements in memories of the past. (Masalha 2008: 143)

Nostalgic-folkloric novels included in this section might be considered as a variation on the theme of these memorial books. In fact, Palestinian nostalgic-folkloric novels provide a detailed description of social and cultural life in Palestine before 1948. It is impossible, in the limited space of this book, to address the great quantity and quality of such a folkloric resource. There is need for further and comprehensive research to address the many questions relating to Palestinian folklore in novels in this corpus. I will, in the following, however, present a sample of the folkloric themes to be found in novels from this group. The presentation of folkloric themes here is central not only to our understanding of novels in this group, but also to the novels discussed in the second and third sections below.

Nostalgic-folkloric novels provide what anthropologists call 'thick description' of Palestinian folklore, social life, and traditional social figures.[5] Novels in this group collate numerous tales, myths, songs, proverbs, poetry (*shiʿr*; *zajal*), as well as traditional medicine.[6] Palestinian food, clothing and numerous household items, tools and equipment as well as animals, birds, wild plants, herbs, trees and insects are all part of the folkloric narrative appearing in these novels. Events in the plots, moreover, are immersed in the 'space' of the village. Streets, alleys, gardens (*ḥawākīr*), the village square (*al-sāḥa*), the spring (*al-ʿayn*), *al-bayādir* (the threshing grounds), *al-maqāthī* (the watermelon fields), and the houses are described in detail (both as private and as public spaces). The social interactions associated with these spaces are also described.

Novels involving childhood memories include details of childhood games,[7] their rules and other activities.[8] In *Dhakirat al-Ayyam* (*Memory of the Days*, 2003), by Jiryis Tannus, a game called *al-ʿawātīl* is described in detail: two players, both bearing a collection of sticks, compete against one another. The goal of the game is to defeat the opponent by obtaining all of his or her sticks. The first player must throw his or her stick with enough force so that it holds erect in the mud. The objective for the second player is then to strike this stick down with his or her own stick. If the stick of the second player lands in the ground and holds erect, he or she wins the round and can claim the stick of the first player.[9]

There are various similarities and differences between nostalgic-folkloric novels and village memorial books. First, the plots in the novels are fictional (although they refer to stories occurring in reality – a point that will be addressed below). Secondly, unlike memory books, novels do not include maps of the villages (which tend to be hand drawn by Palestinian refugees in the case of memorial books), lists of possessions or locations. Conversely, both nostalgic-folkloric novels as well as memorial books

> tell of [...] collective history, not [of] individualised experiences. In most of the books written by people [...] originally from the village, the stories told about places in the village are not framed within personal recollections or personal experiences that give meaning to a place. The stories are collective [...] (R. Davis 2007: 64)

Moreover, Palestinian nostalgic-folkloric novels, like memory books, describe the events of the 1948 war in the villages. Since these are village memoirs, the plots are not, in many cases, concerned with an individual character or a group of characters, but rather with the village itself. Nostalgic-folkloric novels constitute a new literary genre, which Davis terms 'collective auto-biographies' (R. Davis 2007: 64). The appearance of these two new genres – both the nostalgic-folkloric novel and the village memorial book – reflects a new phenomenon in the Palestinian national narrative. In both genres:

> the same kind of story is repeated; the details sometimes different, often similar; the local outcome occasionally variable, as between those who survived and those who were killed, those who managed to return and those who ended up as refugees. But in all, a shared collective fate: the loss of community, the disaster of collective dispossession and radical displacement. (L. Jayyusi 2007: 113)

Like memory books, moreover, some nostalgic-folkloric novels refer to events that occurred outside the boundaries of the novel. *Dhakirat al-Ayyam* (2003), by Jiryis Tannus, for example, deals with the childhood memories of the protagonist, who lives in the 1940s in a fictional Palestinian village. In the introduction to this novel, the author states that *Dhakirat al-Ayyam* is not an autobiography, but 'a series of events taking place in every neighbourhood of our [Palestinian] villages in the first half of the past century' and 'the story of a neighbourhood that symbolises all the villages in the homeland (*al-waṭan*)'. Tannus adds that the 'events of the [1948] war are based on what had taken place in my village *Al-Mghār* and that "in essence" (*bi-jawharihā*) they describe what has happened, shedding light on the story of this homeland'. This novel, along with the others in this group, is intended to work as a collective narrative of a lost homeland.

Furthermore, the choice of a fictional village emphasises the collective character of the novel. Literary critic Catherine Gallagher suggests that 'the stories of fictive individuals can create the sense of shared experience best' (quoted in Wagner 2004: 24). Whereas novels in the second period (1967–87) reflect various manifestations of the differentiation in Palestinian society in Israel (anomie, individualisation and social disintegration), nostalgic-folkloric novels being a form of collective autobiographies represent a new tendency: that of de-differentiation, or, collectivisation. Although novels from the earlier period critically address Palestinian disintegration and anomie, aiming to combat it, the discourse in novels in the later period (1987–2010) shifts from the social to the national level. The novels and narratives of the group under consideration in this section signify a process by which Palestinians in Israel recollect their fragmented identities, aiming to reconstruct and revive an authentic Palestinian self. This section aims to elucidate the collectivisation process of Palestinians in Israel after 1987.

The historical narrative embedded in nostalgic-folkloric novels pays close attention to a number of aspects of the 1948 war: the military assistance of the Arab countries (seen more as a burden than a blessing); the occupation of villages; Israeli massacres and brutalities against civilians; the expulsion of Palestinians; and the return, or attempted return, of Palestinian refugees to their homes. The historical narrative presented in these novels is comparable to narratives presented in history books concerning the Nakba, or testimonies of people who witnessed and survived its events. The similarity between the accounts of experiences of witnesses and survivors and the accounts of characters in the novels is evident in two ways.

First, it is evident in the retelling of the historical account of the events, the methods and patterns of expulsion by the Israeli forces. Secondly, in the recounting of the nostalgic view of a past that has been lost and destroyed (see also: R. Davis 2007). In the following discussion, I will present a handful of examples of such narratives, focusing on the occupation of villages and its aftermath. My intention is not to handle the historical narrative as such but to point to the folklorification of these events in Palestinian novels in Israel since 1987 as markers of Palestinian collectivisation in this period (1987–2010).

The concept of the 'folklorification of the Nakba' refers to the writing of folkloric narratives about Palestinian life before 1948 while 'injecting' these narratives with historical accounts of the war in 1948, in an attempt to offer a collective narrative. The folklorification of the Nakba, as a narrative technique, has been identified by Dina Matar in her book *What It Means to Be Palestinian*, collating Palestinian memory narratives from across the Middle East:

> almost all [interviewees], irrespective of who they were and where they ended up, had a personal story to tell about the focal date of 1948 and insisted on telling it. A similar structure of telling, in which personal stories converge on and intermesh with the collective (nationalist) Palestinian narrative of dispossession and loss [...] (Matar 2011: 25)

The following excerpt from *Awja' al-Bilad al-Muqaddasa* (*Sorrows of the Holy Land*, 1997), by Hanna Ibrahim, reflects both the historical narrative of the events of the 1948 war and the folklorification of the Nakba. Here the protagonist, Ziyad, and the inhabitants of the village are ordered by the occupying army to gather in the village square.

> Wa-ḥanat minhu iltifāta fa-ra'ā akhāhu akram yanhaḍ wa-kan yaq'ud ayḍan 'alā al-arḍ qarīban min abīh wa-yasūqahu al-jundiyy ilā ḥayth yaqif thalātha ākharūn 'arifa fīhim aḥmad al-kharbush 'āzif al-arghūl al-shahīr wa-fawzī al-as'ad ibn akhī al-mukhtār wa-shābban masīḥiyyan yud'ā hanna al-farran. Awqaf jundiyyān al-arba'a amām jidh' zaytūna rūmiyya ḍakhma kānū yusammūnaha 'amūd al-'ursān ḥaythu kānū yujlisūn al-'arīs qabl al-ghadā' wa-tarquṣ al-nisā' wa-l-ṣabāyā wa-yughannīn wa-yanṣib al-shubbān al-dabka ḥattā yaḥīn maw'id tanāwul al-ṭa'ām. Wa-ba'da dhālik yakūn al-ṭawāfu bi-ṣaffi saḥja yaṣil ilā al-bayādir wa-ya'ūd ilā dār al-'arīs. Wa-idhā kān al-'arīs masīḥiyyan ya'ud al-ṣaff ilā al-kanīsa ḥaythu tajrī al-marāsīm al-kanasiyya al-mu'tāda. Jaffa rīq ziyād idh andharahu qalbahu bi-khaṭar washīk. Wa-taḥaqqaqat aswa' tawaqqu'ātihi wa-huwa yarā al-arba'a yasquṭūn bi-raṣāṣ rashshāshatayn khafīfatayn uṭliqa 'alayhim bi-damm bārid. Wa-adraka anna al-qaṣd lam yakun 'iqāban yuqṣadu bihi unās mu'ayyanūn bal wasīla li-ikhāfat al-nās wa-daf'ahum ilā al-raḥīl. (pp. 102–3)
>
> He turned his gaze and saw his brother Akram stand up, he was sitting on the ground next to his father and led by the soldier to the spot where three others stood. He recognised Ahmad al-Kharbush, the famous Arghul player, and Fawzi al-As'ad, the Mukhtar's nephew, and a Christian guy called Hanna al-Farran. The two soldiers positioned the four in front of a huge Roman olive tree, which they used to call the grooms' pole. This is where they used to seat the groom before lunch while the women and girls danced and sang, and the young men danced the Dabka until it is lunch time. After that they roam with the Sahja until they reach the threshing grounds, then back to the groom's home. If the groom was Christian, the Sahja would return to the church, where the regular wedding ceremony would take place. Ziyad's throat became dry as he felt the danger. And his worst predictions became true, as he saw the four drop to the ground by the shooting of two light machine guns in cold blood. He realised that this was not a punishment to particular persons, but a means to scare the people and push them to flee. (pp. 102–3)

With regards to the way the text describes the events of the 1948 war and the occupation of the village, the story in *Awjaʿ al-Bilad al-Muqaddasa* closely resembles testimonies and memories of Palestinians who witnessed and survived the events of the 1948 war (e.g. see: Nazzal 1974; Pappé 2006; Sayigh 2007; Masalha 2008).[10] Like village memorial books, this paragraph tells the story of the village, rather than an individual character. Thus, in order to present the narrative in collective terms, the narrator pays little heed to the execution of his brother in cold blood (*bidam bārid*). The description of the execution focuses on the death of four men and the collective implications of this incident: the terrorisation of Palestinians, which forced them to leave the village (*dafʿahum ilā al-raḥīl*). This is especially true since the narrator indicates that he did not know each of the four men well (*ʿarifa fihim*), thus their execution surpasses the personal grief he feels for any one of them. This collective discourse reflects the folklorification of the Nakba, in which a folkloric narrative is injected into the description of the occupation of the village and the execution of four of its men.

In what follows, I will analyse the different aspects of folklorification expressed in the excerpt. My treatment of folklorification is presented in two steps. The first step, described in light of this excerpt, aims to show Palestinian folklore and folklorification as depicted in the novels. The presentation of the folkloric narrative below lays a significant basis for our understanding of the connection between folklorification and the nostalgic-folkloric narrative. This is the case because nostalgic-folkloric novels 'compare' present-day life in Israel with what has been lost of Palestinian folklore. The second step of my analysis will be concerned with understanding Palestinian identity in this period in light of the folklorification of the Nakba.

The execution of the four men is incorporated into the scene of a folkloric Palestinian wedding. In order to understand the implications of combining the two scenes, it is important to understand the social and public-ceremonial aspects of traditional Palestinian weddings. In the excerpt quoted above, the four men are lined up under a vast, ancient olive tree (*rūmiyya*, dating from the time of the Roman Empire), which is known in the village as *ʿamūd al-ʿirsān* (the pole of grooms), under which all the couples of the village are married. The wedding venue is the village itself, as the parade ferrying the bride and the groom to the village square proceeds along the streets of the village, accompanied by *ṣaff saḥja*, a Palestinian wedding procession performed by participants standing shoulder to shoulder, which would progress down the village streets.

The wedding moves along the streets, coming to a final halt at the village square. This marks the holistic relationship between the inhabitants of the village and their space. In other words, the creation of each new family occurs in the whole of the village space, involving the participation of a large number of families from the village. Folkloric narrative stresses the pride of Palestinians in their village: the song 'this is the water-spring square and we are its men' (*hāy saḥit al-ʿayn w-niḥnā rjālhā*) is sung in *ṣaff al-saḥja* (*Asiyy al-Damʿ*, p. 8). The lyrics emphasise that the village square precedes the men (*rjāl*) in importance. Instead of saying 'we are the village men, and this is *our* village square', the song gives primacy to the square, to which the men belong (*rjāl**hā***), and the square becomes their reference point for identity.

The centrality of the village to the rural Palestinian lifestyle is reflected in the use, for the wedding, of the entire space of the village: the village 'was the most important unit in the fellah's life. Its functions were not only social and economic, but, in the broadest sense political as well' (J. Ruedy quoted in Sayigh 2007: 5). This relation between 'person' and 'village' has, of course, a social dimension. The social cohesion in Palestinian villages is best described by Palestinian anthropologist Rosemary Sayigh, who sees the village as '"a family of families", closely linked by a common history and continuous intermarriage' (Sayigh 2007: 6).

Another folkloric feature that appears in the excerpt above, and also extensively in other novels, is the use of nicknames. *Al-Kharbush* could be Ahmad's family name, but it is more likely to be a nickname attached to this character, whose appearance in the novel is restricted to this scene. Nicknames are very common in Palestinian as well as in Arab culture and they are used extensively in nostalgic-folkloric novels. Many of the main characters had nicknames, for example the novel *Asiyy al-Damʿ* (*Unable to Cry*, 1997), by Suhil Kiwan, has characters bearing the following nicknames: *al-ḥardhūn* (stellion);[11] *al-naʿsān* (the sleepy); *Abū qurq* (a man whose penis was stung by a bee, after which it grew to huge dimensions); *umm-qāfyi* (for a woman who repeatedly used the phrase *balā qāfya*, which means 'no bad connotation intended'); or a man who was named *al-ṭawwāsha* ('floaty') to mock his impotency.

Nicknames attached themselves to people with little chance of shaking them off, a fact which is commented on in the novels themselves (*Asiyy al-Dam*ʿ, pp. 42–3). The social function of nicknames is to reflect 'the intimate knowledge each villager possesses of the personal habits and life histories of others' (Antoun 1968: 165). The use of nicknames also has a levelling dimension. Since '[e]veryone with a nickname is the object of laughter [, i]t is this idiom of abusive equality that defines each man as a member of the community and, hence, subject to its norms' (Antoun 1968: 166).

The choice of including Hanna al-Farran and his explicitly mentioning that he was a Christian relates both to Palestinian folklore and the Nakba. First, with regards to folklore, Palestinians celebrated weddings in similar ways, regardless of whether they were Muslims or Christians, differing only as to where their religious ceremonies were held, yet sharing the same locations and customs for the celebration. Thus the single 'core' value of Palestinian culture, shared by Muslims and Christians, resides in the similar way they celebrate weddings, which symbolises national continuity as will become clear below.[12] Secondly, with regard to the Nakba, the inclusion of a Christian character aims to emphasise that both Christians and Muslims shared a similar fate. Such a discourse reflects the collectivisation and de-differentiation in nostalgic-folkloric novels.

What can we discern about Palestinian identity transformation in Israel in this period from the folkloric narrative described above? The execution scene is suggestive of Israeli 'execution' of Palestinian culture and folklore. The documentation of Israeli war crimes during the 1948 war delivers the message that the occupation of Palestinian land also meant the execution of its culture and folklore. This is a moment that signifies an abrupt discontinuity of Palestinian culture. I use the term 'discontinuity' because it better reflects what the nostalgic dimension of nostalgic-folkloric narrative aims at, this being not only a destruction of culture, but an event that *aimed* to stop continuity, symbolised by the wedding, a ceremony of family formation and continuity of society. The wedding with all its cultural, public and collective significance is terminated at the moment of the occupation of Palestine.

In the excerpt above from *Awja*ʿ *al-Bilad al-Muqaddasa*, discontinuity of Palestinian culture is expressed on different levels: (1) the site: including 'the grooms' pole', the village square and its collective social significance, used to be a location dedicated to ensuring continuity; the site of family formation, has become a locus of death and discontinuity symbolised by the execution; (2) the participants: the executing of young men marked the circumscription of future generations; (3) the ceremony: the lining up of the men for execution contrasts with the way Palestinian men line up to participate in the *ṣaff al-saḥja* and the *dabka* at the village square to celebrate a wedding. Moreover, the execution of the flute player (*ʿāzif al-arghūl*), who leads *ṣaff al-saḥja* with music, aimed to eliminate Palestinian culture by killing those who perform and maintain it.

The contrast between continuity and discontinuity is a central feature of novels in this period (1987–2010). This is reflected in the two ceremonies that appear in the entire corpus of novels in this period: weddings and funerals. In the next section dealing with Intifada novels, we will see how Palestinian martyrs during the first Intifada were treated like grooms and families insisted on holding weddings rather than funerals for their dead sons (Pitcher 1998: 26). Thus, the process of transforming a funeral into a wedding aims to affirm the continuity of Palestinians alongside resistance to Israeli erasure. Other expressions of the continuity–discontinuity dichotomy are to be found in reference to issues relating to the masculinity of Palestinian men. In nostalgic-folkloric novels, impotency parallels discontinuity, death and defeat (a concrete example will be discussed below). In Intifada novels, continuity (defiance of death) is associated with potency, vitality and rite of passage from childhood to adulthood (this will be elaborated in the following section). Nostalgia and folklore in the Palestinian case in Israel are related in terms of their temporality. While nostalgia is associated with discontinuity (as it laments a lost past) and folklore associated with continuity (it being the preservation and transmission of culture to future generations), Palestinian Nakba folklore of the 1990s and 2000s is nostalgic, thus representing an attempt to revive or recreate such discontinued folklore (see also: Matar 2011: 25).

So far, I have introduced how nostalgic-folkloric novels depict Palestinian life up to and including 1948, aiming to highlight how such life was abruptly stopped and destroyed with the occupation of Palestine. Nonetheless, nostalgic-folkloric novels emphasise the magnitude of the loss and that it was not a momentary event, but a continuous practice inherent in Zionism. This is evidenced in the fact that many novels in this group do not end their plots in 1948, but continue to describe Palestinian life in Israel.

Palestinian nostalgic-folkloric novels that take their plots into the years after 1948 deal with the transformations occurring in Palestinian society in Israel since this date. The narrative provided therein resembles, to some degree, the evolutionary processes outlined in Chapters 1 and 2 of this book. In other words, Palestinian novels in the third period not only outline the history of Palestinians in Israel since 1948, but they also rethink and reassess Palestinian discourse in earlier 'periods', or stages, since the Nakba. One of the main issues occupying the novels in this period is rethinking the modernisation discourse prevalent during the first period (1948–67). It is true that novels in the second period also offered a reassessment of Palestinian modernisation in Israel, but they focused on social aspects of modernisation (differentiation, in its various manifestations) while presenting a 'unified' response to the political aspects (Zionism), in the form of counter-erasure and un-erasure. In contrast, nostalgic-folkloric novels focus on Zionism and what they see as manifest Israeli attempts to erase Palestinian history and continuity. The following scene from *Asiyy al-Dam*ʿ depicts the formation of a village council and some first encounters with the Israeli establishment.

> Wa-ṭalab al-ḥākim min al-raʾīs fī awwal liqāʾ ʿalā taslīm balāṭ al-ʿayn li-l-ḥukūma, wa-hiya sa-taqūm bi-l-muqābil bi-tazfīt al-sāḥa, wa-lam tuwājih al-fikra ayy iʿtirāḍ illā min mkhimar, wa-ʿindamā suʾil ʿan tafsīr li-iʿtirāḍih qāl: liʾanna al-zift ḥār bi-l-ṣayf ghayr muḥtamal, thumma ʿalaynā al-iḥtifāẓ bi-l-ṭābiʿ al-qadīm li-l-balad, fa-ḍaḥik al-aʿḍāʾ wa-l-raʾīs wa-l-jumhūr al-fuḍuliyy, wa-baʿd ayyām ibtadaʾa awwal mashrūʿ fīʿ ʿinba munthu qurūn ḥaythu qāl al-raʾīs (al-mukhtār): āmal an yakūn hādhā al-mashrūʿ fātiḥa, kay narfaʿ ruʾūsina jamīʿan bi-l-shawāriʿ wa-l-sāḥat al-muzaffata. Surra al-nās kathīran min kalimat al-mukhtār, wa-taqaddam mkhimar (abū khālid) bi-ṭalab li-iqāmat qunn, fa-waʿadahu al-mukhtār bi-iʿdād taṣrīḥ min ḥākim al-liwāʾ liʾanna tarbiyat al-dawājin min ikhtiṣāṣ al-kibūts wa-l-mūshāf. (p. 159)

> The governor asked the mayor in their first meeting to deliver the tiles of the village square to the government, and in return it will pave the square with

> asphalt. The idea was met with no objection, apart from Mkhimar, who explained his objection saying: the asphalt is unbearably hot in the summer, and we need to keep the old character of the village. The municipality members, the mayor and the curious crowd laughed at this reply, and a few days later the first project to be carried out in Inba for centuries was launched. The mayor (Mukhtar) said: I hope this project becomes a starting point, so we can all be proud of our paved streets and squares. The people were very pleased, and Mkhimar (Abu Khalid) submitted a request to establish a chicken coop, and the Mukhtar promised him to prepare a permit from the district governor, because rearing chickens is the specialty of the kibbutz and the moshav. (p. 159)

The above excerpt resonates with the Palestinian modernisation narrative of the first period (1948–67), discussed in Chapter 1. The *mukhtar*, appointed as the head of the village council by the Israeli district governor (*ḥākim al-liwāʾ*), is delighted to accept the proposal of the Israeli governor to modernise the village square and to replace the old cobbles (*balāṭ al-ʿayn*, translates as the 'cobbles of the water-spring', referring to the main square in the village) with asphalt. The appointed *mukhtar*, and the role he leads, is reminiscent of Hasan from *Qalb fi Qarya* (1963), who was constantly reminded of the great humanistic responsibility, laid on his shoulders by the instructors in the kibbutz, to modernise his village. In the above excerpt from *Asiyy al-Damʿ*, the rest of the villagers are contented with the modernisation of the village, aside from Mkhimar, who is laughed away when he objects to the proposal. The reference to the centuries before modernising Palestinian culture (*qurūn*) is also reminiscent of those sentiments expressed in modernisation novels, depicting Palestinian backwardness as 'centuries old' (*qurūn ṭawīla*).

However, the above excerpt reflects a shift in Palestinian discourse in Israel. The request of the military governor from the council members to remove the old cobbles from the village square is depicted in a comparable way to the execution of the four men under the Roman olive tree, both of which are centuries old. The removal of the cobbles is portrayed as an order to 'hand in' (*taslīm*) the cobbles to the government, which resembles the handing in of weapons or activists (to be executed) to the occupying forces in 1948. Since the cobbles that make up the village square have the potential to preserve Palestinian history and identity, they are treated as a site of resistance against Israeli occupation. For this reason, it is important for the Israeli governor to have the cobbles 'handed in'.

The transformation that nostalgic-folkloric novels reflect is both the rejection as well as the exposure of Israeli erasure practices. The removal of the cobbles marks the erasure not only of Palestinian history and physical existence, but also suggests the dismantling of the village square's social role along with all its sentimental associations. Mkhimar opposes the use of asphalt, exposing its ugliness and impracticality, it being too hot in the summer. Timeworn Palestinian cobbles were better suited to the Palestinian climate, also bearing greater aesthetic value. These cobbles had remained untouched for centuries precisely *because* they performed their function so well. Thus, replacing these cobbles with asphalt was an imposed modernisation: alien and aiming to destroy Palestinian culture.

A second parallel between modernisation and nostalgic-folkloric novels relates to the proscription against Palestinians from pursuing any forms of growth and development. Whereas in modernisation novels, Jewish-Israeli instructors in a kibbutz are depicted to 'love to help Palestinians' to develop, in the above excerpt, the military governor is portrayed as voicing the opposite tendency. According to the governor, Palestinian farmers are unqualified to keep chickens, as chicken rearing is a specialist skill reserved for the kibbutzim and the moshavim. This is, perhaps, a laughable way in which to hide the true and racist justification for the denial of such a licence, especially as Palestinians have always reared chickens. Moreover, impeding Palestinian growth and economic development is not restricted to 'heavy industry', but to basic agricultural enterprises like rearing chickens, which is almost inseparable from Palestinian rural life. To put it differently, whereas modernisation discourse emphasised the interrelatedness of economic growth and development with peace and coexistence, the narrative in *Asiyy al-Dam*ʿ reverses such proclaimed intentions: Israel does not allow Palestinian citizens in Israel to develop, thereby impeding their integration into Israel.

In addition to negating modernisation discourse, certain symbolic features in the above excerpt from *Asiyy al-Dam*ʿ shed further light on the discourse of nostalgic-folkloric novels: first, Mkhimar is known throughout the novel by the nickname *ṭawwāsha* (floaty), mocking his impotency, which became known to the inhabitants of the village due to his failure to prove the virginity of his wife on the night of their wedding. The impotency of Mkhimar denotes the impotency and collective humiliation of Palestinians in 1948 at their failure to protect their villages. Sexual impotency relates not only to issues of masculinity and manhood, but also resonates with the depiction of Palestinian continuity, which is symbolised by family creation: the inability of Mkhimar to reproduce symbolises Palestinian discontinuity.

However, although Mkhimar is ridiculed for his impotency throughout the plot, in later stages he takes the name of Abu Khalid. Abu Khalid was the nickname of the Egyptian president Gamal Abdel Nasser, which is an expression of affinity, since Abdel Nasser symbolised Arab national pride due to his especially successful, potent stance against imperialism, in the 1956 war with Israel, France and Britain. Starting to call Mkhimar Abu Khalid and attributing to him the role of opponent to Israeli erasure of Palestinian culture and history marks the shift in the Palestinian discourse that these novels depict.

Secondly, the name Mkhimar is derivationally connected to the word *khamr* ('wine') in Arabic. This name has a direct relationship with the name of the village, Inba, meaning in Arabic 'a single grape'. As wine is produced from grapes, Mkhimar by this analogy is the son of the village (*ibn al-balad*), a term in Arabic which implies a strong connection to the village, and hence reinforces the responsibility vested in Mkhimar to protect and defend it. Moreover, it is also possible that choosing to call the village Inba, a single grape, may refer to it as one unit belonging to a larger cluster of similar units. According to this analogy, in the same way that one grape can represent the whole cluster, in taste and through other characteristics, one village can represent a cluster of, or indeed all, Palestinian villages. This reading is reminiscent of the statement provided by Jiryis Tannus in the introduction to his novel *Dhakirat al-Ayyam*, stating that the story is 'in essence' (*bi-jawhariha̅*) similar to other Palestinian cases. The above two aspects (that of national pride and of collectivity) constitute the collectivisation discourse in nostalgic-folkloric novels: an individual story which speaks for a collective.

In nostalgic-folkloric novels, the implications of Palestinian modernisation within the Israeli framework are depicted in terms of spatial change. The village square is a worthy example of this: until 1948 it used to be a site where ceremonies of continuity (weddings) were held. In 1948, it became a site of death and terror. Then, later, it was removed altogether (as cobbles were replaced with asphalt), stripped of its social significance as a public space. The following excerpt depicts the impact, on Palestinian society, of Israeli erasure:

> Wa-lam yaṭra᾽ ayy taghyīr ʿalā ʿinba bi-istithnā᾽ tazfīt baʿḍ al-shawāriʿ, wa-iqtuliʿat ghābāt min ashjār al-zaytūn wa-l-tīn wa-kurūm al-ʿinab, wa-trākamat al-abniya al-ismantiyya fawq baʿḍiha al-baʿḍ bidūn niẓām walā jamāl, wa-ṣār al-tilfizyūn huwa al-waḥīd al-qādir ʿalā al-nuṭq fī hādhihi al-balda, huwa yatakallam wa-l-jamīʿ yunṣit, wa-mā ʿudt tarā fallāḥ fī arḍih, laqad ḍāʿat al-arḍ bīʿat aw nuhibat bi-sabab al-ḍarā᾽ib al-bāhiẓa, wa-izdādat qā᾽imat al-mamnūʿat, wa-l-judrān al-silkiyya wa-l-ismantiyya wa-l-shā᾽ika, wa-ṣārat ʿinba aqdhar buqʿa fī-l-ʿālam, wa-aktharuhā ḍīqan, qayẓ khāniq lā yuḥtamal fī-l-ṣayf wa-bard qāris fī-l-shitā᾽, wa-taḥawwal nasuhā ilā ālāt tarkuḍ layl nahār fī-l-maṣāniʿ al-baʿīda, wa-taqqaṭaʿat awṣāl ʿilāqātihim bi-baʿḍ wa-bāt al-jār lā yadkhul bayt jarih wala fī-l-aʿyād, bal tamurr al-aʿyād dūn an yashʿurū bihā li-annahum nasaw anfusahum. (p. 177)

> Nothing changed in Inba, apart from paving some roads, with forests of olive and fig trees and vineyards uprooted, and cement buildings piled on top of each other without any order or beauty. Television has become the only thing capable of speaking in this village. It speaks and everyone listens. And you no longer could see a farmer in his land, since the land has been lost, either sold or pillaged [*nuhibat*] through extortionate taxes. And the list of illegalities has grown, as well as the barbed wire and cement walls. And Inba has become the dirtiest spot in the world, and the narrowest. Unbearable heat in the summer, and freezing cold in the winter, and its people have become machines rushing day and night to the faraway factories, and their family bonds have been torn, and neighbours have stopped visiting each other, not even in holidays. Holidays pass without them feeling them because they have forgotten themselves. (p. 177)

This excerpt utilises a similar logic to that represented in the earlier discussion regarding Palestinian modernisation in Israel. For example, the way in which the uprooting of the trees and the theft of land (*nahb*) are depicted resembles the 'handing in' of the cobbles: by equating the land with 'illegal commodities' (*mamnūʿāt*), such as weapons, cobbles or national identity, the land was confiscated from the villagers. Moreover, framing the theft of land in legal terms, such as in the form of taxes (*ḍarāʾib*), is comparable to the preceding extract in which Mkhimar was prohibited from building a chicken coop – 'wrapping' racism in legal or administrative formulas.

In addition to this, the above excerpt shows the price that Palestinians were forced to pay for modernisation in Israel, and this is depicted in terms of quality and quantity. In exchange for asphalt-paved roads, Palestinians lost fruit trees (olives, figs and grapes). While, in gaining a better 'quality of life', as Palestinians are regularly reminded in Israel, they lost elements integral to their culture. This is evident in the contrast between the barren and black asphalt (denoting Israeli modernisation) and the fruit trees, which symbolise Palestinian culture in all its colour, flavour and vitality. The barren asphalt and the vitality of the fruit trees resonate with the impotency–discontinuity and potency–continuity themes. In terms of quantity, the price of modernisation was high: in return for paving 'some roads' (*baʿḍ al-shawāriʿ*), 'forests' of trees (*ghābāt*) were removed.

The spatial modernisation of Palestinian villages is evident in the reference to cement, a modern building material that replaced local mud brick for building houses. Modern cement houses are piled one on top of the other in chaos, ruining the landscape of the village (*bidūn jamāl*). Other additions to the village space are the barbed wire and cement fences. These barriers denote the fragmentation of Palestinian society. As a result, inhabitants of the village no longer visit one another.

The removal of the village square as a social space resulted in the fragmentation of people (*taqqaṭaʿat awṣāl*). *Awṣāl* in Arabic means 'limbs' or bodily parts: thus *taqqaṭaʿat awṣāl* here refers to the dismembering of the 'Palestinian body' by modernisation, which is reminiscent of the impeding of Palestinian continuity and weddings by military force. According to this analogy, the private (wedding) corresponds to the public: Palestinian citizens in Israel even forgot the social and religious events that used to bring them together, such as religious holidays (*aʿyād*). The end result of Palestinian modernisation is that Palestinians have become mute (discontinued communication): only the television set 'speaks' in the village. The people tuning in to their television sets have forgotten how to socialise, have forgotten themselves (*nasaw anfusahum*), and have become passive consumers, with little to talk about.

In Chapter 2, I quoted the nostalgic narrative in *Ikhtayya* (by Emile Habiby) on neighbourhood life in Haifa. Habiby recalls that neighbours used to be considered members of the family, reflecting the cohesion of Palestinian society prior to 1948. The narrator in *Ikhtayya* yearns for a lost Palestinian life in which everything was 'legitimate' (*ḥalāl*) or morally uncontaminated: the neighbourhood, the life (*al-dunyā*) and all those who lived in it (*al-ʿaysh fihā*). The above excerpt from *Asiyy al-Dam*ʿ voices similar nostalgic sentiments. The village of Inba has become, after 1948, a claustrophobic, cluttered and an unbearable space. The destruction of the collective square, which had previously brought its inhabitants together, and the erection of fences between people's houses, rendered the inhabitants of this village unsociable and mute.

The difference between the two novels lies in the fact that in *Ikhtayya*, Habiby laments the lost, good (*ḥalāl*) past, while *Asiyy al-Dam*ʿ criticises the bad present. Below I will analyse another example of the negative portrayal of the present in nostalgic-folkloric novels. In the following dialogue, which takes place between two characters in *Awja*ʿ *al-Bilad al-Muqaddasa* in the 1990s, Asim – who left the village to study abroad – wonders why the traditional Palestinian wedding no longer takes place:

– Lākin bi-aiyy ʿudhr taghīb al-dabka wa-l-arghūl wa-l-mijwiz wa-ṣaff al-saḥja?

Wa-qāl ʿabdallah:

– Hādhī mūḍa qadīma.

– Wa-l-dīn mūḍa qadīma! Hal natakhallā ʿanhu? Wa-hal natakhallā ʿan kull ʿādātina al-ḥasana liʾannahā qadīma, mujarrad qadīma?. (p. 252)

– But with what excuse did the Dabka and Arghul and Mijwiz and Sahja disappear?

Abdallah said:

– They're old-fashioned.

> – And religion is old-fashioned! Should we give it up? And should we give up all our good traditions only because they're old, simply old? (p. 252)

Asim, criticising modernisation discourse promoted by Palestinian citizens in Israel, is wondering whether it really is the case that Palestinians in Israel must replace their traditions merely because they are old. The absence (*ghiyāb*) of the *dabka*, the *ṣaff al-saḥja* and the processions which form a major part of the Palestinian wedding were attributed to their outdatedness (*mūḍa qadīma*). New Palestinian weddings are no longer held under an olive tree, in village squares paved with centuries-old cobbles. Instead, Palestinians imitate Jewish-Israeli weddings, which are held in wedding halls. The new Palestinian weddings resemble the new Palestinian asphalt-paved village squares. The old authentic (*aṣīl*) and innocent (*sādhaj*) wedding has been replaced with that which is fake (*zayf*) and pretentious (*taṣṣannu*ʾ) (*Awja*ʿ *al-Bilad al-Muqaddasa*, p. 251).

Palestinian 'modernisation' is an imitation of Israeli culture, and it is a result of the hollowing out of Palestinian culture. The imitation of Israeli culture is enacted 'by default' to replace an absence (*ghiyāb*) rather than out of conviction. The reply, in the above excerpt, that tradition was 'merely old' (*mujarrad qadīma*) reflects the lack of prior consideration with which the 'old' was replaced by the 'new'.

In effect, Asim criticises Palestinians in Israel for abandoning (*natakhallā*) their culture and all that is good in it (*kull* ʿ*ādātinā al-ḥasana*), which includes the *dabka* dance, *al-arghūl* (a type of Palestinian flute), *al-mijwiz* (another type of Palestinian flute), *ṣaff al-saḥja* and religion (*al-dīn*). Equating religion with Palestinian folklore (ʿ*ādātinā*) is interesting because it parallels Palestinian folklore with morality. Moreover, being 'old-fashioned' does not mean, according to Asim, incompatibility with contemporary, modern life. In the same way cobbles were used for centuries because they fulfilled their purpose, traditions and values can also be in use in modern times.

So, how do the nostalgic narratives regarding the Palestinian past and the folklorification of the Nakba reflect Palestinian identity in the 1990s and 2000s? The answer to this question lies in the comparative dimension of nostalgia between past and present. The following excerpt from *Siraj al-Ghula* (1996), the memoirs of Emile Habiby, clarifies the links between past and present components of nostalgia. Habiby recalls a meeting with a couple of Palestinian refugees who are originally from his village, Shafa-Amr, in the Galilee. Their parents fled to Lebanon during the 1948 war and the meeting with Habiby takes place in Europe, since Palestinian citizens in Israel cannot travel to Arab countries (with the exception of Jordan and Egypt):

> Al-lājiʾūn al-ladhīn ṭuridū min qarya falasṭīniyya ilā ṣaḥārī al-ghurba ḥamilū maʿahum ʿādātahum wa-taqālīdahum al-khāṣṣa bi-qaryatihum al-aṣliyya. Sakanū sawiyya fī-l-mukhayyam al-wāḥid wa-fī ḥāra aw ruqʿa wāḥida fī dhālik al-mukhayyam wa-aʿānū baʿḍahum al-baʿḍ wa-tazāwajū fīmā baynahum wa-ḥāfaẓū ʿalā turāthahum al-khāṣṣ bi-qaryatahum al-aṣliyya bimā fī dhālik al-turāth min lahja khāṣṣa wa-ghinwat al-nuṭq al-khāṣṣa bi-qaryatihum. Wa-law lam yafʿalū hādhā al-amr lama kān fī maqdūrihum taḥammul ḥayāt ghayr muḥtamala. Ammā mā ḥadath li-sukkān al-mudun al-falasṭīniyya fakāna mukhtalifan jiddan. Fa-badaʾtu, mudhu tilka al-layla, fī-l-tafkīr bi-riwāyatī 'Ikhṭayya' ʿan madīnatī ḥayfā wa-ʿammā jarā li-abnāʾihā al-ʿarab. Kana mujtamaʿunā al-ʿarabiyy al-madaniyy qad qatāʿ shawṭan marmūqan fī sullam al-taṭawwur al-ḥaḍāriyy bi-mafāhīm dhālika al-zamān, min niqābāt mihaniyya wa-min ḥayāt thaqāfiyya ijtuth-that kulluhā min uṣulihā wa-buddidat shadhara madhara. Kānat maʿsāt al-shaʿb al-ʿarabiyy al-filisṭīniyy maʾsāt shāmila. Aṣābat ʾūlāʾika al-ladhīn iḍṭurrū ilā tark al-waṭan kamā aṣābat ʾūlāʾika al-ladhīn turikū fī waṭanihim. (pp. 36–7)
>
> The refugees who have been expelled from a Palestinian village to the deserts of foreignness carried with them the unique customs and traditions of their original village. They lived together in the same refugee camp or in a neighbourhood or a spot in that camp, they helped each other and married amongst themselves and preserved their unique folklore from the original village, including the unique accent of their original village. Had they not done that, they would have not been able to bear an unbearable life. But what happened to the inhabitants of the Palestinian cities was very different. So I started from that night to think about my novel *Ikhtayya* – which is about my city of Haifa and what has happened to her Arab sons. Our urban Arab society has come a long way in civilisational development, as it was perceived at that time, from professional unions and cultural life, all

of which was completely uprooted and dispersed widely. The disaster of the Arab Palestinian nation was a comprehensive disaster. It hit all those who were forced to leave their homeland, and it hit those who were left in their homeland. (pp. 36–7)

Habiby distinguishes between two 'types' of Palestinians: Palestinian refugees and Palestinian citizens in Israel (focusing on urban Palestinians in this case). The Palestinians who were expelled to the 'deserts of banishment' (*ṣaḥārī al-ghurba*) carried their culture with them. Palestinian refugees settled in camps and neighbourhoods according to their village of origin, and maintained the heritage (*turāth*) of their village, continuing to marry among themselves, 'a custom so strong that it is still the marriage that the camp families prefer' (Sayigh 2007: 9). In contrast to Palestinians who preserved their culture, Palestinians in Israel, even though they have remained in their homeland and have not had to preserve their small societies as refugees have done, have lost their culture and identity. According to Habiby, Palestinian urban society until 1948 was greatly modernised (*qad qaṭaʿa shawṭan marmūqan fī sullam al-taṭawwur al-ḥaḍārī*)[13] in the scale of those times (mid-twentieth century). This advanced society was deracinated (*ijtuththat*) and shattered (*buddidat shathara mathara*), with the creation of Israel. Thus, the Palestinian disaster (*maʾsāt*), the Nakba, as expressed by Habiby and the rest of the nostalgic-folkloric novels, struck a comprehensive (*shāmila*) blow, affecting both Palestinians who became refugees and Palestinians who remained in their homeland.

Palestinian refugees lost their homes, villages and homeland but they deployed their 'traditions as a means of maintaining their sense of self-respect[,] value' and identity (Abrahams 1993: 5). Habiby suggests that the reason for the survival of Palestinian refugees, despite their unbearable conditions (*ghayr muḥtamala*), was *because* they had clung to their culture. However, Palestinians who were allowed to stay in their homeland (*turikū fī waṭanihim*) have been stripped of their culture and folklore. The violent birth of Israel constituted a blow, tearing apart the fabric of Palestinian society. Even the accents or dialects of villages (*lahja khāṣṣa wa ghinwat al-nuṭq al-khāṣṣa*) transformed and altered. The loss of the past is, of course, equivalent to the loss of identity (Lowenthal 1985: 197), which is why nostalgic-folkloric novels lament the displacement of Palestinian culture and identity.

Palestinian citizens in Israel lived in isolation from Palestinians outside of Israel for two decades (1948–67), having both parts of the Palestinian nation 'evolve' in different circumstances. The renewed encounter of the two parts of Palestinian society after 1967 highlighted the cultural differences between them. Whereas Palestinians in Israel have undergone a process of modernisation, ridding themselves of obsolete traditions (*al-taqālīd al-bāliya*) under which, they thought, Palestinian society toiled, Palestinian refugees outside Israel have preserved their culture, heritage and identity. Moreover, from a political point of view, Palestinians across the border also preserved their national struggle for liberation and independence, a discourse which was wiped out among Palestinians in Israel due to their de-nationalising modernisation within the Zionist framework, as we saw in Chapter 1. This contrast, the social-cultural and the political, between the two parts of the Palestinian nation, could explain the doubly contradictory identity reflected in novels published after 1967.

If folklore is concerned with the continuity of culture, and nostalgia marks the discontinuity of culture and identity, the folklorification of Palestinian history in nostalgic narratives is an attempt to bridge a gap in the (dis-)continuity of Palestinian national memory. The act of writing nostalgic-folkloric novels is an act of un-erasure, reaffirming Palestinian identity. Moreover, the act of writing about the Palestinian Nakba maintains the battle over Palestine. The Palestinians who witnessed the Nakba, writing about it sixty years later, reflect a process of realisation that inaction could lead to complete identity wipe-out. Whereas the conflict between Israel and the Palestinians is generally perceived in terms of the occupation of land and the imposition of barriers that prohibit the Palestinian refugees from returning to their homes, Palestinian novels in Israel reflect a realisation that Israeli erasure and Palestinian un-erasure are another site for the battle over Palestine.

Since the Intifada transferred the centre of gravity of the Palestinian conflict to the Occupied Territories, both Palestinian nostalgic narratives and the rewriting of Nakba folklore is an attempt to emphasise that the Palestinian conflict began in 1948, not 1967. It is a way of restoring the Nakba as the primary event in the Palestinian national ethos: an event that unites all Palestinians everywhere. The fact that nostalgic novels continued to be published well into the 1990s and the 2000s indicates that it was not the Intifada alone that removed the Nakba and Palestinian citizens in Israel from the Palestinian conflict. The peace process also planted the seed of this belief among Palestinians, Israelis and the international community. The exclusion of Palestinian citizens in Israel from the historic reconciliation has had serious implications for the identity of Palestinians in Israel.

The attempt of Palestinian citizens in Israel to un-erase their history is paralleled by NGOs such as Zochrot (Remembering), which aims to obtain historical acknowledgement of the Nakba, seeing this recognition as a stage in the political reconciliation of the Middle East, which should include the Palestinian citizens in Israel:

> Zochrot ('Remembering') seeks to raise public awareness of the Palestinian Nakba, especially among Jews in Israel, who bear a special responsibility to remember and amend the legacy of 1948. The principal victims of the Nakba were the Palestinians, especially the refugees, who lost their entire world. But Jews in Israel also pay a price for their conquest of the land in 1948, living in constant fear and without hope.[14]

Indeed, the work of Zochrot should be understood 'in the historical and contemporary context of a larger Zionist project of spatial obliteration and active historical amnesia, a project which works to erase Palestinian presence from the land and to construct Palestinians as "absentees"' (Weaver 2007: 127).

In the novels analysed for this section, Palestinian memories of the Nakba question the status quo and provide a nagging counter-narrative (R. Davis 2007: 6). Palestinian nostalgic-folkloric novels function, in the Palestinian national memory, in some ways comparably to village memorial books. Like nostalgia, memory is understood as articulating the past from the viewpoint of the present (L. Jayyusi 2007), which is reflected in what Rosemary Sayigh defines as the 'continuing Nakba', that is, the memory narrative of the Palestinian Nakba. In nostalgic-folkloric novels, the Nakba for Palestinians in Israel is omnipresent because it alludes not only to the erasure of space, but to the erasure of culture as well.

Remembering the Nakba provides a narrative 'of continuity that marks not only the past within the present, as legacy, scar, outcome, wound, and so on, but also the past *still at work* within the present, still actively re-engendering it in its own shape [...]' (Yaqub 2007: 114; italics in original). The fact that the 'past is still at work in the present', to use Yaqub's formulation, leads me to conclude that nostalgia is a more accurate concept than 'memory' through which to understand Palestinian novels in Israel. The importance of the 'present' dimension of nostalgia novels was mentioned earlier and will be discussed at the end of the chapter, when I compare the common characteristics of all novels in this period. In short, while memory narrative *ends* in the past, nostalgia novels deliver a message about the present, because they make implicit comparisons between past and present.

Palestinian citizens in Israel are deeply concerned with their present situation in Israel. Emile Habiby 'admits' in the above excerpt that Palestinians in Israel have a distorted Palestinian heritage. However, it is important to remember that Palestinian identity and culture in Israel are merely distorted, rather than utterly lost or forgotten. Since the erasure of Palestinian identity was characterised by the absence of anything to fill its place, the Palestinians have taken on a veneer of Israeli identity that has no solid basis and thus cannot replace their Palestinian identity. Resort to a prior, undistorted past is a way of attenuating this distortion, even if it cannot completely reverse this process. The folklorification of the Nakba in Palestinian novels in Israel in this period reflects the fact that 'in recent decades there has been an intense relationship between the Nakba and the articulation of Palestinian national identity' (Masalha 2008: 142). Parallel to resorting to an undistorted past, in the following section I will deal with Palestinian novels that focus on the present, but in a space that is outside Israel.

Intifada Novels

This section will focus on novels containing plots concerning the Palestinian Intifada in the West Bank and Gaza Strip, and, more generally, on the Palestinian struggle for independence *outside* Israel since 1987. The discussion in this section will be based, to a large degree, on a comparison between the narrative in Intifada novels and the narrative expressed in nostalgic-folkloric novels. This is so because Intifada novels[15] and nostalgic-folkloric novels are part of the collectivisation tendency outlined in the first section. Rather than merely reflecting Palestinian divisions (both internally in terms of social disintegration, and externally through differentiating between groups of Palestinians), these groups of novels in fact mark an effort to reunite all Palestinians in one national struggle.

Intifada novels provide thick description relating to Palestinian life in the Occupied Territories, to folklore, through to near-ethnographic accounts of daily life during the Intifada, to the role of women and children in resistance. A discussion on these issues, as interesting and important as they may be, tells us little about identity transformation among the Palestinian citizens in Israel. To elaborate, then, I will present the themes that help convey Palestinian identity in Israel. One of the first questions that arises regarding Intifada novels relates to the reasons that induce Palestinian authors in Israel to write about Palestinian life in the Occupied Territories during this period.

The impact of the Intifada on Palestinian citizens in Israel is connected to the centrality of the Intifada in the Palestinian national struggle. The Intifada proposed a solution that 'no longer seemed remote to the Palestinians, and one that was on the international agenda as the key to settlement of the Arab-Israeli conflict' (Peretz 1990: 113). Peretz refers to a two-state solution, according to which a Palestinian state could be established alongside Israel in the territories occupied in 1967. This proposed solution excluded the Palestinian citizens in Israel, requiring them to define their status and identity as 'Palestinians residing in Israel' (Rouhana 1997: 73).

Since the eruption of the Intifada in 1987, the question of the future of the Palestinian citizens in Israel has become a central issue for both Palestinian and Israeli academics and politicians. Articles such as Ghanem and Ozacky-Lazar's (2003), subtitled 'Part of the Problem but not Part of the Solution', dealt with this issue. Rouhana (1997, 1998), Peleg (2004) and others (such as the edited volume of Gavison and Hacker 2000) also discuss future political options for Palestinians in Israel. Novels in this period could be considered literary participants in the debate on Palestinian identity and its future, as we will see later.

The impact of the Intifada on novels is evident in the fact that it is only after the outbreak of the Intifada that Palestinians in Israel began to write about life in the Occupied Territories. Until 1987, Palestinian citizens in Israel 'erased' the Palestinians outside Israel, something that reflected their 'doubly contradictory' identity. Since 1948, only a few novels by Palestinians in Israel have had their plots, or part of their plots, situated outside Israel, while never straying into the West Bank or Gaza Strip. Plots never revolve around life in these places, nor describe their struggle against Israeli occupation.

Intifada novels are similar to nostalgic-folkloric novels in a number of ways. Firstly, novels in this group tell the collective story of a village, or a refugee camp, rather than a single individual. Secondly, most of the novels in this group are folkloric in the sense that they record Palestinian folklore in the West Bank and Gaza Strip. However, this similarity also marks one of the differences between this group and the nostalgic-folkloric group. Whereas nostalgic-folkloric novels lament the lost Palestinian folklore in Israel, Intifada novels show a continuation of Palestinian folklore in the West Bank and Gaza Strip. This is due to the resistance of the Palestinians in the Occupied Territories to Israeli erasure since the occupation in 1967. These measures of erasure are similar to the policies imposed on Palestinians in Israel since 1948. However, because of Palestinian increased politicisation in the Occupied Territories, these policies were resisted:

> During and immediately upon the conclusion of the [1967] war, a slogan became popular among the Palestinians, al-Ard qabl al-ʿArd [*sic.*], or 'land before honour'; it reversed the sentiment that in 1948 led to massive flights of Palestinians into exile. For the Palestinians this slogan expressed the recognition that the loss of land would mean the final destruction of their society, their dispossession, loss of identity, and dispersed exile. It was as if the motto expressed a collective will, a determination to stay put, grit one's teeth, and persevere. This collective determination, infused by the collective memory of 1948, undoubtedly undergirded the spirit of resistance so pivotal to fighting the war of possession against dispossessive Israeli colonialism. (Farsoun and Landis 1990: 29–30)

Since 1948, Palestinian novels in Israel have recorded the 'destruction of their society, their dispossession, and loss of identity'. For Palestinians outside Israel, increasing political awareness led to a realisation that, in order to preserve their identity and society, they needed to resist Israeli erasure. In *Yad al-Qadar* (*Hand of Fate*, 2005), Jiryis Tannus (also author of *Dhakirat al-Ayyam*, which I examined in the preceding section) attributes the 1948

Nakba to the ignorance (*jahl*) and lack of political awareness of Palestinians at that time (*Yad al-Qadar*, p. 52). The fact that Tannus (and Ilyas Majid Munib) wrote novels that belong to the category of both nostalgic-folkloric novels and Intifada novels indicates the ideological link between them, as I will show below.

Intifada novels mark a further step in the transformation of Palestinian identity in Israel. This transformation can be seen in terms of 'active' and 'passive' narratives. As the terms 'active' and 'passive' are contextual, it is important to distinguish between the different active and passive narratives identified in Palestinian literature elsewhere in this book. In the second period (1967–87) I described Palestinian novels as 'passive' because they *called for* passive perseverance and steadfastness. In *Al-Mutasha'il* (1974), as part of a call for non-violent resistance, Habiby preferred to keep Sa'id, the protagonist, seated atop an impalement stake, rather than to take any action. In this novel, Habiby portrayed those who took action in a negative light. He later admitted that he wrote the novel in order to prevent active resistance among Palestinians in Israel. However, in *Ikhtayya* (1985), Habiby realises that the passive approach resulted in a loss of identity.

Novels in the third period present both passive and active narratives. The passive–active differentiation stems from the contrast between past and present in the two groups of novels, providing another dimension of the discontinuity–continuity contrast. It is important to note that the folklorification aspect in nostalgic-folkloric novels represents an active effort to un-erase the Nakba and to implant it into Palestinian folklore. Nostalgic-folkloric novels depict Palestinians in the past (in 1948 to be accurate) to be passive, while in the present they are active in reviving their identity. It is the same for Intifada novels, which reflect active Palestinian effort to resist occupation and reunite Palestinians. In the following I will show how Intifada novels portray this active narrative by comparing them with the passive narrative of nostalgic-folkloric novels. My aim in using the passive–active distinction is ultimately to understand how Intifada novels reflect Palestinian identity in Israel in this period, through a contrast between the narratives in these two groups.

Zagharid al-Maqathi (*Ululations of the Watermelon Fields*, 1988), by Muhammad Watad, is a novel concerning the inhabitants of Khirbat al-

Zibdawi village in the West Bank, and their resistance to Israeli occupation. In the scene preceding the quotation below, Abu al-Abid, an elderly man from the village, is accidentally drawn towards an Israeli army roadblock and then harassed by one of the soldiers. Abu al-Abid does not succumb to this humiliation, standing up to the insults of the soldier. Soon, a fight starts between the soldiers and Abu al-Abid. One of the soldiers shoots him, and the excerpt below describes the final moments of Abu al-Abid's life.

> Tadaffaq al-dam shallālan min ṣadr abī al-ʿabid … Kāna rāfiʿan raʾsahu ʿan al-turāb yushāhid fuṣūlan min sīrat ḥayātihi fī damihi al-nāzif. Ayyām al-taḥaddī … ʿindamā kāna shahr shbāṭ 'yshabbiṭ w-ykhabbiṭ' ḥāmilan rāʾiḥat al-ṣayf, kāna shabāb al-zibdāwī yakhrujūn ilā al-bayādir. Yaḍaʿūn al-ḥadīd fī yadayhā kay lā tabtaʿid kathīran wa-tarukūnaha tuqaṭmish al-ʿushb, fīmā yanṣarifūn ilā al-lahw wa-l-laʿib.
>
> Majmūʿat abī al-ʿabid kānat tafūz daʾiman … kāna yaḍrib al-daqqa bi-l-ḥāb, fa-taghīb ʿan al-ʿayn. Wa-kāna min al-mustaḥīl ikhtirāq khaṭ difāʿahu ʿan jurat al-kūra. Saʾima hādhā al-lahw marra, fa-rāhana ʿalā annahu yastaṭiʿa an yanṭaḥ al-ḥiṣān arḍan … Ijtamaʿa ahālī al-khirba kullahum ʿalā al-bayādir … Lam yabqa fī-l-buyūt 'lā ʿarja wa-lā ʿūra' illā wa-atat li-tatafarraj. Faqaṭ nfūs takhallafat, li-amrin mā, ʿan al-majīʾ …
>
> Sāl damahu ʿalā al-arḍ masāfa aṭwal min qāmatahu …
>
> Awqafū al-ḥiṣān fī wasaṭ al-baydar … ibtaʿad khamsin khuṭwa ʿan al-ḥiṣān wa-rakaḍ naḥwahu muqawwisan ẓahrahu, māddan raʾsahu … Iṣṭadam bi-baṭn al-ḥiṣān, tarannaḥ al-qdīsh wa-saqaṭ … Imtaṣṣat raqabat abī al-ʿabid al-ṣadma wa-kaʾannahā zunbarak, wa-hā tarfaʿ raʾsahu al-muthqal bi-l-ṣuwar wa-huwa yaḥtaḍir wa-kaʾannahā jidhʿ sindyāna.
>
> Asbal jifnayhi wa-lam yaʿud yarā …
>
> Kānat ʿuyūn ṣaghīra turāqib al-maʿraka … wa-kānat aydin ṣaghīra qad jamaʿat al-banādiq min al-sayyāra wa-sallamathā li-shāb kān yakmun fī-l-maghāra … Bakā sāmiḥ – min ghayẓahu – wa-huwa yarā abā al-ʿabid yaḥtaḍir, mumaddadan ʿalā al-arḍ, rāfiʿan raʾsahu …
>
> Innahu awwal mayyit yarāh …
>
> *Wa-qad taʿallam minhu anna al-rijāl yamūtūn marfūʿī al-ruʾūs.* (pp. 48–9)

The blood gushed from Abu Al-Abid's chest like a waterfall … He held his head above the ground, while he was watching chapters from his life story in his seeping blood. The days of challenges … when February was going wild, carrying the scents of the summer, the young men of Al-Zibdawi used to take their mares to the threshing grounds. They used to cuff them, lest they stray, and would let them graze there, while they [the men] play and have fun.

Abu al-Abid's group used to always win … He used to hit the *daqqa* with *al-ḥāb*, and it would disappear. And it was impossible to penetrate his defence line of the ball's hall. One day he got bored of these games, so he bet that he could head-butt the horse to the ground … the people of the *khirba* gathered on the threshing grounds … no one left in their home, and all came to watch. Only Nfus, for some reason, failed to come …

His blood seeped on the ground a distance longer than his body …

They placed the horse in the middle of the threshing ground … He stepped away some fifty steps and ran towards the horse arching his back and stretching his head … he collided in the horse's belly, it swayed and fell … Abu al-Abid's neck absorbed the shock as if it was a spring, and here it is like the trunk of an oak tree lifting his head, full of images, while he is dying …

He closed his eyes and no longer could see …

Small eyes were watching the battle … and small hands collected the rifles from the car and handed them over to a young man hiding in the cave … Samih cried – angrily – as he watched Abu al-Abid die, lying on the ground, his head lifted …

He is the first dead person he sees …

And he learned from him that men die with their heads lifted up … (pp. 48–9)

This excerpt demonstrates some of the similarities between Intifada and nostalgic-folkloric novels. The depiction of the life of the village in the West Bank during the late 1980s (throughout the Intifada) is reminiscent of the depiction of Palestinian village life before 1948 in nostalgic-folkloric novels.

The excerpt above is an example of the preservation of Palestinian culture outside Israel. The description of games on the threshing grounds (*bayādir*), a public space comparable in function to the village square, bears many similarities. I will not expand on the games, or the other folkloric features included in the above text, as they add little to what has already been offered to our understanding of Palestinian identity in this period. When comparing the two groups of novels from the point of view of passive–active differentiation, there are, however, a number of points worth considering. These points are easier to elaborate if we contrast the death of Abu al-Abid with the execution of the four men under the olive tree in *Awjaʿ al-Bilad al-Muqaddasa.*

First, one of the major differences between the two scenes is that in nostalgic-folkloric novels, Palestinians during the Nakba are portrayed as passive victims of a brutal execution,[16] while in the Intifada in the Occupied Territories, Palestinians die actively resisting. This reflects a discourse that aims to invert weakness into strength. The fact that Abu al-Abid is an old man fighting by himself a group of young (strong) armed Israeli soldiers, contrasts with the depiction of young Palestinian men during the 1948 war, hand-picked by a few Israeli soldiers, and 'led' to be executed in the village square. Young Palestinian men in 1948 neither resisted nor fought for their lives. Abu al-Abid, however, did not accept his fate passively, and fought a losing battle against a group of soldiers. Such a depiction of Palestinian unwillingness to capitulate to Israeli power is true of almost all deaths in Intifada novels. Thus, Intifada novels stress the honour of resistance, since men die proud (*al-rijāl yamūtūn marfūʿī al-ruʿūs*).

The inversion of weakness into strength is also evident in the last scene that Abu al-Abid 'sees' before he dies. It is not his defeat in a fight against Israeli soldiers, but that of his memorable victory in the challenge to head-butt a horse to the ground. Therefore, Abu al-Abid dies victorious, since he replaces his defeat to the Israeli soldiers with his glory at the village threshing grounds. The success of Abu al-Abid to head-butt a horse to the ground, witnessed by the entire village, contrasts with the public executions of defeated men in the village squares in nostalgic-folkloric novels. Another example for Palestinian empowerment narrative is evidenced in the portrayal of the bleeding Abu al-Abid: 'the blood gushed like a waterfall from the chest of Abu al-Abid' (*tadaffaqa al-damu shallālan min ṣadr abī al-ʿabid*). This depicts the vitality and energy of the old man, rather than weakness or illness.

Another difference regarding the passive–active distinction refers to the observation of death. Whereas in Nakba narratives the observers of death remained passive, in the scene above, during the soldiers' fight with Abu al-Abid, the young children steal the weapons of the soldiers, and hand them over to a fighter hiding in a cave. Thus the children of the Intifada are seen to be heroic, since, by stealing weapons from the soldiers, they have taken the initiative and turned the loss of Abu al-Abid to a Palestinian advantage. Moreover, by this, they invert their powerlessness to strength.

The depiction of children is another site of difference in the two groups of novels along the passive–active divide. In nostalgic-folkloric novels, some of which included childhood memories, children are inert and politically unaware. In comparison, children are highly praised in Intifada novels. For example, in *Al-Jarad Yuhibb al-Battikh* (*The Locust Loves Watermelon*, 1990), by Radi Shhada, one character says that the activity of the children during the Intifada surpassed what the Arab countries did for the Palestinians: '*illī ʿimlūh al-awlād fi-l-intifāḍa kūm willī ʿimlūh kull al-ʿarab kūm*' (p. 267). Since 1948, Arab armies have been depicted negatively in Palestinian novels, due to their association with defeat in the wars with Israel. However, armed only with rocks and Molotov cocktails, the Palestinians, youth and children, managed to put Israel 'on the defensive' (Lustick 1993: 564).

Both in reality and in the novels, the participation of children in the resistance marks the deep nationalisation of Palestinian society. During the Intifada, the children in the West Bank and Gaza Strip were called *aṭfāl al-ḥijāra* ('children of stones'), who were 'raised in an environment with all the symbolism and slogans of Palestinian nationalism permeating their daily lives from infancy' (Peretz 1990: 83). In the above excerpt from *Zagharid al-Maqathi*, the message that 'men die proud' (*al-rijāl yamūtūn marfūʿī al-ruʿūs*) has been clearly transmitted to, and learned (*taʿallam*) by, the spectating children. The relationship between manhood and political discourse was indicated in a number of occasions earlier. Peteet describes, furthermore, how resisting Israeli occupation has become 'a rite of passage into manhood' (Peteet 1994: 31).

Palestinian active discourse, denoting continuity, is further expressed in other ways in Intifada novels. The following quotation from *Al-Jarad Yuhibb al-Battikh* describes the funeral-wedding of Nassur, a student at Birzeit University in Ramallah, who was killed during a demonstration against the Israeli occupation. When the inhabitants of Al-Shabura refugee camp in the Gaza Strip, in which he lived, find out about his death they launch a mock funeral, which lasts until Nassur's body is brought back to the Gaza Strip from the West Bank.

> Al-hitāfāt tataḍāʿaf, al-zaghārīd tazdād, al-muhāhāt, al-ṣurākh, wa-l-ʿarīs waṣal. Yatajaddad al-ḥamās wa-yataḍāʿaf ʾīqāʿ al-masīra, wa-nabaʿith al-rūḥ wa-l-ḥayawiyya ilā al-jasad al-bashariyy al-kathīf wa-qad nasaw taʿab yawm kāmil min al-dawarān ghayr al-mutakāmil ḥattā waṣal al-shahīd fa-ḥawwal masīrat al-naʿsh al-wahmiyya ilā janāza ḥaqīqiyya. Al-shabāb yatadāfaʿūn li-akhdh ḥiṣṣa bi-naql al-shahīd min al-sayyāra ilā al-naʿsh [...] yarfaʿūnahu fawqa aydīhim, baynamā rāḥ shābb yashudd aṣābiʿ al-ʿarīs li-yaʿmal minhā shakl 'fi' wa-ʿindamā yanjaḥ fi dhālik yuṭliqhā fi-l-hawāʾ. Naṣṣūr yaʿtalī naʿshahu, ʿarshahu. (p. 155)

> The cheers double, the ululations increase, the shouting – the groom has arrived. The energy is renewed and the marching rhythm is doubled, and this dense human gathering is filled with energy and vitality, forgetting a full day of marching aimlessly until the martyr has arrived, turning the fake casket funeral into a true one. The young men struggle to take part in moving the martyr from the car into the casket [...] carrying him above their hands, while one of them stretched the groom's fingers into a V shape, and then lifted it up in the air. Nassur rises to his casket, his throne. (p. 155)

In nostalgic-folkloric novels, the site of continuity (weddings) has become a site of discontinuity and death. In Intifada novels, in contrast, the site of discontinuity and death (funerals) becomes a site of continuity and 'vitality' (*tanbaʿith al-rūḥ wa-l-ḥayawiyya*). The funeral-wedding during the Intifada defied Israeli attempts to eradicate the Palestinians and to disperse them. Thus, the Intifada became a display of Palestinian unity (see: Farsoun and Landis 1990: 16; Peretz 1990: 78), and this unity took the form of collective weddings. The cohesion of Palestinian society is further cemented in its representation as a 'dense human body' (*al-jasad al-basharī al-kathīf*), when defiance of Israeli erasure is expressed in the parallel between Nassur as martyr (*shahīd*) and as a person treated as a groom (*ʿarīs*). Moreover, the death of Nassur, the political activist, which takes place among his friends/comrades during demonstrations that express Palestinian united struggle against Israeli occupation, contrasts with the anomic, lonely death of Muhammad from *Al-Juththa al-Majhula*, on a beach in Tel-Aviv. This contrast highlights the collectivisation of Palestinian discourse in this period vis-à-vis the differentiation of Palestinian society reflected in earlier novels.

In contrast to dying passively and being buried quietly, as nostalgic-folkloric novels portray Palestinian death in 1948, Intifada novels turn death in combat into a public and collective celebration of continuity and glory. Nassur, the martyr, is lifted onto the shoulders of his people and carried around the refugee camp, just as grooms are lifted in Palestinian weddings. Moreover, the ululations (*zaghārīd*) and the marching in the streets of the refugee camp closely resemble the proceedings of Palestinian weddings outlined in the preceding section: 'This celebratory spirit is also evident in the funeral of the martyr, a manifestation of the glory that martyrdom brings' (Peteet 1991: 107). Thus, the coffin (*naʿsh*) becomes a throne (*ʿarsh*), since there is nothing shameful in death: death is a sign of courage. The similar sound of these two words in Arabic further highlights the contrasts between them.

Firstly, the coffin resembles the ultimate human 'powerlessness', death, while the throne signifies supreme power. Whereas in 1948 Palestinian powerlessness meant flight and defeat, resistance to occupation in the Intifada marks for the enemy that Palestinians defy their powerlessness by their willingness to die in an unmatched combat. Secondly, whereas normally the throne is elevated above 'the common people' and the coffin is buried in the ground, Palestinian martyrs are elevated to the status of kings. Thirdly, as happens when kings die, the coronation of a new king marks the continuity of the kingdom. However, while the slogan 'the king is dead, long live the king' refers to two kings, the deceased and his successor, in the funeral-wedding the Palestinian martyr is both the deceased and the successor at the same time, marking the idea that Palestinian continuity is preserved through resistance to occupation. To be a martyr, in other words, means elevation to the status of kings, stressing power and continuity.

While in 1948 death and massacre were used to terrorise the Palestinians into flight, Palestinians are, in 1987, no longer afraid of death. To acknowledge the bravery that Nassur demonstrated in resisting Israeli occupation, one of the participants uses Nassur's fingers to form the 'V' sign, for victory: a symbol of the Intifada. Death in resistance is thus perceived as a source of pride, and the celebration of death in resistance, or martyrdom, defies the Israeli attempted erasure of Palestinians, conveying the message that the Zionist myth of 'a land without a people' cannot be realised through the executions of Palestinians (Peteet 1994: 33).

Intifada novels not only reflect the unity of Palestinian society in the West Bank and Gaza Strip, they call for Palestinian unity across all borders. *Yad al-Qadar*, by Jiryis Tannus, tells the story of five Palestinian citizens in Israel who were separated during the military rule (1948–66) as a result of their political activities as high school students. The friends became dispersed throughout the Middle East. Amjad stays in Jordan and becomes a lawyer after his deportation from Israel; Fadi moves to Ayn al-Hilwa refugee camp in Lebanon, immersing himself in the Palestinian resistance movement there; Walid manages to return to Israel, becoming a teacher and a loyal citizen who opposes Palestinian national activism; Ra'id remains in Israel and maintains his nationalistic political views; and Amira, Amjad's beloved girlfriend, is not deported but rather stays in Israel and continues to be politically active. The stories of the different characters represent different sections of Palestinian society, or different political orientations. The novel focuses mainly on Palestinian citizens in Israel, since only two characters live outside Israel. However, having the plot take place both inside and outside Israel illustrates the collectivisation role of Intifada novels, as I will discuss below.

Yad al-Qadar, as well as other Intifada novels, aims to present a unified Palestinian discourse. The novel begins with the separation of Amjad and Amira as a result of his deportation to Jordan. This is another example of the ruptures caused in Palestinian society as a result of Israeli prevention of the creation of new families. However, the closing scene in the novel is that of a wedding. Hiba, Fadi's daughter, marries Haytham, Walid's son. This wedding stands in contrast to the failed love of Amjad and Amira, signifying the discontinuity of Palestinian society in the Nakba. The final paragraph in the novel reflects the message of an all-Palestinian reunification:

> Qām rāʾid min makānahu wa-ʿaynāh talmaʿān faraḥan wa-taṣmīman. Jamaʿa aṣdiqāʾ al-māḍī wa-ʿāʾilātahum fī wasaṭ al-qāʿa wa-fī ḥalabat al-raqṣ wa-ṭalab min al-firqa an taʿzif maʿzūfat al-mijwiz li-yarquṣū ʿalā anghāmihā. Tashābakat al-aydī wa-ishraʾabbat al-aʿnāq wa-sukibat al-dumūʿ, dumūʿ al-faraḥ bi-l-liqāʾ al-mujaddad. (p. 152)

> Ra'id stood up, his determined eyes shining happily. He gathered his friends of old and their families in the centre of the hall in the dance floor and asked the band to play the *mijwiz* so they could dance. The hands interlocked and the heads stretched upwards and tears fell, the tears of happiness in this reunion. (p. 152)

This excerpt exemplifies the evolution of Palestinian identity in Israel. The wedding in *Yad al-Qadar* is an act of defiance against Israeli erasure of Palestinian identity. While Amjad and Amira accepted their separation with passivity, Palestinians in the present (the novel was published in 2005) will not succumb to this, and the wedding is an assertion of Palestinian unified continuity. The wedding in this novel contrasts with the doubly contradictory identity expressed in the previously discussed *Ila al-Jahim Ayyuha al-Laylak* (1977), by Samih al-Qasim, in two ways: the unachieved meeting of Samih with Dunya from the final scene of the novel, as well as the temporary nature of the encounter with Palestinians in Jerusalem. The renewed encounter (*al-liqāʾ al-mujaddad*) of Palestinians in *Yad al-Qadar* is neither unachieved nor temporary: rather it is cemented in an eternal bond of marriage.

Moreover, although the wedding takes place in a wedding hall instead of the village square, Ra'id asks the band to play the '*mijwiz*' (Palestinian flute), restoring one aspect of 'old' Palestinian culture. This instrument was traditionally played at Palestinian weddings, and its erasure has been lamented by nostalgic-folkloric novels. In the preceding section, the execution of the flute player was discussed as a symbol of the eradication of Palestinian culture and an attempt to prevent Palestinian continuity by inhibiting Palestinian weddings from taking place. Asking to play the *mijwiz* revives, or resurrects, the 'assassinated' *mijwiz* player, hence music, described earlier in this chapter.

The fragmentation of Palestinian society due to the Nakba in 1948 is further defied by the act of holding hands (*tashābakat al-aydī*), symbolising the collectivisation of all Palestinians, the happy tears with the reunification (*dumūʿ al-faraḥ bi-l-liqāʾ al-jadīd*), and the fact that the bride and the groom are from across the border (Haytham is a Palestinian citizen in Israel, and Hiba is from Ayn al-Hilwa camp in Lebanon). The fact that this reunification and its defiance of the continuation of the passive Palestinian existence take place in Israel reflects the Palestinian conviction that the refugees should be able to return to Palestine.

Another difference between Intifada and nostalgic-folkloric novels, on the line of continuity–discontinuity, is that in the former, the outlook is future focused and aims at liberation, while the latter is pessimistic and concerned with the lost past. The conclusion of *Yad al-Qadar* is a positive one, in that it posits a joint Palestinian future through the new family that has formed. Two other novels contain open-ended closures. *Zagharid al-Maqathi* (1988), by Muhammad Watad, is said to be a '*riwāya fī thalāthat ajzāʾ*', a novel of three parts. The second part ends with a note that a third part 'will follow'. The same is true of *Al-Jarad Yuhibb al-Battikh* (1990), by Radi Shhada. The final sentence states that the novel 'has not been concluded and that the nation has the final decision (*al-qarār al-akhīr*) in the form and content (*shakl wa-maḍmūn*) of its ending' (p. 489). These endings exemplify the active narrative that I spoke about at the beginning of this section. Intifada novels defy Israeli erasure of all that is Palestinian, and according to this discourse, only the Palestinians themselves can determine their future. This call contrasts with the nostalgic narrative that lamented the lost past. In comparison with nostalgic-folkloric novels, Intifada novels do not deal with the Palestinian past at all, since the orientation of these novels is towards the future.

According to the novels addressed here, and contrary to what Rouhana claims, the Intifada did not 'resurrect the Green Line in the consciousness of both Palestinian communities' (Rouhana 1997: 75). It resurrected, rather, a Palestinian national awareness among Palestinians in Israel, adapted to the structural limitations of the Israeli political and administrative system. At the beginning of this chapter, I quoted Rouhana as saying that Palestinian citizens in Israel expressed no more than 'sentimental identification' with Palestinians across the border. However, the two groups of novels analysed above demonstrate the depth of identity transformation among Palestinians in Israel in the aftermath of the Intifada. This stands in contrast to Rouhana's dismissal of such 'verbal and artistic' expressions of identification. Thus,

Intifada and nostalgic-folkloric novels demonstrate a notable identity transformation among Palestinians in Israel, one that calls for a united national struggle. That it was only after the Intifada that Palestinians in Israel started to write novels about Palestinian life outside Israel is a further indication of the effect that the Intifada had on Palestinians in Israel.

The 'doubly contradictory' identity of Palestinians in Israel, which was prominent among novelists during the second period (1967–87), echoes a political orientation that was led for many years by the communist party in Israel:

> the idea that the Arabs in Israel are Israeli citizens and [at] the same time part of the Palestinian Arab people – a complete rather than a split identity – is a cornerstone of the Communist [party] viewpoint. It is fully in keeping with their attitude toward the future of the Arabs in Israel even after a resolution of the Palestinian problem – namely, that the Arabs will remain citizens of Israel with an Israeli identity superadded to their Palestinian identity. (Ghanem 2001: 84)

Nostalgic-folkloric novels and Intifada novels mark a shift away from such an approach and a stronger association with the Palestinian national struggle. Mahmud Ghanayim arrives at a similar conclusion that 'despite the double identity evinced by [Palestinian literature in Israel], there have been many attempts to shift decisively toward a distinctive identity that would break the tie with Israeli reality' (Ghanayim 2009: 196). In political terms, national currents among Palestinians in Israel began to strengthen after the Intifada, reflecting their collectivisation:

> In 1992 an Arab-dominated political movement – The Equality Covenant – called for the first time for the transformation of Israel from an ethnic state into a democratic state for all its citizens, and articulated in sharp focus the need for equality and state transformation. Towards the 1996 Israeli elections, this movement was organised into a political party – The National Democratic Alignment [...] thus bringing the issue of equality to the fore of Arab politics. (Rouhana 1998: 287)

This political direction of the National Democratic Alignment (NDA) is essentially different from the line that the communist party took for many years. Azmi Bishara characterised the activity of the communist party in Israel as one of struggling against discrimination, not *for* equality. Bishara argues that it was 'a struggle which defined equality negatively as an absence of discrimination, rather than according to a positive definition which would see Israel as a state of all its citizens' (Bishara 1993: 11). The contrast between the communist party and the NDA is similar to the contrast between the passivity of the novels from the second period, and the active tone that characterises novels in the third period.

The NDA ideological basis 'rejected the status quo and called for the establishment of a secular democratic state in the entire territory of Mandatory Palestine, and called for the return of the refugees who left their homes in 1948' (Ghanem 2001: 117). The transformation in political activity among Palestinians in Israel is reflected in the massive expansion of their civil society struggle after the Intifada. This is evident in the fact that, until 1990, there were 'about 180 public societies among the Palestinian Arab minority in Israel. In the last nine years since 1990 a new 656 Arab societies were established' (Ghanem 2001: 172). The expansion of Palestinian civil society NGOs in Israel marks the realisation of the need to take an active role in shaping the lives and future of Palestinians living in Israel:

> The wide network of Arab NGOs forms a counterpublic where the interests of the Arab community are represented in such areas as urban planning, health services, educational infrastructure, legal rights and services, and human rights monitoring. The NGOs serve an important function, providing goods and services much needed in the neglected Arab community. (Jamal 2006: 12)

The civil society activity, which aims at granting equal rights to Palestinians in Israel, reflects nationalist sentiments rather than the mere struggle of a minority for equality of budget. Rouhana (1997) distinguishes between the sentimental and the instrumental levels in Palestinian identity in Israel. To demonstrate that the identification of Palestinians in Israel with the Intifada was merely sentimental, Rouhana mentions the passivity of Palestinians in Israel with regard to their military and political participation in the Palestinian struggle for statehood outside Israel (Rouhana 1997: 78).

However, the effect of the Intifada on the Palestinian citizens in Israel should not be seen merely in terms of sentimental solidarity with the Palestinian struggle against Israeli occupation. Palestinian citizens in Israel, by being exposed to the Intifada discourse of freedom, liberation and dignity, also adapted their own struggle inside Israel. This adaptation refers to Palestinians in Israel providing a contextualised definition of their struggle in search of equality. Thus the contextualisation of the Palestinian struggle in Israel needs to be viewed not only in terms of passive or active discourses, but also in terms of collective or individual rights. In a survey conducted by Ghanem (2002), on the individual and collective orientations of Palestinian citizens in Israel, he concludes that

> an overwhelming majority of the Palestinian citizens of Israel are satisfied with their level of individual advancement, that is, the individual and personal modernisation they have achieved. On the other hand, they are generally not happy with the advancement of the Arabs as a group, with regards to their conditions and achievements, the ability to influence their own future, take decisions, integrate on the countrywide level, and attain an appropriate collective status. (Ghanem 2002: 145)

The works of Ghanem and Rouhana are important to an understanding of the political orientations of Palestinians in Israel. They do not, however, distinguish between national identification, pragmatic political choices, and the relationship between them. Palestinians in Israel, according to the survey conducted by Ghanem, were reluctant to take part in Palestinian politics in the West Bank and Gaza Strip and their struggle for statehood. However, the majority of respondents in the survey 'feel closer to the Palestinians in the West Bank and Gaza Strip'. The contrast between these two orientations can be understood in terms of emotional affinity versus pragmatic political choice, determined by the prevailing political discourse during the period of the Oslo peace process. Indication of this is found in the fact that the majority of Palestinian citizens in Israel believe that their struggle for full equality in Israel and the Palestinians' struggle for statehood should be advanced simultaneously.

In other words, Palestinians in Israel in the period 1987–2010 see their situation in national terms 'rather than a problem of budget discrimination against a minority' (Ghanim 2009: 142). The quest for full equality with

Jewish-Israelis in Israel substitutes the quest for national determination, based on political pragmatism. The political vision of Palestinian citizens in Israel in the 1990s is based on a strategy of compromise as the means to achieve long-awaited peace in the Middle East. This vision includes the establishment of a sovereign Palestinian state within the 1967 borders, involving the right of return for the refugees, as well as the granting of full civil rights to Palestinians in Israel. Full equality with Israeli-Jews in Israel means turning Israel into a state of all of its citizens – a bi-national state – which would amount to self-determination for Palestinian citizens in Israel, because it would mean the de-Zionising of Israel. This is a situation that Palestinian citizens in Israel are willing to accept (see: Bishara 1993; Ghanem 2000; Ghanim 2009).

Nostalgic-folkloric and Intifada novels portray a significant transformation in the symbolic and sentimental identification of Palestinians in Israel, especially when compared with novels from previous periods. This transformation, the collectivisation of Palestinians in Israel, is consistent with the work of political and civil organisations that also challenged the Zionist discourse in Israel, since these organisations evolved in tandem with the political transformations in the Middle East.

Nostalgic-folkloric and Intifada novels represent the movement in Palestinian society in Israel towards a nationalist Palestinian narrative. This should not, however, be understood as a complete representation of the Palestinian political map in Israel. In the following section, I will analyse the narrative of more than twenty novels published in Israel since 1987, whose plots are situated both in the present and inside Israel.

Novels of Perplexity

Palestinian citizens in Israel are present-absentified. This has been expressed in various ways in Palestinian novels. Novels in the group under consideration in this section deal with the experience of being present-absentified, namely, with Palestinian alienation in Israel.

The two groups we have discussed so far in this chapter share a number of common characteristics. These common characteristics relate to the way they address Palestinian alienation in Israel, as well as the 'solutions' offered to this problem. The discourse of collectivisation in both groups expresses the same logic, but is manifest in two dimensions, either temporal or spatial.

The underlying logic of such discourse is to connect with non-Israeli space or time. In both groups, Palestinians in Israel solve the problem of their alienation in Israel by connecting with a Palestinian past ('then'), or with a Palestinian present outside Israel ('there'). While nostalgic-folkloric novels aim to implant the Nakba as the uniting event of all Palestinians, Intifada novels 'cross the border' and focus on the Palestinian struggle against the Israeli occupation in the West Bank and Gaza Strip. In contrast, novels in the third group, under discussion in this section, are situated inside Israel ('here') and in the present ('now'). Apart from the spatio-temporal contrast with the other two groups, the third group differs in terms of the way its novels 'read' and analyse Palestinian alienation in Israel. However, although plots in this group are situated inside Israel, they devote a great deal of attention to the relationship with Palestinians outside Israel.

Palestinians in Israel start to deal directly with issues relating to their identity and status in Israel, in light of the political developments taking place in this period (1987–2010), such as the Intifada and the peace process. Novels in this section are preoccupied with similar issues that novels in the other two groups are. Like nostalgic-folkloric novels, these novels deal with Palestinian erasure in Israel, while also addressing the relationship between Palestinians in Israel and Palestinians outside Israel, as was apparent in Intifada novels. Unlike the first two groups, however, novels in this section do not offer a clear 'solution' to Palestinian alienation in Israel. Above all they reflect a perplexed position (*ḥīra*) with regard to this issue.

In this section, I will explore the clashing forces that create this perplexity: these include the duality of the 'presence *and* absence', or alienation of Palestinian citizens in Israel both in Israel, on the one hand, and regarding the Palestinians outside Israel, on the other. The resultant 'double-alienation' felt by Palestinians in Israel mirrors the effects of the peace process between Israel and the PLO on Palestinian citizens in Israel. During the peace process, the two parties excluded Palestinian citizens in Israel from the solution to the Palestinian problem. In other words, two alien and alienating entities set out to design the future of Palestinians in Israel without including them in the process of decision-making. Both the PLO and the Palestinian National Authority (PNA) are alien to Palestinian citizens in Israel because neither body has representatives from Palestinians in Israel: Palestinian citizens in Israel were not included in the political movement that created them. The PLO and the PNA are, therefore, deemed to be alienating to the Palestinians in Israel because the former excludes them from its political agenda. Additionally, Palestinian citizens in Israel had excluded themselves from Palestinian political activity outside Israel, as shown earlier (Rouhana 1990: 59–60). Israel was, moreover, alien and alienating to Palestinian citizens in Israel because of its erasure and exclusive discourse, discussed elsewhere (see Chapter 1). Thus, Israel, too, excluded its Palestinian citizens from the political decision-making regarding the solution to the Palestinian problem.

What we will see in this section is that Palestinian citizens in Israel do perceive themselves in collective terms, but, as the novels of perplexity reveal, they are uncertain about the 'direction' in which they should head. Moreover, they do not reflect a discourse of collectivisation, highlighting, instead, Palestinian alienation in Israel. Perplexity novels problematise such alienation. They break it down to its component parts and try to understand it. To elaborate, there are a number of complementary characteristics, common to perplexity novels, which we should mention at this stage of the discussion.

Firstly, perplexity is evident in the disjointed narratives or plots. In comparison, nostalgic-folkloric and Intifada narratives are mostly linear in their temporal progression, which adopts a historical, or a 'documentary'-style narrative. Moreover, perplexity plots usually express the thoughts and recollections of their protagonists. Thus they do not necessarily progress in a linear way, since we sometimes do not know the length of the lapse of time between each 'episode' or scene in the narrative.

This characteristic is related to the second common feature in this group: just as the discourse is 'fluid' in temporal terms, this is also the case spatially. Although most plots take place inside Israel (as names of cities and other plot-related information suggest), 'space' is described 'thinly', in comparison to the thick description of the other two groups. The third, and related, characteristic of perplexity novels is that the narrative is 'phenomenological'. Through this characteristic, novels in the group address Palestinian existence in Israel. Novels in this group do not deal with 'events'; they deal with the meanings and implications surrounding such events. Thus, while the first two characteristics are difficult to demonstrate here, we will see later in the chapter that the discussion regarding the third characteristic is intertwined with aspects of the first two.

Thus, the two-stage analysis in this section will focus first on levels of Palestinian alienation inside Israel, and later on the mutual alienation both of Palestinians inside and outside Israel, as expressed in perplexity novels.

Palestinian Alienation in Israel

Al-Hamishiyy (*The Marginal*, 1992), by Riyad Baydas, is a good example of the explicit expression of Palestinian alienation in Israel. The speaker, Samih, is a Palestinian citizen in Israel who lives in Haifa. He comes to study at the University of Haifa from a village in the Galilee. Samih works in a bookshop owned by a Jewish-Israeli and lives with Lamya', his girlfriend, in a shared apartment. The novel is about Samih, his life and work in the city, as well as his relationships with some of its inhabitants, both Palestinians and Jewish-Israelis. Due to the socio-political situation in which Palestinians in Israel live, Samih feels alienated and marginalised in Haifa, hence the title of the novel. At the end of the novel he sees the return to his village as the solution to his alienation.

However, apart from the direct expression of alienation in the title of the novel, *Al-Hamishiyy* also depicts, in claustrophobic terms, Palestinian alienation in Israel more generally:

> Hākadhā aṣbaḥat ḥayfā wa-ḥattā al-amākin al-ukhrā bi-l-nisbati lī. Makān yanghaliq ʿalā dhātihi yawman baʿda yawm. (p. 38)

> This is how Haifa, and even the other places, have become for me, a place that closes onto itself day by day. (p. 38)

'Claustrophobic alienation' in the excerpt is expressed in two ways, both explicitly and implicitly. The claustrophobia that Samih experiences is depicted in the description of Haifa in the above excerpt, while conveyed elsewhere in the novels by the use of terms such as 'foreignness' (*ghurba*), 'prison' (*sijn*), 'suffocation' (*ikhtināq*), 'ghetto', 'loneliness' (*wiḥda*), the feeling of being 'stuck' (*ʿāliq*), and a sense of 'disharmony' (*ʿadam insijām*) in life. Claustrophobic alienation is evoked implicitly when Samih seems to detach himself from the description of Haifa. For him, Haifa is a place that closes in on itself (*makān yanghaliq ʿalā dhātihi*), rather than a place that closes in on him, even though he lives in(side) this city. This is so because Haifa here does not relate to a physical place, but to Israeli discourse; which Samih, due to his alienation, observes as an outsider.

As a means to overcome his claustrophobia, Samih forms the habit of loitering in the streets (*yatasakkaʿ*). By walking in the streets of the city, he attempts to 'open it', '*al-tasakkuʿ yuwallid ladayya shuʿūran bi-l-ittisāʿ*' (p. 20). 'Loitering', as a theme, also appears in the novels *Let It Be Morning* (2004) and *Second Person* (2010), both by Sayyed Kashua, where this theme is used to express the alienation and loneliness of the characters. The keynote of walking aimlessly in the streets of Haifa also appears in *Ikhtayya* (1985), by Emile Habiby, discussed in Chapter 2. We have already seen that *Ikhtayya* was concerned with the 'passage of time', and the way Palestinians in Israel lose their identity, or become alienated, if they remain passive towards it. *Al-Hamishiyy* is a more recent account of the alienation felt by Palestinians in Israel towards their space. The passage of time is expressed in the excerpt above: Haifa is closing in on itself 'day by day' (*yawm baʿda yawm*).

Moreover, alienation is expressed in the title of an article that Samih wanted to write, '*al-bilād al-latī kānat lī, al-bilād al-latī lam taʿud lī*' (p. 39), which translates as: 'The country that used to be mine, the country that ceased to be mine'. The title expresses alienation by stating that the country has been taken from him – that it is no longer his. Thus, Samih does not say that he does not belong to the country, but that the country was appropriated through acts of erasure, which is why Samih says it 'no longer belongs to' him. Emile Habiby expresses a similar concern when in *Siraj al-Ghula* he describes how Palestinians in Israel lost their culture and folklore, though they remained in their homes and villages. Contrary to Habiby, Samih does not stress his ownership over the country, nor does he attempt to undo its erasure, or assert Palestinian ownership over Palestine. Similarly, Raef Zreik proposes that 'the Palestinians [in Israel] have lost not only their rights and their land, but also the context that enables them to demand these rights in a way that makes sense' (Zreik 2004: 78). This is true of most perplexity novels. They point to the problem (erasure and alienation), but do not offer a 'solution' to it.

The return of Samih to his village is important in two ways. First, it corresponds to the 'return' to Palestinian identity in this period, also reflected in writing folkloric narratives and village history books. The return (*al-ʿawda*) is also evocative of the aspirations of Palestinian refugees to return to their homeland, symbolised in *Al-Hamishiyy* by the village, since being alienated in Israeli space parallels the experience of refugees being forced out of their homeland. A similar allusion to the return of the refugees to Palestine is expressed in *Yad al-Qadar*, discussed in the preceding section. The second important point regarding Samih returning to his village stands in opposition to novels of the second period (in which characters escape from their villages and refuse to return as a means towards individualisation); thus, reflecting a rethinking of the process of differentiation, which results from modernisation. All further discussion of these points will focus on the aforementioned novel, *Let It Be Morning*, by Sayyed Kashua.

Unlike *Al-Hamishiyy*, *Let It Be Morning* begins with the return of the protagonist to his village, rendering this issue one of the central themes in the novel. Moreover, this text is pivotal to our analysis, due to the centrality of Palestinian double-alienation to it, which, as mentioned above, refers to the alienation of Palestinians both inside and outside Israel.

Let It Be Morning is the first-person narrative of a Palestinian citizen in Israel who returns to his village in the Triangle area after having tried to live in Jerusalem for ten years. It begins with his difficulties reintegrating back into village life. Soon after his return, an unexplained siege is imposed on the village by the Israeli army. Thus, the majority of the plot revolves around the reactions of the villagers to this unexpected Israeli action. At the close of the novel, the siege is lifted and villagers discover that the borders have been moved to incorporate it into the Palestinian state, which has been established according to a peace agreement between Israel and the Palestinian Authority.

This plot expresses the fears of Palestinians in Israel that they may be transferred from Israel through a land swap within a peace agreement, and, more importantly, that they have no say in their own fate. In the following discussion I will deal with the two sides of double-alienation as expressed in *Let It Be Morning*. First, I will discuss Palestinian alienation inside Israel, having the return to the village as a keynote that reflects one dimension of Palestinian alienation in Israel. Afterwards, I will focus on Palestinian mutual alienation – between those inside and outside Israel.

The theme of returning to the village aids our understanding of novels of perplexity in two ways. First, perplexity novels, which include this theme, seem to express a logic similar to that deployed by the first two groups: a (re)turn to Palestinian space/time. (Re)turn to a Palestinian time or space also involves the choice of existing in a non-Israeli space. Secondly, return to the village problematises this logic, reflecting the idea that going back to a Palestinian space is impossible inside Israel, since Palestinian spaces have been subject to erasure. As a result, Palestinians in Israel are unable to 'escape' to a Palestinian space inside Israel, leading to their ultimate alienation.

Return to the village in the third period (1987–2010) offers a 'follow-up' to modernisation discourse (first period: 1948–67) where Palestinian integration in Israel is tied to their modernisation there. Counteraction novels in the second period (1967–87) 'warned' of the loss of identity that would result from living in Israeli space. Novels in the third period suggest that both collective modernisation and individual Palestinian attempts to integrate into Israeli society have failed. Thus, Palestinian citizens in Israel are presented in perplexity novels as alien in Israeli as well as in (what used to be) Palestinian space. The following excerpt from *Let It Be Morning* exemplifies this alienation of Palestinians inside Israel:

> How I hate them now, how I hate myself for trying to believe I was really one of them, for trailing after them on lunch breaks, for trying to kid around with them, to make them laugh. I never managed to feel like I was one of them. They always made me feel like an outsider[17]. I hate myself now for not doing a thing about it all this time, for letting things get this way. Didn't I realise we'd find ourselves in a situation like this sooner or later? Not that I really know what kind of a situation this is exactly.
>
> I hate myself for thinking that coming back to the village would solve everything. For some reason, I thought that if I was surrounded by people like myself, my own people, nothing bad could happen to me. I thought that in the village I'd be much more sheltered than I was in the Jewish neighbourhood. I thought the village would make a good guesthouse for me to come back to at the end of my working day, like everyone else. I'd go off to work and I'd come back to sleep, safe and sound. But now I have no choice but to admit that there's nowhere to run away to anymore. I hate myself for

> not getting out of here at the right time, for finding comfort in the thought that everything would work out soon. I hate myself for not getting my wife and daughter out of here as soon as I felt the danger approaching, as soon as the hatred began getting to me, day in and day out, at work, in the street, at home, in restaurants, in the malls and in the playgrounds. (pp. 170–1)

This excerpt shows that erasure of Palestinians in Israel takes personal and collective forms. Palestinians in Israel are also prevented from integration, through the erasure of Palestinian collective identity, and through emphasis on Palestinian individual identity. In this way, Palestinian individuality in Israel is rendered collective, since national identity is imposed on each individual: an attitude which, after all, collectivises Palestinians. Palestinian integration in Israel, achieved only

> on an individual basis is a fictive integration, requiring the abandoning of the collective identity [...] collective-cultural Israelisation is not provided as an option, and indeed it could not be provided [...] Israelisation as a political cultural option results in marginalisation, or, in other words, the decision to live without an identity, at the margins of a society that makes religious conversion [to Judaism] or security-driven patriotism a criteria for belonging to the collective. (Bishara 1993: 13, see also: Bishara 2001: 58)

Thus, Palestinians are, on the individual level, alienated through the prohibition of individual integration, since they are always the 'Other' and paradigmatically Palestinian, as they try to evade, or even conceal their identity. The preceding excerpt from Kashua suggests that the protagonist 'self-erased' himself through the quelling of his Palestinian identity in an attempt to assimilate among his colleagues at the newspaper workplace. This was despite his being employed by the newspaper precisely *because* of his Otherness, since he was a Palestinian who could speak Arabic (p. 23).

Collective erasure is, in *Let It Be Morning*, exemplified in the fragmented way in which society deals with collective problems, and with threats that view them as a cohesive group: such as the Israeli siege on the village. The looting and violence that begins to occur in the village after a few days of siege contrasts with the firm social cohesion expressed in the Intifada novels. When a Palestinian village or refugee camp was placed under Israeli military siege, regularly accompanied, as it was, by military violence, Palestinians, as expressed in Intifada novels, used unity and cooperation as a tactic with which to withstand Israeli policies against them. The sharing of food supplies and money between people was a central theme in such novels (e.g. see: *Zagharid al-Maqathi*).

Moreover, the above excerpt reflects the alienation that Palestinians feel in their villages inside Israel. The speaker describes the shock of his return to 'my home, to a new place' (p. 20). His reaction to this return is alienation on arrival at what seems to be a 'new place'. Those Palestinians who could not bear the individual alienation affixed to them in Israeli space, discover that the place to which they return has also been subjected to collective alienation.

Another level of alienation expressed in *Let It Be Morning* relates to Palestinians from the West Bank. *Let It Be Morning* highlights the distinction between Palestinian citizens in Israel and Palestinians outside Israel. In contrast to Palestinian society outside Israel, Palestinians in Israel still held faith in Israel, which was not seen as an aggressor until the later stages of the siege and the novel. By not seeing Israel as an aggressor or justifying her actions in terms of her security needs, Palestinians from the West Bank are 'Othered'. For years, Palestinians in Israel believed they had a 'doubly contradictory' identity. This doubly contradictory identity contains components of 'Othering' and alienation since it has, at its centre, the idea that Palestinians in Israel are a 'special case', which suggests that they are different from Palestinians outside Israel. This 'self-Othering', or dissociation, was a mutual process since, as Palestinians outside Israel accepted the 'special' status of Palestinians in Israel, this excluded Palestinian citizens in Israel from the political discourse and activity of Palestinians outside Israel. This point will be further elaborated below.

Mutual Palestinian Alienation

In this period, Palestinians outside Israel take a central role in Palestinian novels in Israel, as is the case in Intifada novels. The appearance of Palestinians from outside Israel in the third group of novels is depicted in a theme that I will call the 'returning-absentee', or '*al-ghāʾib al-ʿāʾid*'. This theme appears in eleven novels. The 'returning-absentee' keynote relates to the duality of presence and absence of friends and family members in the plots.[18] There are a number of manifestations of this theme, but generally plots describe the return of a character to the life of the narrator and the way this return changes the narrator's life.

In *Hazim Ya'ud Hadha-l-Masa'* (*Hazim Returns This Evening*, 1990), by Nabil Uda, the narrator, Nabil, recalls meeting a friend whom he had not seen for a long time. For Nabil, this encounter was unexpected and dumbfounding (*ṣa'aqatnī*; see excerpt below). When he approaches his friend, Hazim, he does not recognise Nabil, but later a conversation between the two develops. Nabil recounts memories from times prior to the departure of Hazim, eight years before the meeting; one of which is the relationship of Hazim with Amina.

To understand Palestinian mutual alienation as expressed in this novel, I will discuss a characteristic of perplexity novels mentioned earlier: the 'phenomenological' and fragmented narrative of the novels in this group. The fragmented nature of perplexity plots is evident in the fact that in *Hazim Ya'ud Hadha-l-Masa'*, the narrative alternates between present thoughts and memories of the past interchangeably. Perplexity novels do not describe historical events as such but deal with issues relating to them. The novel deals more with the problematic nature of the encounter between Hazim and Nabil, and less with its unfolding events. See, for example, the following excerpt, where Nabil recounts what happened on first re-encountering Hazim:

> Kān al-waqt qabl al-ẓuhr. Hādhā mā adhkuruhu tamāman. Wa-lā adrī in kān li-dhālik qīma mā. Kuntu 'ā'idan min al-sūq bi-ba'ḍ akyās al-khuḍra wa-l-fawākih. 'Alā al-aghlab kunt liwaḥdī, fa-mā 'aliqa bi-dhākiratī lā yashmalnī illā anā wa-huwa. Anā bi-jiha … wa-huwa bi-jiha ukhrā, wa-mā yuḥīṭunī wa-mā yuḥīṭahu lam ya'laq bi-dhihnī minhu shay'. Ẓahar bilā sābiq tawaqqu'. Mufāja'atī bihi kānat tāmma, istaḥwadhat 'alā ḥawāssī, ṣa'aqatnī. Arbakatnī. Fajjarat mi'āt al-tasā'ulāt fī dhihnī, dakhaltu li-a'māq nafsī ḥa'iran. Wa-lam astaw'ib illā ḥaqīqa wāḥida … innī aqif bi-muwājahatihi, anā hunā wa-huwa hunāk. (p. 9)

> It was before noon. This is what I remember exactly. And I don't know if this has any value at all. I was on my way back from the market with some shopping bags filled with vegetables and fruits. Most probably I was on

> my own, because all that stuck in my memory includes only me and him. Me on one side … and him on another, and nothing else around me and him stuck in my memory. He appeared unexpectedly. My surprise was complete. It took over my senses, it shocked me. Confused me. It exploded hundreds of questions in my head and left me deeply perplexed. And I realised only one truth … that I am standing opposite him … I am here, and he is there. (p. 9)

Nostalgic-folkloric novels describe life in pre-1948 Palestine in detail, including the events of the Nakba. Intifada novels deal with resistance to Israeli occupation of the West Bank and Gaza Strip in a somewhat documentary style, providing 'thick description' of childhood memories; the events of the Nakba; life in one Palestinian village; as well as resistance in a Palestinian refugee camp. Novels in the third group give less attention to the details of events, relative to the other two groups. The excerpt above demonstrates the 'phenomenological' narrative displayed in novels in this group. What matters in the narrative is the *event* of meeting Hazim, rather than the *context*. Nabil recalls that he saw Hazim just before noon, but he is unsure whether this detail adds any value (*qīma mā*) to his narrative. He also recalls that he was carrying shopping bags as he was returning home from the market (*sūq*). The time of the encounter between Nabil and Hazim is a minor detail in the narrative, in the same way that the shopping bags are. The spatial details of the encounter are also marginal. The speaker is not even sure whether or not he was by himself at that time.

Two things only are important for Nabil: firstly, the memory of the encounter excludes all potential interlocutors other than the speaker and Hazim, rendering the possibility of other people being present at the encounter insignificant. Secondly, the spatial division between Nabil and Hazim stands out: the two men are opposite one another, a detail which is mentioned twice, both at the beginning and at the end of the excerpt ('… me and him. Me on one side … and him on another'; 'I am standing opposite him … I am here, and he is there'). In other words, the spatial details of the encounter are marginal to the narrative. Instead, what matters is the meaning of the encounter: the encounter between the two men and their opposing positions is, quite literally, the main subject of the novel, as I will outline below.

The novel starts with the speaker, Nabil, who catches sight of Hazim as he is walking in the street. The first twenty pages of the novel include a monologue by Nabil, which describes his shock at seeing Hazim, an old friend of his, who left long ago. The monologue not only describes the feelings Nabil experiences as a result of the sudden encounter but describes *the way in which* Hazim appears to him, even offering impressions as to what Hazim might be feeling. Hazim himself sits in a bar. The bar belongs to a mutual friend of Hazim and Nabil, but Hazim does not, according to Nabil's narration, interact with anyone. In other words, throughout the first twenty pages, it is Nabil who 'speaks for' Hazim, who is silent, and whose take on the occasion is not included in the description. Hazim himself is thus present-absent in the text for the first twenty pages (symbolising almost two decades of Palestinian detachment: 1948–67), and it is Nabil who sets the tone and the scene. However, mutual erasure is expressed in the novel by the fact that Nabil is unsure whether Hazim recognises him, something which is confirmed later when Hazim admits that this is the case. The following paragraph provides further insight into this mutual Palestinian erasure:

> Kunt lā azāl ataḥarrak amāmahu muḥāwilan lafta intibāhihi. Yanẓur li-jihatī wa-li-amr ghayr mafhūm lā yuḥarrik sākinan. Rubbamā lā yarāni?! Yuthīrunī bi-burūdatihi ghayr al-mutawaqqaʿa. Yurbikunī bi-tajāhulihi ghayr al-mafhūm. Huwa wa-laysa huwa!! Akādu afqidu thiqatī bi-nafsī. Mā yaʿtarī hādhā al-rajul? Hal ʿāda jasadan bilā rūḥ?! Faqada dhākiratahu? Faqada ṣilatihi bi-māḍīhi? Nasiya mā yarbiṭhu bi-l-aṣḥāb? Talāshat dhākiratahu, inmaḥā al-māḍī min dhihnihi?! (p. 25)

> I was still moving in front of him, trying to catch his attention. He looks in my direction, and for an unfathomable reason remains unmoved. Maybe he can't see me?! His unexpected coldness annoys me. He confuses me with his unfathomable disregard. It's him and not him!! I almost lose my confidence. What is wrong with this man? Did he return as a soulless body?! Lost his memory? Lost his connection with his past? Forgot what connected him to his friends? His memory diminished, the past erased from his mind?! (p. 25)

The excerpt above demonstrates how characters can be represented as both present and absent at the same time. Nabil was erased as he stood in front of Hazim trying to attract his attention, yet Nabil also erased Hazim by speaking for him during the first twenty pages. Furthermore, while, in the excerpt above, Nabil is the subject of the sentence when moving about (‘*ataḥarrak amamahu*’), trying to attract the attention of Hazim, in the rest of the paragraph Hazim is the subject. Moreover, Hazim is the agent who conducts erasure on Nabil, to which Nabil can only react with discomfort: ‘he annoys me’ (*yuthīranī*); ‘he confuses me’ (*yurbikanī*). Hazim ignores him (*tajāhal*); he has returned as a body without a soul (*ʿāda jasadan bilā rūḥ*); lost his memory (*faqada dhākiratahu*); lost his connection to his past (*faqada ṣilatahu bi-māḍīhi*); and forgotten his connections with his friends (*nasiya mā yarbuṭuhu bi-l-aṣḥāb*). Here there is a sense of accusation. Nabil, for his part, is certain of his perception of history, of his own memory. He is also certain that this man is Hazim, his friend from the past. The use of the passive at the end of the paragraph (*talāshat dhākiratuhu*, ‘his memory was made to fade away’, and *inmaḥā al-māḍī min dhihnihi*, ‘the past has been erased from his mind’) refers to Hazim. In other words, it is Hazim’s memory that should be accounted for in this situation, rather than Nabil’s. By wondering whether Hazim has lost his memory, and has therefore lost contact with his past, Nabil indicates that he is the sole retainer of past memories. If Hazim has forgotten his past, then it is Nabil who possesses the complete history, both for himself and for Hazim.

The mutual erasure of Hazim and Nabil is a perplexing situation in which past and present interchange, in which there are two pasts and two presents, both of which are present and absent at the same time. The mutual absentification, or erasure, gives new meaning to the term ‘present-absent’ with regard to the relationship between Palestinian citizens in Israel and Palestinians outside Israel. Since for both communities, the ‘Other Palestinian’ has, since 1948, been both present and absent at the same time, the ‘encounter’ of two Palestinian voices that used to mutually erase each other is bound to create confusion represented in this novel by twenty pages that describe the shock resulting from the renewed encounter. Moreover, perplexity occurs as a result of the discursive ‘debate’ over ‘who owns the past’, and who owns the authentic Palestinian narrative. The historical debate is evident in the following dialogue between Nabil and Hazim. In this excerpt, Nabil is trying to break the silence by asking Hazim about a woman called Amina:

– Hal tadhkur amīna yā ḥāzim?!

– Āh … zawjatī!!

Raghma mufāja'atī lahu bi-l-su'āl, illā anna jawābahu jā'a tilqā'iyyan wa-bishakl 'ādiyy.

– Wa-lakinnakumā lam tatazawwajā?!!

– Amīna kānat da'iman zawjatī!

Yaqīnahu hazza thiqatī bi-nafsi, wa-ja'alanī atasā'al baynī wa-bayn nafsī: 'mā bāl al-insān yatajāhal wa-yata'āmā wa-yadda'ī mā lam yaḥṣul. Wa-yuffaḍil al-ẓalām 'alā al-nūr, wa-l-ghumūḍ 'alā al-wuḍūḥ?!'

'Udtu as'alahu, ghayr qādir 'alā ikhfā' istihjānī wa-ḥiratī min al-mufāraqāt al-gharība allatī taḥduth ma'ī:

– Amīna nafsahā …? Al-yāfawiyya ibnat al-turkī?!

– *Ajal zawjatī … da'iman kānat zawjatī!?* (pp. 38–9)

– Do you remember Amina, Hazim?!

– Yes … My wife!!

Despite me surprising him with this question, his answer was spontaneous and normal.

– But you did not marry?!!

– Amina was always my wife.

His certainty shook my confidence and made my think to myself: 'what is the matter with this man, ignoring and claiming things that never happened, and preferring darkness to light, and vagueness to clarity?!'

I asked him again, unable to hide my deploring and perplexity from the strange paradoxes that are happening with me:

– The same Amina …? The Yaffan daughter of the Turk?!

– Yes, my wife … was always my wife?! (pp. 38–9)

The issue of the relationship between Amina and Hazim is a 'historical' question, because the above dialogue suggests that the nature of their relationship might be debatable. The exchange between Nabil and Hazim reflects two contradictory narratives. This begins with the question 'Can you remember Amina, Hazim?'. This question suggests that Amina is a person known to the two men from their past, but that she is so insignificant that she could be forgotten. The reply 'yes … my wife' contradicts this assumption, as it is difficult to assume that anybody would forget his own wife. Furthermore, if we break down Hazim's answer we see that in addition to replying positively to the question, Hazim indicates that she was his wife, suggesting that he opposes the assumption implied in Nabil's question: Hazim concurs that he remembers Amina in the first part of his answer: (*āh* [yes]). In the second part of his answer, Hazim offers unelicited additional information: *zawjatī* (my wife). Since Hazim was not asked for this information, his supply of it after a pause, represented by the aposiopesis separating the two parts of his answer, suggests that he intended to contradict Nabil, who assumes that Hazim has forgotten Amina. This is evident in the proceeding comment by Nabil, reflecting his surprise at Hazim's spontaneous reply.

The exchange that follows further highlights the contradiction between the two narratives. As far as Nabil is concerned, Hazim and Amina never married, yet Hazim replies that she was *always* his wife. The use of 'always' (*dā'iman*) indicates that Hazim is aware of the other narrative (about not being married), but he wants to stress its fallacy. This is apparent in the second use of *dā'iman* at the end of the quotation. By saying that Amina was always his wife, Hazim asserts *his* 'historical' narrative. It is possible to say that the use of 'always' marks a change in the narrative of Hazim, because if Amina was his wife, he would have said 'Amina *is* my wife', not 'Amina was always my wife'. Saying that she 'was always' his wife implies that Hazim is trying to impose this notion retrospectively. 'Marriage' for him refers to the strong bond and relationship he always had with Amina, even if they did not actually marry.

Nabil, nonetheless, believes that Hazim ignores and denies the facts, thus fabricating history (*yadda'ī mā lam yaḥṣul*). The clash between the two narratives is evident, moreover, when Nabil acknowledges that the confidence (*yaqīn*) Hazim has in his answer has shaken Nabil's own confidence (*thiqatī bi-nafsī*). The clash is then between two people, both confident in their own positions. Furthermore, the clash between the narratives is expressed in the contradiction between confidence (*yaqīn*) and the 'fabrication of history' – which is the only way for Nabil to resolve the clash for himself. Thus, Hazim, by his firm position on this question continues to baffle Nabil, who tries, for his part, to clarify the issue by offering further details about Amina and her family.

The clash between characters in the plot represents a clash between two Palestinian narratives or identities. Palestinians both inside and outside Israel mutually excluded one another for decades. If Amina symbolises Palestine, as she does, it is possible to understand the narrative presented by Nabil as an accusation that the Palestinian refugees abandoned Palestine in 1948. However, Hazim says that they were always part of (married to) Palestine. Later, Nabil acknowledges the organic relationship (*al-rābiṭa al-ʿuḍwiyya*) between Hazim, his love for Amina, and its relation to Palestine (p. 61).

If we return to the mutual alienation of Palestinians, the excerpt above includes the exchange between Nabil and Hazim and the reaction of the former to it. As this novel is a monologue by Nabil, we hear only about his experience of any given event and learn little about what Hazim is thinking. In other words, even after Nabil and Hazim are engaged in a dialogue and are no longer erasing each other, Hazim remains unknown and 'Other' to Nabil. This 'Othered' Hazim contrasts with the nostalgic image that Nabil depicts of their collective past:

> Kunnā naḥnu ʿāʾilatuk wa-dunyāk, lā taṭīb laka al-ḥayā bidūnina wa-lā taṭīb lanā al-ḥayā bidūnik. (p. 22)
>
> We used to be your family and world. You didn't like life without us, and we didn't like life without you. (p. 22)

Note the collective tone in this nostalgic expression (*kunnā naḥnu ʿāʾilataka wa-dunyāk*, 'we were your family and your world'). Nabil here uses the first-person plural and addresses Hazim directly in the second person, in contrast to his use of the third person in the preceding excerpt. The transition in persons, from third to second in this case, is a technique called *iltifāt*, which is widely used in the Quran, but not only there. There are a number of functions for the use of *iltifāt*, for example to raise the interest of the listener being the most known (Abdel-Haleem 1992: 432). Other functions that Abdel-Haleem suggests refer to 'showing a particular interest in something at which [a] shift takes place' and 'showing others by a change from 2nd to 3rd person how badly the original addressees have behaved, so that they are turned away from' (Abdel-Haleem 1992: 432).

In the case of the above excerpt the speaker, Nabil, turns from third to second person, expressing his sense of yearning for a lost past and marking his 'particular interest' in this issue. Nabil and Hazim, according to the excerpt, no longer enjoy their lives (*taṭīb al-ḥayāt*) because they are no longer like a family, as they used to be in the past. In the present, however, even with the return of Hazim and the supposed reunification of this 'family', the old representation of their relationship is not true anymore, as indicated by the *kunnā* at the beginning of the quotation – portraying all that proceeds it as belonging to the past. After the departure of Hazim, the group disintegrates, denoting the fragmentation of Palestinian society (or 'family' to use the terms of the excerpt).

The end of *Hazim Yaʿud Hadha-l-Masāʾ* is perplexing. The roots of the perplexity of the closure lie in the introduction to the novel. In the introduction, the author indicates that the novel is based on his personal experience and that he 'refused … to change the details or the names of the characters' in order to retain as much of the authenticity of the story as possible. The author acknowledges, however, that he made changes as part of the artistic writing process and the needs of 'novelistic amazement' (*al-dahsha al-riwāʾiyya*). On the face of it, these two somewhat contradictory statements make the understanding of the ending of the novel more difficult. The novel closes with the speaker, Nabil, waking up and realising that the encounter with Hazim was but a dream. Thus, it is hard to determine whether this final twist is part of the 'real' story or belongs to the artistic-novelistic component. There is, however, supporting evidence that this novel is based on a dream. During the dialogue between the two, Nabil, in fact, tells Hazim about his funeral, indicating that Hazim has already died by this point:

> Lā ziltu adhkur janāzatuk ḥattā-l-yawm … kull al-ladhīn karihtahum jāʾū. Lam tataʿarraf ʿalayhum bi-ḥayātik. Fa-tawallū amrak bi-mamātik. Ammā

naḥnu … aṣḥābak, fa-sirnā ka-l-ghurabāʾ, kunnā nushayyiʿu juzʾan minnā. Kān al-ḥuznu ḥuznunā. Wa-l-faqīdu faqīdunā.

– Lā adrī ʿan dhālik shayʾan?!

– Kayfa tadrī wa-anta al-faqīd?!

– Wa-lākinnī amāmuk!!

– Mawtuk kān ṣadma lanā, naḥnu aṣḥābak …

Inqalab wajhahu ghāḍiban wa-amaranī:

– Iṣmit. Ayy mawt tataḥaddath ʿanhu. Innī ḥayy kamā tarā!?

– Anta ḥayy?!

– Bi-l-ḍabṭ!!

– Wa-tuṣirr anna amīna kānat zawjatuk?!

– Tamāman.

– Lam tamut amīna?! Wa-lam tamut anta?!

– Zawjatī lam tamut … wa-anā lam amut!!

– *Lā tanfaʿil yā ṣaḥbī lā tanfaʿil. Anta tuḥayyrunī. ʿAwdatuka muḥayyira wa-ẓuhūrika lī muḥayyir!! Kalāmak muḥayyir!! Mā alladhī aʿadaka liʿālamina? Ayyat quwwa hādhihi?! Hal ḥaqqan yaʿūd al-amwāt ilā al-ḥayā?!* (pp. 106–7)

I still remember your funeral until this day … All those you hated came. You ignored them all your life, and they took over your affairs after your death. As for us, your friends, we walked like strangers, burying a part of ourselves. The sadness was our sadness. And the deceased is ours.

– I know nothing about this!?

– How would you know and you're the deceased?!

– But I'm in front of you!!

– Your death was a shock to us, your friends …

His face turned angry and ordered me:

– Shut up. What death are you talking about. I'm alive as you can see?!

– You're alive?!

– Exactly!!

– And you insist that Amina was your wife?!

– Exactly.

– Amina didn't die?! And you didn't die?!

– My wife did not die … and I did not die!!

– Don't overreact, my friend. You perplex me. Your return is perplexing, and your re-emergence is perplexing!! Your words are perplexing!! What brought you back to our world? What power is that?! Do the dead really come back to life?! (pp. 106–7)

The dialogue between the two men reflects the perplexity and opposing narratives that they represent. After years of focusing on their 'doubly contradictory identity', Palestinian citizens in Israel had come to believe that Palestinians outside Israel had, in fact, ceased to exist (or rather had 'died'). They mourned the death of such Palestinians in 1948 but forgot about them later. 'Those who hated them' came to their funeral. This seems to refer to the Arab states that failed to help in the 1948 war and are accused of collaborating with the Zionist forces. This construction alludes to the Palestinian saying (*qatal al-qatīl wa-mashā bi-janāzatu*), which relates to the hypocrisy of the person 'who murdered the victim and attended his funeral'.

Hazim, however, asserts that neither he nor Amina (both of whom may symbolise the Palestinian problem and Palestinians outside Israel) had died. Regarding whether Uda was dreaming or not and whether Hazim could or could not be considered dead, our understanding of this novel as a representative case of perplexity novels does not rest on a clarification of this functional ambiguity. In fact, the author indicates in the introduction that all the liberties he took in writing the novel were justifiable according to the needs of the subject (*mawḍū'*): the relationship between Palestinians in Israel and Palestinians outside Israel.

The duality of the death of Amina and Hazim in the excerpt above may represent the two discourses of Palestinians: both inside and outside Israel. The return of Hazim, which ushers in a new discourse, perplexes Nabil (*muḥayyir*, a term which is used four times in the above excerpt). Novels of perplexity reflect, in fact, the challenge to notions of 'doubly contradictory' identity and the 'Othering' of Palestinians outside Israel, which Palestinians in Israel attributed to themselves and to their erstwhile counterparts for years. In the excerpt above, Nabil is baffled by the determination with which Hazim refutes Nabil's claim that he and Amina had died. The resurrection of the dead in the excerpt corresponds to the reappearance of Palestinians outside Israel as well as their un-Othering. We have seen the motif of resurrection of the dead as a signifier of the resurrection of Palestinian identity in Israel in novels in the second period.

The contrast between perplexity novels and the first two groups in the period under consideration in this chapter is evident in the different ways in which the novels end. Some Intifada novels discussed in the preceding section (like *Yad al-Qadar* by Jiryis Tannus) also represented a returning absent character. In this case, the return marked reunification, continuity and the beginning of a new future represented by the wedding and the creation of a new Palestinian family, making use of people who were previously absentified from each other and who are now both present in Israel. By situating the creation of the new Palestinian family inside Israel, Tannus is asserting the Palestinian refugees' right of return to their homeland.

While Intifada novels had definitive endings, indicating Palestinian unity, endings in perplexity novels do not point clearly towards a clear future. *Hazim Ya'ud Hadha-l-Masa'* ends with the voice of Hazim calling Amina's name. The final word in the novel, 'Amina', contrasts with the first twenty pages in which Nabil silenced Hazim – and by extension the Palestinians outside Israel. The ending of the novel is 'open', since it can be interpreted in different ways, but it does strongly suggest that Amina, or the Palestinian national question, both inside and outside Israel, had returned to the Palestinian discourse inside Israel. This renewed Palestinian national awareness starts to play a role in the discourse of Palestinian citizens in Israel. This conclusion applies to other novels in this group. For example, in *Al-Hamishiyy*, Samih returned to his village, but we do not know what happened to him afterwards. Moreover, we learn in *Let It Be Morning* that the border was moved to incorporate the village into the Palestinian state established in the peace agreement. Nonetheless, there is no indication about what happens next.

This chapter began at the scene of an execution at a site where weddings used to take place, marking the discontinuity of Palestinian existence in 1948. Intifada novels, however, celebrated two types of wedding – a funeral-wedding that asserts the continuity of Palestinian presence through the resistance of Israeli erasure; and weddings that depict Palestinian reunification. Finally, in *Hazim Ya'ud Hadha-l-Masa'*, the prospective couple remain unmarried, and their wedding is left for a future reunification. To summarise, perplexity novels have no clear orientation regarding the future of Palestinians in Israel.

Perplexity novels are part of the attempt of Palestinian citizens in Israel to work out their relationship with Israel, and their future status as Palestinians, non-Palestinians, Israelis and non-Israelis. This is the 'issue' at the centre of these novels: a sense of ambivalent identity. These novels are situated in the awakening of Palestinian identity, in a political context that excludes and marginalises such an identity.

Conclusion

The Palestinian Intifada in the West bank and Gaza Strip had profound effects on Palestinian citizens in Israel, both in their 'sentimental identification', to use the words of Nadim Rouhana, as well as in their political participation. Palestinian novels in the period 1987–2010 convey shared Palestinian awareness, reflecting, thus, a process of collectivisation that contrasts with processes of fragmentation and differentiation that were evident in earlier periods. Palestinian novels since 1987 stress a Palestinian identity that is linked to a Palestinian past and present, both inside and outside Israel, seeing the Palestinian citizens in Israel as part of the Palestinian problem, both in the past (the Nakba) and in the present (the Intifada). As seen in nostalgic-folkloric as well as Intifada novels, the unification of Palestinian past and present is seen in some novels as part of the solution to Palestinian alienation. Perplexity novels, on the other hand, point to the same problem of alienation, but do not offer a solution to it.

Novels of perplexity contrast with novels from the first two groups in this chapter: they differ in their structure and narrative. One other difference that might mark the perplexity of Palestinian identity in Israel in this period is borne out in the contrast between the thick and thin descriptions of Palestinian 'life' – tradition and folklore. The thick description of the first two groups contrasts with the thin description of the third group, which emphasises the alienation and de-Palestinisation of Palestinians in Israel.

There are, however, a number of common characteristics that 'unite' all groups. One central characteristic of novels in this period is that they are all situated in, or derive from, contemporary conditions. This is true also of nostalgic-folkloric novels. In fact, the three groups are linked by the perplexed identity of Palestinians in Israel. With regards to the way in which they address Palestinian alienation in Israel, the contrast between the three groups is also an indication of the perplexity of Palestinian identity in Israel in this period. Two groups have 'clear answers' as to what will resolve the issue of Palestinian alienation in Israel. The largest group only expresses perplexity. If we want to look at this from the 'alienation' point of view, it is possible to say that as novels in the third group express their alienation explicitly, novels in the first two groups express their alienation implicitly. It is this shared alienation that causes Palestinians in Israel to search for identity in the past or across the border.

Aside from dealing with, or being the product of, the 'present', the most common characteristic of novels in this period, appearing in almost 57 per cent of the novels (26 of 45), is the use of monologue or first-person narration. Monologue novels 'are novels in which monologue is the major, if not the sole, means of narration. In such novels the author provides a voice or voices which he has created as "I" speakers, and the voice(s) can be either mimetic or rhetorical' (Clews 1985: 59). It is possible to categorise nostalgic-folkloric and Intifada novels as 'mimetic' because they provide 'accurate representations of individual perceptions of the observed world' (Clews 1985: 16). Perplexity novels, as we have seen above, however, can be considered, due to their phenomenological style, 'rhetorical'. This does not mean, however, that such novels do not provide 'accurate representations' of Palestinian alienation in Israel. I will address the phenomenological style of perplexity novels later. Nevertheless, monologue is the single common denominator of novels in this period, signifying the state of Palestinian identity in Israel: a state of alienation and perplexity. This is so because in monologues, presence and absence define the relationship between the narrator/author and narratee/reader.

> The monologue [...] in both drama and poetry, is addressed to a listener whose presence is overtly acknowledged by the speaker. In drama, this silent listener is either physically present [...] or assumed to be present [...] by both speaker and audience. (Clews 1985: 15)

Presence and absence in Palestinian monologue not only mark alienation, they also mark an attempt to overcome it. This is especially true in nostalgic-folkloric and Intifada novels. In writing about a shared past and present, about a shared problem, the speaker and the listener, who had been previously alienated, are in the same way united.

If we look at this from a different angle, it is possible to say that Palestinian identity in Israel as represented in these groups, is part of the problem and part of the solution, since the 'two' Palestinian identities clashing in this period are in fact products of the same perplexity debate. This relates to the duality both of Palestinian presence and of Palestinian absence in Israel. Such duality relates to the different levels at which Palestinians are present and absent both in and from Palestine, since even those living in their native villages in historic Palestine do not feel that they belong to its new environment. When the absent Palestinians start to 'appear' in the consciousness of Palestinians in Israel, they begin to re-extend their discourse to a Palestine across the border. While novels in the first two groups try to bridge spatial and temporal boundaries, novels in the third group deal with the problematics of Palestinian alienation in Israel, and also vis-à-vis Palestinians outside Israel.

The phenomenological, or rhetorical, 'style' of perplexity novels hints at the answer to the question regarding the reason for the prominence of first-person narrative in Palestinian novels during this period. Phenomenological philosophy addresses questions relating to 'self-awareness' and phenomenology. Existential phenomenology could, thus, 'provide insights into literature, especially into contemporary literature with its preoccupation with the loneliness of individual experience' (Calhoun 1963: 5). Although Calhoun did not refer to Palestinian literature, his statement holds true in this case.

Contemporary Palestinian literature is preoccupied with the 'loneliness' of Palestinians in Israel. From a phenomenological point of view, one that focuses on the psychological dimensions of individual self-awareness, the use of the first-person pronoun reflects self-awareness. In other words, 'the very mastery of the first-person pronoun presupposes possession of self-conscious thoughts' (Zahavi 2004: 10). It is possible to say that Palestinian novels, being collective autobiographies, as noted earlier, reflect *collective* self-awareness, or 'collective first-person' narrative. Thus, although most novels are written in the first-person singular, we have seen that they refer to a collective experience. The use of a 'collective first person' in Palestinian novels reflects collective self-conscious thoughts about the future of the collective, which were analysed in this chapter.

Table 3.1 Novels published between 1987 and 2010

Group		Novel	
III	M	Ḥaṭūm, Muʿīn (1987–8 [1996]), *Al-Nabiyy Raʾiʿ al-Filsrāliyy*, Dālyat al-Karmil: Manshūrāt Muʿīn Ḥaṭūm.	1
I+III		Ilyās, Mujīd Munīb (1987), *Al-Bandūq*, al-Nāṣira: Shahrazād li-l-Nashr wa-l-Tawzīʿ.	2
II		Shḥāda, Idmūn (1988), *Al-Ṭarīq ilā Bīrzīt*, al-Nāṣira: al-Maktaba al-Ḥadītha.	3
II		Watad, Muḥammad (1988), *Zaghārīd al-Maqāthī*, Jath, al-Muthallath: al-Barq.	4
III	M	Shiblī, Āsyā (1989), *Al-Jazzār*, n.p.	5
III	M	ʿŪda, Nabīl (1989 [2001]), *Imraʾa fi-l-Ṭaraf al-Ākhar*, al-Nāṣira: Daʾirat al-Thaqāfa al-ʿArabiyya fī Wizārat al-Maʿārif wa-l-Thaqāfa.	6
III	M	ʿŪda, Nabīl (1989 [1995]), *Al-Mustaḥīl*, al-Nāṣira: Maṭbaʿat Firās.	7
III	M	ʿŪda, Nabīl (1990 [1994]), *Ḥāzim Yaʿūd Hādhā-l-Masāʾ*, al-Nāṣira: Daʾirat al-Thaqāfa al-ʿArabiyya fī Wizārat al-Maʿārif wa-l-Thaqāfa.	8
III	M	Baydas, Riyāḍ (1990 [1992]), *Al-Hāmishiyy*, al-Quds: Manshūrāt Ghassān Kanafānī.	9
I	M	Habiby, Emile (1991 [2006]), *Sarāyā Bint al-Ghūl*, Ḥayfā: Dār ʿArābesk.	10
*	M	Ḥalabī, Muṣbāḥ (1991), *Yomana shel Tsi'ira Druzit*, n.p.: Hotsaat Asia. [Hebrew]	11
II		Darwīsh, Zakī (1989), *Aḥmad, Maḥmūd wa-Ākharūn*, Shafā ʿAmr: Dār al-Mashriq.	12
II		Shḥāda, Rāḍī (1990), *Al-Jarād Yuḥibb al-Baṭṭīkh*, al-Qāhira: Maṣriyya li-l-Nashr wa-l-Tawzīʿ.	13
III	M	ʿArāydī, Naʿīm (1992), *Tvila Katlanit*, Tel-Aviv: Bitan. [Hebrew]	14
*		Ḥalabī, Muṣbāḥ. (1992), *HaKfar HaHatzuy*, n.p.: Hotsaat Asia. [Hebrew]	15
III	M	Baydas, Riyāḍ (1992 [1993]), *Bāṭ Būṭ*, al-Nāṣira: Daʾirat al-Thaqāfa al-ʿArabiyya fī Wizārat al-Maʿārif wa-l-Thaqāfa.	16

Table 3.1 (continued)

Group		**Novel**	
I+III	M	Shḥāda, Idmūn (1994), *Al-Ghīlān*, al-Nāṣira: Daʾirat al-Thaqāfa al-ʿArabiyya fī Wizārat al-Maʿārif wa-l-Thaqāfa.	17
II		Yiḥyā, Rāfiʿ (1992 [1994]), *Al-Ṭarīq ilā-l-Ṣabāḥ*, al-Nāṣira: Daʾirat al-Thaqāfa al-ʿArabiyya fī Wizārat al-Maʿārif wa-l-Thaqāfa.	18
II		Ilyās, Mujīd Munīb (1994), *Umarāʾ Khān al-Ṣafā*, al-Nāṣira: Shahrazād li-l-Nashr.	19
I+III		Khamīs, Ṣubḥī (1994), *Yallā Nghannī*, al-Nāṣira: Maṭbaʿat Fīnūs.	20
II+III	M	Bakriyya, Rajāʾ (1995), *ʿIwāʾ Dhākira*, al-Nāṣira: Daʾirat al-Thaqāfa al-ʿArabiyya fī Wizārat al-Maʿārif wa-l-Thaqāfa.	21
I+III	M	Dhyāb, Fāṭma (1996), *Al-Khayṭ wa-l-Ṭazzīz*, Kufr Qarʿ: Dār al-Hudā.	22
III	M	Yiḥyā, Rāfiʿ (1996), *Bayt ʿAlā Waraq*, Yafat al-Nāṣira: Manshūrāt al-Ṭalāʾiʿ.	23
I	M	Habiby, Emile (1996 [2006]), *Sirāj al-Ghūla: al-Naṣṣ/al-Waṣṣiyya*, Ḥayfā: Dār ʿArābesk.	24
I		Ibrāhīm, Ḥannā (1997), *Awjāʿ al-Bilād al-Muqaddasa*, ʿAkkā: Muʾassasat al-Aswār.	25
I		Kīwān, Suhīl (1997), *ʿAṣiyy al-Damʿ*, ʿAkkā: Muʾassasat al-Aswār.	26
III		Kīwān, Suhīl (1998), *Maqtal al-Thāʾir al-Akhīr*, ʿAkkā: Muʾassasat al-Aswār.	27
I+III	M	Naṭūr, Salmān (1999), *Hal Qataltum Aḥadan Hunāk? – Shihāda*, Ghazza: al-Markiz al-Thaqāfī al-Falasṭīniyy.	28
III	M	Kīwān, Suhīl (2000), *Al-Mafqūd Raqam 2000*, ʿAkkā: Muʾassasat al-Aswār.	29
III		Ḥlīḥil, ʿAlāʾ (2001), *Al-Sīrk*, Ramallah: Muʾassasat al-Qaṭṭān.	30
III	M	Ibrāhīm, Ḥannā (2002), *ʿAṣfūra min-l-Maghrib*, al-Nāṣira: Daʾirat al-Thaqāfa al-ʿArabiyya fī Wizārat al-Maʿārif wa-l-Thaqāfa.	31
I+III	M	Kashua, Sayyed (2002), *Aravim Rokdim*, Ben Shemen: Modan. [Hebrew]	32
III		Shiblī, ʿAdaniyya (2002), *Massās*, Bayrūt: Dār al-Ādab.	33
I	M	Ṭannūs, Jiryis (2003), *Dhākirat al-Ayyām*, ʿAkkā: Muʾassasat al-Aswār.	34
III		Kashua, Sayyed (2002), *VeYihi Boker*, Jerusalem: Keter. [Hebrew]	35
III	M	Shiblī, ʿAdaniyya (2004), *Kullunā Baʿīd bi-Dhāt al-Miqdār ʿan al-Ḥubb*, Bayrūt: Dār al-Ādab.	36
I	M	ʿAlī, Ṭāhā Muḥammad (2004), *Sīrat Banī Ballūṭ*, ʿAmmān: Dār al-Shurūq.	37
II	M	Ṭannūs, Jiryis (2005), *Yad al-Qadar*, ʿAkkā: Maṭbaʿat Abū Raḥmūn.	38
III	M	Bakriyya, Rajāʾ (2005 [2007]), *Imraʾat al-Risāla*, Bayrūt: Dār al-Ādab.	39
III		Bshāra, ʿAzmī (2006), *Ḥubb fī Manṭiqat al-Ẓill*, al-Qāhira: Dār al-Shurūq.	40
*		Bshāra, ʿAzmī (2006), *Al-Ḥājiz*, al-Dār al-Bayḍāʾ: al-Markiz al-Thaqāfī al-ʿArabī.	41
III		Bshārāt, ʿŪda (2007), *Sāḥāt Zatūnya*, Ḥayfā: al-Shajara.	42
III		Ḥlīḥil, ʿAlāʾ (2008), *Al-Ab wa-l-Ibn wa-l-Rūḥ al-Tāʾiha*, al-Qāhira: Dār al-ʿAyn.	43
III	M	Kashua, Sayyed (2010), *Guf Sheni Yahid*, Jerusalem: Keter. [Hebrew]	44
III	M	Siksik, Ayman (2010), *El Yafo*, Tel-Aviv: Yediot Sfarim. [Hebrew]	45

Groups: I Nostalgic-folkloric novels; II Intifada novels; III Novels of perplexity.
* Novels that do not belong to any of the groups. M = Monologue.

Notes

1. These are: (1) the National Committee for the Heads of the Arab Local Authorities in Israel; (2) the Supreme Follow Up Committee for the Arabs in Israel; (3) Mossawa Centre – The Advocacy Centre for Arab Citizens in Israel; Adalah – The Legal Centre for Arab Minority Rights in Israel; (4) Mada al-Carmel – Arab Centre for Applied Social Research.
2. In this section, 'present' will refer to the time frame of the period under consideration in this chapter, 1987–2010, unless stated otherwise.
3. It is important to note that the categorisation of novels in these groups is not definite. Some novels include themes that are related to more than one group (see Table 3.1 for more details).
4. An academic parallel to this 'trend' is evident in the increased interest of Palestinian academics in Palestinian folklore in this period. See, for example, Min'im Haddad (1986), who wrote about *Palestinian Folklore: Between Obliteration and Revival* [*Al-Turath al-Falastiniyy: Bayn al-Tams wa-l-Ihya'*] (Taybeh: Markiz Ihya' al-Turath al-ʿArabi). Another Palestinian citizen in Israel who wrote about Palestinian folklore is Shukri Arraf (1982), who among other things wrote: *Land, Man and Effort: Deals with Material Culture* [*Al-Arḍ, al-Insān, wa-l-Juhd: Dirāsa li-Ḥaḍāratinā al-Māddiyya ʿalā Arḍina*] (Acre: Matbaʿat Abu Rahmun).
5. Figures featuring in these village novels include *al-mukhtār*, the leader of the village; *al-rāʿī* and *al-ʿajjāl*, the herders of the livestock; *al-nāṭūr*, the village guard, who protects the fields from thieves and announces messages to the people; *al-mukhaḍḍar*, the guard of grazing fields; *ḥāris al-ʿayn*, the guard and operator of the water-spring; *al-ḥadhdhāʾ*, the farrier; and *al-ḥallāq*, the barber, who in many cases acts as the village 'doctor' as well. The social and public role of these figures is portrayed through the descriptions of daily life, in these novels, which include family and public disputes (*ṭuwash*), gossip, swear words and insults.
6. Folk medicine appearing in the novels includes treatments such as boiled nettle (*maghlī al-qarrāṣ*) for kidney stones; the consumption of bullock testicles to fend off impotency; use of ground coffee beans to staunch a wound; and the use of leeches to treat haemorrhoid (*al-bāṣūr*). Also mentioned are *al-tashṭīb* and *al-faṣd*, a treatment which cuts the skin to induce bleeding; *kāsāt al-hawā* (smoke glasses), using vacuum-pressure through the burning of paper in a glass placed on the skin of the patient; the treatment of warts (*thaʾālīl*) with boiled barley and lentils; giving of urine to babies to treat measles (*al-ḥaṣba*); and *al-tarqiya*,

the use of incense in prayer; and breast milk to treat conjunctivitis (*al-ramad*).

7. Other games include: *al-zuqqīṭa* (catch); *al-awtād* (the sticks); *al-ssibirki* (the broom); *kassārat al-ʿuṣī* (stick breakers); *al-banānīr* (marbles); *al-ḥajj* (a game with a cloth ball); *al-dajāja al-ʿamyāʾ* (the blind chicken – which involves hiding an item that a player is then asked to find, while blindfolded, with the assistance of other players); and *al-iks* (the X).
8. Another folkloric activity related to children is termed *al-taghyīth* ('calling for rain'). In years when the rainy season is late to arrive, the children of the village meet on the *baydar* (the village threshing ground, which is also a playground for children). Each child carries a long stick wrapped in cloth and proceeds around the neighbourhood singing the *taghyīth* song. On arrival at each new house, the house mistress is expected to pour water from a height onto the cloth hanging from the children's sticks, drenching both the cloth and the children. The children recite the customary song in praise. If a woman chooses not to take part in the *taghyīth* she will be greeted instead with the customary song of reproof (*Dhakirat al-Ayyam*, pp. 25–7). All songs are included in the text of the novel. The Palestinian geographer Shukri Arraf quotes a number of *taghyīth* songs in his book on Palestinian folklore (Arraf 1982: 238). The songs that appear in the novel (from the Galilee) and in Arraf's work (from Nablus), are very similar. *Taghyīth* songs from Gaza, mentioned in Arraf's book, are different from the other two.
9. There are a number of types of sticks used in this game according to their characteristics and 'value': a dry stick with a sharp rounded edge is named after the beak of the *zāgh* bird, 'which is similar to a pigeon', and called *zuqum zāgha* (*Dhakirat al-Ayyam*, pp. 152–3); a short, thick, dry stick is a *dukmar*; a long, dry and thick stick is *dukrab*; a long, thin, green stick is called *sharṭīṭa*. The *sharṭīṭa* 'is a flexible stick that is very hard to beat' (*Dhakirat al-Ayyam*, pp. 152–3).
10. See, for example, the following account from a person from the village of al-Bassa, near the border with Lebanon: 'The day the village fell, Jewish soldiers ordered all those who remained in the village to gather in the church. They took a few young people […] outside the church and shot them dead. Soon after, they ordered us to bury them. During the following day, we were transferred to al-Mazraʿa … There we met other elderly people gathered from the surrounding villages' (Nazzal 1974: 67).
11. <http://bit.ly/2vgjqXA> (last accessed 24 April 2019).
12. For example, *Dhakirat al-Ayyam* gives a detailed description of the Palestinian *fallāḥ*'s complex relationship with religion.

13. The construction of 'levels of civilisation' (*sullam al-taṭawwur al-ḥaḍārī*) is reminiscent of modernisation formulations depicting societies to move on a unidirectional path to become modernised (*qaṭa'a shawṭan*). This is an example of how modernist constructs have penetrated Palestinian ways of thinking, and are used even when criticising the effects of modernisation itself.
14. <https://www.zochrot.org/en> (last accessed 24 April 2019).
15. Many of the novels in this period, especially earlier ones, were affected by the Intifada. The title of this section, 'Intifada novels', does not mean that only novels in this group are affected by it. The novels in this group situate their plots in the Intifada context.
16. See, for example, Atallah Mansur's *Wa-Baqiyat Samira* (1962). The main protagonist in this novel, Riyad, refuses to fight during the occupation and expulsion of the city of Haifa, saying that he 'sees no cause to die for in Haifa' (*Wa-Baqiyat Samira*, p. 89).
17. In the original text in Hebrew he uses the word *Zar*, which translates to 'alien' or 'foreign'.
18. The theme of an absent character appears in two novels from the second period (1967–87). The first is Anton Shammas's *Arabesques*, where the plot revolved around the search for the absent Other-Palestinian. If we contrast *Arabsques* with perplexity novels, it is noticeable that in *Arabesques*, the Other-Palestinian was 'elusive' and 'hard to catch'. On the other hand, as it appears at the end of *Arabesques*, the Other-Palestinian, Michael Abyad/Anton Shammas, was also searching for his lost cousin. The encounter between the two left their 'identity crisis' unresolved. The second novel is Samih al-Qasim's *Ila al-Jahim Ayyuha al-Laylak*, where the meeting with Hasan takes place at the end of the novel. This meeting was brief, just like the narrator's meeting with his family in 'occupied Jerusalem'. He then 'returned' to (non-occupied) Haifa. I dealt with this quotation from *Ila al-Jahim Ayyuha al-Laylak* when I discussed the double contradictory identity of Palestinians in Israel. The third novel that has this theme is *Ikhtayya* by Emile Habiby. In this novel, which is about the passage of time, the sudden appearance of a childhood friend who had been 'gone' for almost four decades, requires the narrator to remember and rethink unresolved issues from his childhood. It is only with the passage of time that the narrator can assess the significance of these events.

REFLECTIONS: EVOLUTION OF PALESTINIAN IDENTITY IN ISRAEL

The identity of Palestinian citizens in Israel has undergone a long evolution since 1948. In the Introduction, I referred to the use of the 'evolution' metaphor to indicate the 'undesigned identity evolution' of Palestinians in Israel. Undesigned evolution should not be misinterpreted as being random. Identity, according to Anthony Smith, is 'a product of both "natural" continuity and conscious manipulation. Natural continuity emerges from pre-existing [...] identity and community; conscious manipulation is achieved via commemoration, ideology, and symbolism' (Cerulo 1997: 390–1). The above chapters show that Palestinian identity evolution is based on pre-existing identity and community, as well as 'conscious manipulation'. Palestinian novels reflect a process by which Palestinian citizens in Israel (re)considered and (re)evaluated their contemporary life conditions in the light of existing conditions.

Novels published during the first twenty years of Palestinian life under Israeli rule show the gradual adaptation and evolution of Palestinian identity. Palestinian adaptation takes into consideration the balance of power between this community and Israel; for example, the defeat in the 1948 war, with the devastating effects it had on Palestinian society, as well as life under military rule. The writings of Tawfiq Mu'ammar express the remnants of Palestinian national discourse prior to the Nakba, documenting the horrors of the war and expressing the notion that Palestinians, as the indigenous people of the country, should be allowed to take part in ruling themselves. The balance of power between Israel and its Palestinian citizens, also emphasised in Zionist-Israeli discourse, brought the Palestinians to adopt a modernising approach, aiming to close the gaps between the two societies. As we have seen in Chapter 1, proponents of the modernisation approach express the idea that such a process is multifaceted and comprehensive, including social, political and economic modernisations. The aim of closing the gap between Palestinians and Jewish-Israelis, according to both Palestinian and Israeli modernists, was to facilitate Palestinian integration into Israel. Such an approach marks an evolutionary phase from the earlier discourse, that of Mu'ammar, also aiming at Palestinian integration in the country. The difference between the two stages of this evolution lies in their respective attitudes towards the political and historic relations between Israel and the Palestinians. Whereas Mu'ammar aimed to preserve Palestinian history and memory, Palestinian modernisation discourse inherently erased them.

Towards the late 1960s, Palestinians in Israel realised that the exclusivist nature of Zionism could not accommodate Palestinian equal integration into Israel. Such an attitude is expressed in Atallah Mansour's *In a New Light*, a novel that negates the modernist discourse in matters relating to Palestinian life in Israel. In light of their realisation of their inability to integrate into the country, Palestinian citizens in Israel turned to dealing with the implications of their modernisation.

Palestinian postmodernist discourse addresses the two facets of modernisation: the socio-cultural and the political. Palestinian responses to the socio-cultural aspects were diverse, addressing the differentiation of this society from a variety of perspectives, from the religious to the secular, and from the individual to the collective. Discourse relating to the political dimensions of Palestinian life in Israel reflects Palestinian disappointment at not being able to achieve integration, pointing to exclusivist Zionism as the culprit for such a failure. Moreover, Palestinian citizens in Israel carried a doubly contradictory identity, according to which they were not fully Palestinian, nor completely Israeli. Counter-erasure of Jewish-Israelis is an extreme version of the doubly contradictory identity. This is so because by erasing the

Jewish-Israeli, counter-erasure reflects both Palestinian alienation in Israel as well as the lack of a positively defined identity – in the sense that counteraction novels depict Palestinians as non-Israeli, without offering an alternative for such 'non-identity'. Doubly contradictory identity differentiated Palestinians in Israel from Palestinians outside Israel in terms of their political activity, even though some (like Emile Habiby and Samih al-Qasim) emphasised the national-historical links between the two parts of this nation.

However, from the late 1980s onwards, the differentiation between the political and the socio-cultural aspects in Palestinian discourse starts to diminish. The socio-cultural becomes the political in nostalgic-folkloric, as well as Intifada, novels. These two groups emphasise the notion that the political occupation of Palestine, both in 1948 and 1967, might mean the obliteration of Palestinian society and culture. Thus, political resistance to such obliteration starts with clinging to the history and memory of Palestinian culture. The atomisation of Palestinian society in Israel during the first four decades is now replaced with Palestinian collectivisation, emphasising all-Palestinian national identity, history and memory. Nevertheless, Palestinian citizens in Israel are left perplexed in light of political processes and events that are beyond their control. The Oslo process was a primary initiator for this perplexity, bringing to the fore questions of identity not only versus the Jewish-Israelis, but also with regards to Palestinians outside Israel.

With regards to its methodology, this research differs from other studies on Palestinians in Israel on two levels: first, the study of literature provides an 'insider look' into Palestinian discourses in Israel. Traditional sociological or political research on this community is either ideologically driven (as is the case with modernist approaches), or primarily structural – focusing on the status of Palestinians in Israel through the lens of institutional, legal or ideological systems. Such research, as already pointed out, tells us more about Israel and less about Palestinian identity.

The second level on which this study differs from other literature-based research on the Palestinians in Israel relates to the volume of literary works included. The methodological decision to include as many novels as possible (seventy-five in total) had a direct effect on the book, in terms of its weaknesses and strengths. On the one hand, analysing such a large number of literary works in such a limited space allows little margin for in-depth analysis of each of the works. On the other hand, the inclusion of the majority of novels allows a 'macro' prism on the common trends in both Palestinian literature and discourse, which, in fact, serves the initial intention of this book with regard to outlining the transformations (the macro), rather than focusing on specific case studies (the micro). Such trends are evident in the grouping of novels in 'bundles', discussed in separate sections in the chapters above.

Another reason in favour of incorporating this large volume of novels relates to my intention to avoid any straight-jacketing that the notion 'canon' may impose on us. This is so because the canon is a small selection of literary works that are recognised due to certain political-national or artistic criteria. In a study designed to understand the national identity of a minority, as is the case in this book, use of the canon – assuming that one does unproblematically exist – would have a limiting, narrowing and indeed distorting effect on the findings. In addition, since this book provides discourse analysis, the artistic or literary value of the novels is not a criterion for selection. In other words, this study utilises novels as historic documents. Thus, the analysis of literary themes, as we have seen above, aimed to understand the political discourse and identity, rather than to decipher the literary or artistic genre or themes per se. This is evident, for example, in focusing the discussion on Palestinian postmodern themes to understand how they reflect political or national orientations.

The decisions described above had a direct effect on the course of my work with the novels. This is so because, in effect, my approach aimed to overcome the shortcomings of both sociology as well as the canon-focused literary study of Palestinians in Israel. Being free from the limitations of these two disciplines, the lack of disciplinary guidelines posed some 'problems' in handling the material. The first problem relates to the scarcity of scholarly attention to non-canon novels. As a result, analysis of most of the novels had to be carried out without the benefit of existing research on them. A second problem relates to the lack of research on Palestinian internal discourse. The abundance of research on the status of Palestinians in Israel was very useful to understand the context in which the novels were written; but it could provide scant analytical value regarding Palestinian identification.

However, these problems proved to be a blessing. This is so because while reading the novels I was not restricted to any specific set of evaluation parameters. As a result, I 'followed the texts', which led to the grouping of novels according to the common denominators among them, as is described throughout the book. Because of a lack of existing knowledge on most of the novels, I did not know what to expect in terms of findings. Some findings seemed to be surprising at first. Modernisation novels, discussed in Chapter 1, are a good example of this, because reading the novels that make up this group contrasted and challenged my 'knowledge' of Palestinian literature in that period (1948–67). Such novels are characterised by some to be 'resistance literature' (Ashrawi 1978; Harlow 1990; Hassan 2003). In fact, this term was initially coined by Palestinian journalist and writer Ghassan Kanafani (1966, 1968) in reference to Palestinian poetry in Israel in this period. Such a contrast between my findings and my existing knowledge highlights and raises a number of queries: is it really the case that Palestinian poetry and prose written in the same period could be so different? Or, is this contrast a result of the canonisation of Palestinian poetry? These questions show the need for further research into both Palestinian poetry and prose in Israel.

In addition to challenging existing knowledge on both Palestinian discourse and literature, it is important to address another effect of the choices I have made in this study. Creating groups of novels according to common denominators foregrounds some characteristics over others. Moreover, it may give the false impression that all novels in any one group are uniform. This is not the case. Novels in one group may have slightly different orientations from each other. This is most evident in counteraction novels, discussed in Chapter 2. Despite the close structural similarities between novels in this group, I presented in the above discussion two novels with opposing orientations towards religion (*Al-Juththa al-Majhula* and *Hubb ʿAbir al-Qarrat*). In Chapter 3, in addition, there are many overlapping characteristics between groups of novels, as already outlined.

Indeed, the presentation of characteristics and themes throughout this book does not claim to be conclusive. There are several other dimensions of Palestinian society and discourse reflected in the novels that require further investigation. One example of this relates to religious responses to modernisation, as discussed in Chapter 2. In discussing *Al-Juththa al-Majhula*, I pointed to the possibility that the emergence of Islamic discourse in Israel is a response to Palestinian modernisation. This speculation is relevant in a wider discussion on this issue, including the Christian and Druze communities. This speculation is based on signs of de-rationalisation and re-enchantment evidence in the writings of Christian novelists, such as Atallah Mansour and Salim Khuri. *Ruh fi-l-Butaqa* by Khuri is briefly discussed above, noting the extensive reference to religious discussions among the characters in the novel. Future research on this issue may clarify whether a 'return to religion' is a uniquely Muslim phenomenon, or whether it is a general trend encompassing all religious groups in Palestinian society.

To summarise the discussion of the approach adopted here, it is possible to say that although the sections making up the chapters of this book do not claim to contain the entirety of Palestinian discourses in Israel, they illustrate, in broad strokes, the major trends of identity transformations in this society. Moreover, notwithstanding the limitations of this study, it presents a unique picture of Palestinian life in Israel: from initial adaptation to life under Israeli rule; to the adoption of modernisation discourse; to the ramifications of modernisation on individual, family and societal levels; through to adapting and responding to challenges posed to this society as a result of life in Israel. Above all, in addition to identifying these trends, this book explains the transition between them, thereby highlighting the forces behind identity evolution.

BIBLIOGRAPHY

Abbasi, Mahmud (1983), 'The Development of the Novel and Short Story in Israeli Arabic Literature in the Years 1948–1976 [Hebrew: Hitpathut HaRoman VeHaSipur HaKatsar BaSefrut HaAravit BeYisra'el]', PhD Thesis, Jerusalem: Hebrew University of Jerusalem.

Abdel-Haleem, Muhammad A. S. (1992), 'Grammatical Shift for Rhetorical Purposes: Iltifāt and Related Features in the Qur'an', *Bulletin of the School of Oriental and African Studies* 55 (3): 407–32.

Abdel-Malek, Kamal, and David C. Jacobson (1999), *Israeli and Palestinian Identities in History and Literature*, New York: Macmillan.

Abrahams, Roger D. (1993), 'Phantoms of Romantic Nationalism in Folkloristics', *The Journal of American Folklore* 106 (419): 3–37.

Abu-Manneh, Bashir (2016), *The Palestinian Novel: From 1948 to the Present*, Cambridge: Cambridge University Press.

Aburaiya, Issam (2004), 'The 1996 Split of the Islamic Movement in Israel: Between the Holy Text and Israeli-Palestinian Context', *International Journal of Politics, Culture, and Society* 17 (3): 439–55.

Abu-Remaileh, Refqa (2010), 'Documenting Palestinian Presence: A Study of the Novels of Emile Habibi and the Films of Elia Suleiman', PhD Thesis, Oxford: University of Oxford.

Abu-Remaileh, Refqa (2014), 'The Kanafani Effect: Resistance and Counter-

Narration in the Films of Michel Khleifi and Elia Suleiman', *Middle East Journal of Culture and Communication* 7 (2): 190–206.

Agger, Ben (1991), 'Critical Theory, Poststructuralism, Postmodernism: Their Sociological Relevance', *Annual Review of Sociology* 17: 105–31.

Ajami, Fouad, and Martin H. Sours (1970), 'Israel and Sub-Saharan Africa: A Study of Interaction', *African Studies Review* 13 (3): 405–13.

Alexander, Jeffrey C. (1992), 'Durkheim's Problem and Differentiation Theory Today', in Hans Haferkamp and Neil J. Smelser (eds), *Social Change and Modernity*, Berkeley, LA: University of California Press, pp. 179–205.

Al-Khalili, Ali (2001), *The Narrating Inheritors: From the Nakba to the State* [Arabic: *Al-Waratha al-Ruwa: Min al-Nakba Ila al-Dawla*], Acre: Dar al-Aswar.

Amara, Muhammad, and Izhak Schnell (2004), 'Identity Repertoires among Arabs in Israel', *Journal of Ethnic and Migration Studies* 30 (1): 175–93.

Anderson, Benedict (2006), *Imagined Communities: Reflections on the Origin and Spread of Nationalism*, London; New York: Verso.

Antoun, Richard T. (1968), 'On the Significance of Names in an Arab Village', *Ethnology* 7 (2): 158–70.

Arraf, Shukri (1982), *Land, Man and Effort: Deals with Material Culture* [Arabic: *Al-Ard, al-Insan, Wa-l-Juhd: Dirasa li-Hadaratina al-Maddiyya ʿala Ardina*], Acre: Matbaʿat Abu Rahmun.

Ashrawi, Hanan Mikhail (1978), 'The Contemporary Palestinian Poetry of Occupation', *Journal of Palestine Studies* 7 (3): 77–101.

Bakhtin, Mikhail Mikhaĭlovich (1984), *Problems of Dostoevsky's Poetics*, Manchester: Manchester University Press.

Barakat, Halim Isber (1993), *The Arab World: Society, Culture, and State*, Berkeley, LA: University of California Press.

Barakat, Rana (2018), 'Writing/Righting Palestine Studies: Settler Colonialism, Indigenous Sovereignty and Resisting the Ghost(s) of History', *Settler Colonial Studies* 8 (3): 349–63.

Benvenisti, Meron (2000), *Sacred Landscape: The Buried History of the Holy Land since 1948*, Berkeley, LA: University of California Press.

Bernstein, Henry (1971), 'Modernization Theory and the Sociological Study of Development', *The Journal of Development Studies* 7 (2): 141–60.

Bertens, Hans (2003), *The Idea of the Postmodern: A History*, Ann Arbor, MI: Routledge.

Besnard, Philippe (1988), 'The True Nature of Anomie', *Sociological Theory* 6 (1): 91–5.

Bishara, Azmi (1993), 'On the Question of the Palestinian Minority in Israel [Hebrew: Al She'elat HaMi'uṭ HaFalasṭini BeYisra'el]', *Theory and Criticism* [Hebrew: *Tiorya UBikoret*] 3 (Winter): 7–20.

Bishara, Azmi (2001), 'Reflections on October 2000: A Landmark in Jewish–Arab Relations in Israel', *Journal of Palestine Studies* 30 (3): 54–67.

Bishara, Azmi (2011), 'The Israeli Sociology and Baruch Kimmerling's Contribution: General Comments [Arabic: Ilm al-Ijtima' al-Isra'iliyy wa-Musahamat Barukh Kimirling: Mulahazat 'Amma]', *Al-Mustaqbal Al-Arabi* 394 (Kanun al-Awwal): 7–33.

Bowes, Alison M. (1980), 'Strangers in the Kibbutz: Volunteer Workers in an Israeli Community', *Man (New Series)* 15 (4): 665–81.

Brenner, Rachel Feldhay (2001), 'The Search for Identity in Israeli Arab Fiction: Atallah Mansour, Emile Habiby, and Anton Shammas', *Israel Studies* 6 (3): 91–112.

Calhoun, Richard James (1963), 'Existentialism, Phenomenology, and Literary Theory', *South Atlantic Bulletin* 28 (4): 4–8.

Cerulo, Karen A. (1997), 'Identity Construction: New Issues, New Directions', *Annual Review of Sociology* 23 (1): 385–409.

Chamberlayne, John H. (1968), 'The Family in Islam', *Numen* 15 (1): 119–41.

Clews, Hetty (1985), *The Only Teller: Readings in the Monologue Novel*, Victoria, British Columbia: Sono Nis Pr.

Dallmayr, Fred (1992), 'Modernization and Postmodernization: Whither India?', *Alternatives: Global, Local, Political* 17 (4): 421–52.

Davis, Fred (1979), *Yearning for Yesterday: A Sociology of Nostalgia*, New York; London: Free Press; Collier Macmillan.

Davis, Rochelle (2007), 'Mapping the Past, Re-Creating the Homeland: Memories of Village Places in Pre-1948 Palestine', in Ahmad H. Sa'di and Lila Abu-Lughod (eds), *Nakba: Palestine, 1948, and the Claims of Memory*, New York: Columbia University Press, pp. 53–76.

de Certeau, Michel, Luce Giard and Pierre Mayol (1998), *The Practice of Everyday Life. Volume 2: Living and Cooking*, Minneapolis, MN: University of Minnesota Press.

Degani, Arnon Yehuda (2015), 'The Decline and Fall of the Israeli Military Government, 1948–1966: A Case of Settler-Colonial Consolidation?', *Settler Colonial Studies* 5 (1): 84–99.

de Man, Paul (1983), 'Dialogue and Dialogism', *Poetics Today* 4 (1): 99–107.

Dickinson, Hilary, and Michael Erben (2006), 'Nostalgia and Autobiography: The Past in the Present', *Auto/Biography* 14 (3): 223–44.

Eisenstadt, Shmuel N., and Wolfgang Schluchter (1998), 'Introduction: Paths to Early Modernities: A Comparative View', *Daedalus* 127 (3): 1–18.

Elad-Bouskila, Ami (1999), 'Arabic and/or Hebrew: The Languages of Arab Writers in Israel', in Abdel-Malek Kamal and David C. Jacobson (eds), *Israeli and Palestinian Identities in History and Literature*, New York: St. Martin's Press, pp. 133–58.

El-Asmar, Fouzi (1975a), *To Be an Arab in Israel* [Hebrew: *Lihyot Aravi BeYisrael*], Jerusalem: Prof. Israel Shahak.

El-Asmar, Fouzi (1975b), *To Be an Arab in Israel*, London: Frances Pinter.

Eyal, Gil (2006), *The Disenchantment of the Orient: Expertise in Arab Affairs and the Israeli State*, Stanford, CA: Stanford University Press.

Falah, Ghazi (1991), 'Israeli "Judaization" Policy in Galilee', *Journal of Palestine Studies* 20 (4): 69–85.

Falah, Ghazi (1996), 'The 1948 Israeli-Palestinian War and Its Aftermath: The Transformation and De-Signification of Palestine's Cultural Landscape', *Annals of the Association of American Geographers* 86 (2): 256–85.

Fanon, Frantz (2004), *The Wretched of the Earth*, New York: Grove Press.

Farsoun, Samih K., and Jean M. Landis (1990), 'The Sociology of an Uprising: The Roots of the Intifada', in Jamal R. Nassar and Roger Heacock (eds), *Intifada: Palestine at the Crossroads*, New York: Praeger, pp. 15–35.

Fayyad, Tawfiq (1978), *The Acre Group 778* [Arabic: *Majm'uat 'Akka 778*], Acre: n.p.

Galtung, Johan (1990), 'Cultural Violence', *Journal of Peace Research* 27 (3): 291–305.

Gavison, Ruth, and Dafna Hacker, eds (2000), *The Jewish-Arab Rift in Israel: A Reader* [Hebrew: *HaShesa' HaYehudi-Aravi BeYisrael: Mikraa*], Jerusalem: The Israel Democracy Institute.

Ghanayim, Mahmud (2008), *The Quest for a Lost Identity: Palestinian Fiction in Israel*, Studies in Arabic Language and Literature, Wiesbaden: Harrassowitz Verlag.

Ghanayim, Mahmud (2009), 'A Dream of Severance: Crisis of Identity in Palestinian Fiction in Israel', in Meir Litvak (ed.), *Palestinian Collective Memory and National Identity*, New York: Palgrave Macmillan, pp. 193–216.

Ghanem, As'ad (1998), 'State and Minority in Israel: The Case of Ethnic State and the Predicament of Its Minority', *Ethnic and Racial Studies* 21 (3): 428–48.

Ghanem, As'ad (2000), 'The Palestinian Minority in Israel: The "Challenge" of the Jewish State and Its Implications', *Third World Quarterly* 21 (1): 87–104.

Ghanem, As'ad (2001), *The Palestinian-Arab Minority in Israel 1948–2000: A Political Study*, Albany, NY: State University of New York Press.

Ghanem, As'ad (2002), 'The Palestinians in Israel: Political Orientation and Aspirations', *International Journal of Intercultural Relations* 26 (2): 135–52.

Ghanem, As'ad, and Sarah Ozacky-Lazar (2003), 'The Status of the Palestinians in Israel in an Era of Peace: Part of the Problem but not Part of the Solution', in Alexander Bligh (ed.), *The Israeli Palestinians: An Arab Minority in the Jewish State*, London: Frank Cass, pp. 267–89.

Ghanim, Honaida (2009), *Reinventing the Nation: Palestinian Intellectuals in Israel* [Hebrew: *Livnot Et HaUma MeHadash: Intilektualim Falastinim BeYisrael*], Jerusalem: The Hebrew University Magnes Press.

Ghanim, Honaida (2011), 'The Nakba', in Nadim N. Rouhana and Areej Sabbagh-Khoury (eds), *The Palestinians in Israel: Readings in History, Politics and Society*, Haifa: Mada al-Carmel – Arab Center for Applied Social Research, pp. 17–25.

Graeff, P., and G. Mehlkop (2007), 'When Anomie Becomes a Reason for Suicide: A New Macro-Sociological Approach in the Durkheimian Tradition', *European Sociological Review* 23 (4): 521–35.

Haddad, Yvonne (1992), 'Islamists and the "Problem of Israel": The 1967 Awakening', *Middle East Journal* 46 (2): 266–85.

Halman, Loek (1996), 'Individualism in Individualized Society?', *International Journal of Comparative Sociology* 37 (3–4): 195–214.

Handelman, Don (1994), 'Contradictions between Citizenship and Nationality: Their Consequences for Ethnicity and Inequality in Israel', *International Journal of Politics, Culture, and Society* 7 (3): 441–59.

Harlow, Barbara (1987), *Resistance Literature* New York; London: Methuen.

Harlow, Barbara (1990), 'Introduction to Kanafani's "Thoughts on Change and the 'Blind Language'"', *Alif: Journal of Comparative Poetics*, no. 10: 132–36.

Hassan, Salah Dean Assaf (2003), 'Nation Validation: Modern Palestinian Literature and the Politics of Appeasement', *Social Text* 21 (2): 7–24.

Hatina, Meir (2000), 'On the Margins of Consensus: The Call to Separate Religion and State in Modern Egypt', *Middle Eastern Studies* 36 (1): 35–67.

Heath, Peter (2000), 'Creativity in the Novels of Emile Habiby, with Special Reference to Sa'id the Pessoptimist', in Kamal Abdel-Malek and Wael B. Hallaq (eds), *Tradition, Modernity, and Postmodernity in Arabic Literature: Essays in Honor of Professor Issa J. Boullata*, Leiden; Boston: Brill, pp. 158–72.

Heise, Ursula K. (2011), 'Postmodern Novels', in Leonard Cassuto, Clare Virginia

Eby, and Benjamin Reiss (eds), *The Cambridge History of the American Novel*, Cambridge: Cambridge University Press, pp. 964–85.

Holub, Robert (2001), 'Modernism, Modernity, Modernisation', in Christa Knellwolf and Christopher Norris (eds), *The Cambridge History of Literary Criticism*, Cambridge: Cambridge University Press, pp. 275–88.

Home, Robert (2003), 'An "Irreversible Conquest"? Colonial and Postcolonial Land Law in Israel/Palestine', *Social & Legal Studies* 12 (3): 291–310.

Huschka, Denis, and Steffen Mau (2006), 'Social Anomie and Racial Segregation in South Africa', *Social Indicators Research* 76 (3): 467–98.

Hutcheon, Linda (1994), *Irony's Edge: The Theory and Politics of Irony*, Abingdon: Taylor & Francis.

Hutcheon, Linda (2000), 'Irony, Nostalgia, and the Postmodern', in Raymond Vervliet and Annemarie Estor (eds), *Methods for the Study of Literature as Cultural Memory*, Amsterdam: Rodopi, pp. 189–207.

Huyssen, Andreas (1984), 'Mapping the Postmodern', *New German Critique*, no. 33: 5–52.

Ibn Khaldun, Abd el-Rahman Ben Muhammad (1965), *The Prolegomena of Ibn Khaldun* [Arabic: *Muqaddimat Ibn Khaldun*], Cairo: Lajnat al-Bayan al-ʿArabi.

Inglehart, Ronald (1997), *Modernization and Postmodernization: Cultural, Economic, and Political Change in 43 Societies*, Princeton, NJ: Princeton University Press.

Jamal, Amal (2006), 'The Arab Leadership in Israel: Ascendance and Fragmentation', *Journal of Palestine Studies* 35 (2): 6–22.

Jayyusi, Lena (2007), 'Iterability, Cumulativity, and Presence: The Relational Figures of Palestinian Memory', in Ahmad H. Sa'di and Lila Abu-Lughod (eds), *Nakba: Palestine, 1948, and the Claims of Memory*, New York: Columbia University Press, pp. 107–34.

Jayyusi, Salma Khadra (1999), 'Palestinian Identity in Literature', in Kamal Abdel-Malek and David C. Jacobson (eds), *Israeli and Palestinian Identities in History and Literature*, New York: St. Martin's Press, pp. 167–77.

Jiryis, Sabri (1976), *The Arabs in Israel*, New York; London: Monthly Review Press.

Jiryis, Sabri (1979), 'The Arabs in Israel, 1973–79', *Journal of Palestine Studies* 8 (4): 31–56.

Johnson, Richard (1986), 'What Is Cultural Studies Anyway?', *Social Text*, no. 16: 38–80.

Joseph, Suad (1996), 'Patriarchy and Development in the Arab World', *Gender & Development* 4 (2): 14–19.

Kadman, Noga (2015), *Erased from Space and Consciousness: Israel and the Depopulated Palestinian Villages of 1948*, Bloomington, IN: Indiana University Press.

Kanafani, Ghassan (1966), *Resistance Literature in Occupied Palestine 1948–1966* [Arabic: *Adab al-Muqawama fi Falastin al-Muhtalla 1948–1966*], Beirut: Dar al-Adab.

Kanafani, Ghassan (1968), *Palestinian Resistance Literature under Occupation, 1948–1968* [Arabic: *Al-Adab al-Falastini al-Muqawim taht al-Ihtilal, 1948–1968*], Beirut: Mu'assasat al-Dirasat al-Filastiniyya.

Kayyal, Mahmoud (2008), '"Arabs Dancing in a New Light of Arabesques": Minor Hebrew Works of Palestinian Authors in the Eyes of Critics', *Middle Eastern Literatures* 11 (1 April): 31–51.

Khadduri, Majid (1953), 'The Role of the Military in Middle East Politics', *American Political Science Review* 47 (2): 511–24.

Khalidi, Raja (1984), 'The Arab Economy in Israel: Dependency or Development?', *Journal of Palestine Studies* 13 (3): 63–86.

Khalidi, Raja (1988), *The Arab Economy in Israel: The Dynamics of a Region's Development*, London: Croom Helm.

Khalidi, Walid (1985), 'A Palestinian Perspective on the Arab–Israeli Conflict', *Journal of Palestine Studies* 14 (4): 35–48.

Khalidi, Walid (1988), 'Plan Dalet: Master Plan for the Conquest of Palestine', *Journal of Palestine Studies* 18 (1): 4–33.

Khalidi, Walid (2008), 'The Fall of Haifa Revisited', *Journal of Palestine Studies* 37 (3): 30–58.

Khater, Akram F. (1993), 'Emile Habibi: The Mirror of Irony in Palestinian Literature', *Journal of Arabic Literature* 24 (1): 75–94.

Kidron, Hedva Ben-Israel (2003), 'Zionism and European Nationalisms; Comparative Aspects', *Israel Studies* 8 (1): 91–104.

Kimmerling, Baruch (1992), 'Sociology, Ideology, and Nation-Building: The Palestinians and Their Meaning in Israeli Sociology', *American Sociological Review* 57 (4): 446–60.

Kook, Rebecca B. (2002), *The Logic of Democratic Exclusion: African Americans in the United States and Palestinian Citizens in Israel*, Lanham, MD: Lexington Books.

Korn, Alina (2000), 'Military Government, Political Control and Crime: The Case of Israeli Arabs', *Crime, Law & Social Change* 34 (2): 159–82.

Kvale, Steinar (1995), 'Themes of Postmodernity', in Walt Anderson (ed.), *The Truth About the Truth: De-Confusing and Re-Constructing the Postmodern World*, New York: Jeremy P. Tarcher/Putnam, pp. 18–25.

Landau, Jacob M. (1969), *The Arabs in Israel: A Political Study*, Oxford: Oxford University Press.

Latham, Michael E. (1998), 'Ideology, Social Science, and Destiny: Modernization and the Kennedy-Era Alliance for Progress', *Diplomatic History* 22 (2): 199–229.

Lewis, Barry (2001), 'Postmodernism and Literature (or: World Salad Days, 1960–90)', in Stuart Sim (ed.), *The Routledge Companion to Postmodernism*, London: Routledge, pp. 121–33.

Lorch, Netanel (1963), 'Israel and Africa', *The World Today* 19 (8): 358–68.

Lowenthal, David (1985), *The Past Is a Foreign Country*, Cambridge: Cambridge University Press.

Lowrance, Sherry (2005), 'Being Palestinian in Israel: Identity, Protest, and Political Exclusion', *Comparative Studies of South Asia, Africa and the Middle East* 25 (2): 487–99.

Lustick, Ian S. (1980a), *Arabs in the Jewish State: Israel's Control of a National Minority*, Austin, TX: University of Texas Press.

Lustick, Ian S. (1980b), 'Zionism and the State of Israel: Regime Objectives and the Arab Minority in the First Years of Statehood', *Middle Eastern Studies* 16 (1): 127–46.

Lustick, Ian S. (1993), 'Review: Writing the Intifada: Collective Action in the Occupied Territories', *World Politics* 45 (4): 560–94.

Mahraz, Samiyah (1984), 'Irony in Joyce's Ulysses and Habibi's Pessoptimist [Arabic: Al-Mufaraqa ʿinda James Joyce wa-Imil Habibi]', *Alif: Journal of Comparative Poetics*, no. 4: 33–54.

Makdisi, Saree (2010), 'The Architecture of Erasure', *Critical Inquiry* 36 (3): 519–59.

Makhoul, Manar H. (2018a), 'Palestinian Citizens of Israel – Evolution of a Name', in Nadim N. Rouhana and Areej Sabbagh-Khoury (eds), *The Palestinians in Israel: Readings in History, Politics and Society*, Haifa: Mada al-Carmel – Arab Center for Applied Social Research, pp. 5–17.

Makhoul, Manar H. (2018b), 'Paratexts: Thresholds to Palestinian Identity', in Marta Dominguez (ed.), *Book Studies and Islamic Studies in Conversation*, Kodex 8, Wiesbaden: Harrassowitz Verlag, pp. 105–20.

Mansour, Atallah (1975), *Waiting for the Dawn: An Autobiography*, London: Secker and Warburg.

Mansour, Atallah (2013), *Still Waiting for the Dawn*, n.p.: CreateSpace Independent Publishing Platform.

Masalha, Nur (2007), 'Present Absentees and Indigenous Resistance', in Ilan Pappé (ed.), *The Israel/Palestine Question: A Reader*, London; New York: Routledge, pp. 255–84.

Masalha, Nur (2008), 'Remembering the Palestinian Nakba: Commemoration, Oral History and Narratives of Memory', *Holy Land Studies* 7 (2): 123–56.

Matar, Dina (2011), *What It Means to Be Palestinian: Stories of Palestinian Peoplehood*, London; New York: I.B. Tauris.

Miari, Mahmud (2008), 'The Development of Palestinians' Identity on Both Sides of the "Green Line" [Arabic: Tatawwur Hawiyyat al-Falastinyin ʿala Janibayy "al-Khatt al-Akhdar"]', *Majallat al-Dirasat al-Filastiniyya* 19 (74–5): 41–61.

Mittelberg, David (1988), *Strangers in Paradise: The Israeli Kibbutz Experience*, New Brunswick, NJ: Transaction Books.

Muhawi, Ibrahim (2006), 'Irony and the Poetics of Palestinian Exile', in Ibrahim Muhawi and Yasir Suleiman (eds), *Literature and Nation in the Middle East*, Edinburgh: Edinburgh University Press, pp. 31–47.

Mukherjee, S. Romi (2006), 'On Violence as the Negativity of the Durkheimian: Between Anomie, Sacrifice and Effervescence', *International Social Science Journal* 58: 5–39.

Nakhleh, Khalil (1977), 'Anthropological and Sociological Studies on the Arabs in Israel: A Critique', *Journal of Palestine Studies* 6 (4): 41–70.

Nazzal, Nafez Abdullah (1974), 'The Zionist Occupation of Western Galilee, 1948', *Journal of Palestine Studies* 3 (3): 58–76.

Norberg-Schulz, Christian (2000), *Architecture: Presence, Language and Place*, Milan: Skira.

O'Neill, Patrick (1983), 'The Comedy of Entropy: The Contexts of Black Humour', *Canadian Review of Comparative Literature/Revue Canadienne de Littérature Comparée* 10 (2): 145–66.

Ozacky-Lazar, Sara (2002), 'The Military Government as an Apparatus of Control of the Arab Citizens in Israel: The First Decade, 1948–1958', *The New East* [Hebrew: *HaMizrah HeHadash*] XLIII: 103–31.

Pappé, Ilan (1997), 'Post-Zionist Critique on Israel and the Palestinians Part II: The Media', *Journal of Palestine Studies* 26 (3): 37–43.

Pappé, Ilan (2006), *A History of Modern Palestine: One Land, Two Peoples*, 2nd edn, Cambridge: Cambridge University Press.

Pappé, Ilan (2007), *The Ethnic Cleansing of Palestine*, Oxford: Oneworld.

Peled, Yoav (1993), 'Strangers in Utopia: The Civil Status of Palestinians In Israel [Hebrew: Zarim BaAutupya: Maʿmadam HaIzrahi Shel HaFalastinaim BiYisrael]', *Theory and Criticism* [Hebrew: *Tiorya UBikoret*] 3 (Winter): 21–33.

Peleg, Ilan (2004), 'Jewish–Palestinian Relations in Israel: From Hegemony to Equality?', *International Journal of Politics, Culture, and Society* 17 (3): 415–37.

Peres, Yochanan (1970), 'Modernization and Nationalism in the Identity of the Israeli Arab', *Middle East Journal* 24 (4): 479–92.

Peretz, Don (1990), *Intifada: The Palestinian Uprising*, Boulder, CO: Westview Press.

Peteet, Julie M. (1991), *Gender in Crisis: Women and the Palestinian Resistance Movement*, New York: Columbia University Press.

Peteet, Julie M. (1994), 'Male Gender and Rituals of Resistance in the Palestinian "Intifada": A Cultural Politics of Violence', *American Ethnologist* 21 (1): 31–49.

Pitcher, Linda M. (1998), '"The Divine Impatience": Ritual, Narrative, and Symbolization in the Practice of Martyrdom Palestine', *Medical Anthropology Quarterly* 12 (1): 8–30.

Piterberg, G. (2001), 'Erasures', *New Left Review* 10: 31–46.

al-Qasim, Nabih (1979), *Studies in the Local Story* [Arabic: *Dirasat fi-l-Qissa al-Mahaliyya*], Acre: Dar al-Aswar.

al-Qasim, Nabih (1991), *On the Palestinian Novel* [Arabic: *Fi-l-Riwaya al-Falastiniyya*], Kafr Qara: n.p.

Rekhess, Eli (1989), 'The Arabs in Israel and the Territories' Arabs: Political Orientation and National Solidarity (1967–1988) [Hebrew: HaAravim BeYisrael VeArviyye HaShtahim: Zika Politit VeSolidaryut Leomit]', *The New East* [Hebrew: *HaMizrah HeHadash*] 32 (125–8): 165–91.

Rekhess, Eli (2002), 'The Arabs of Israel after Oslo: Localization of the National Struggle', *Israel Studies* 7 (3): 1–44.

Rinnawi, Khalil (2003), *The Palestinian Society in Israel: An Ambivalent Agenda* [Hebrew: *HaHevra HaAravit BiYisrael: Seder Yom Ambivalenti*]. Rishon LeZion: n.p.

Robinson, Shira (2003), 'Local Struggle, National Struggle: Palestinian Responses to the Kafr Qasim Massacre and Its Aftermath, 1956–66', *International Journal of Middle East Studies* 35 (3): 393–416.

Robinson, Shira (2013), *Citizen Strangers: Palestinians and the Birth of Israel's Liberal Settler State*, Stanford, CA: Stanford University Press.

Rosenhek, Zeev (1998), 'New Developments in the Sociology of Palestinian Citizens of Israel: An Analytical Review', *Ethnic and Racial Studies* 21: 558–78.

Rouhana, Nadim N. (1990), 'The Intifada and the Palestinians of Israel: Resurrecting the Green Line', *Journal of Palestine Studies* 19 (3): 58–75.

Rouhana, Nadim N. (1993), 'Accentuated Identities in Protracted Conflicts: The Collective Identity of Palestinian Citizens of Israel', *Asian and African Studies* 27: 97–127.

Rouhana, Nadim N. (1997), *Palestinian Citizens in an Ethnic Jewish State: Identities in Conflict*, New Haven, CT: Yale University Press.

Rouhana, Nadim N. (1998), 'Israel and Its Arab Citizens: Predicaments in the Relationship between Ethnic States and Ethnonational Minorities', *Third World Quarterly* 19 (2): 277–96.

Rouhana, Nadim N., and Areej Sabbagh-Khoury (2014), 'Settler-Colonial Citizenship: Conceptualizing the Relationship between Israel and its Palestinian Citizens', *Settler Colonial Studies* 5 (3): 205–25.

Sabbagh-Khoury, Areej (2018), 'Settler Colonialism, the Indigenous Perspective and the Sociology of Knowledge Production in Israel [Hebrew: Colonbializm Hityashvuti, Nekoudat HaMabat HaYelidit VeHaSotzyologia Shel Yitsur Yeda' BeYisrael]', *Theory and Criticism* [Hebrew: *Tiorya UBikoret*] 50 (Winter): 391–418.

Sa'di, Ahmad H. (1992), 'Between State Ideology and Minority National Identity: Palestinians in Israel and in Israeli Social Science Research', *Review of Middle East Studies* 5: 110–30.

Sa'di, Ahmad H. (1997), 'Modernization as an Explanatory Discourse of Zionist–Palestinian Relations', *British Journal of Middle Eastern Studies* 24 (1): 25–48.

Said, Edward W. (1979), 'Zionism from the Standpoint of Its Victims', *Social Text* 1 (Winter): 7–58.

Said, Edward W. (1994), *Culture and Imperialism*, London: Vintage.

Sayigh, Rosemary (2007), *The Palestinians: From Peasants to Revolutionaries*, London: Zed Books.

Seeman, Melvin (1959), 'On the Meaning of Alienation', *American Sociological Review* 24 (6): 783–91.

Seliktar, Ofira (1984), 'The Arabs in Israel: Some Observations on the Psychology of the System of Controls', *The Journal of Conflict Resolution* 28 (2): 247–69.

Shalhat, Antun (2003), 'On Culture and Identity: A Genealogical Account [Arabic: Fi-l-Thaqafa wa-l-Hawiyya: Mudakhala Ta'siliyya]', *Al-Adab* 7–8: 27–32.

Sharabi, Hisham (1988), *Neopatriarchy: A Theory of Distorted Change in Arab Society*, Oxford: Oxford University Press.

Sharma, R. K. (1988), *Contemporary Black Humour American Novels, from Nathanael West to Thomas Berger*, Delhi: Ajanta Publications.

Shhada, Yusif (2007), 'Intertextuality and the Balance of the Old and New in the Language of Emile Habiby [Arabic: Al-Tanas wa-Tanasuq al-Qadim wa-l-Hadith fi Lughat Imil Habibi al-Sardiyya]', *Al-Bayan* 441 (April): 40–9.

Shlaim, Avi (1995), 'The Debate about 1948', *International Journal of Middle Eastern Studies* 27 (3): 287–304.

Shlaim, Avi (2000), *The Iron Wall: Israel and the Arab World*, London: Penguin Books.

Simatei, Tirop (2005), 'Colonial Violence, Postcolonial Violations: Violence, Landscape, and Memory in Kenyan Fiction', *Research in African Literatures* 36 (2): 85–94.

Slyomovics, Susan (1998), *The Object of Memory: Arab and Jew Narrate the Palestinian Village*, Philadelphia, PA: University of Pennsylvania Press.

Smooha, Sammy (1990), 'Minority Status in an Ethnic Democracy: The Status of the Arab Minority in Israel', *Ethnic and Racial Studies* 13 (3): 389–413.

So, Alvin Y. (1990), *Social Change and Development: Modernization, Dependency, and World-Systems Theories*, Newbury Park, CA: Sage Publications.

Sone, Abigail (2010), 'Linguistic and Spatial Practice in a Divided Landscape', PhD Thesis, Toronto: University of Toronto.

Sorek, Tamir (2015), *Palestinian Commemoration in Israel: Calendars, Monuments, and Martyrs*, Stanford, CA: Stanford University Press.

Stedman Jones, Susan (2006), 'Durkheim, the Question of Violence and the Paris Commune of 1871', *International Social Science Journal* 58: 63–81.

Stendel, Ori (1996), *The Arabs in Israel*, Brighton: Sussex Academic Press.

Suleiman, Yasir (2004), *A War of Words: Language and Conflict in the Middle East*, Cambridge Middle East Studies 19, New York: Cambridge University Press.

Suleiman, Yasir (2006a), 'Introduction', in Yasir Suleiman and Ibrahim Muhawi (eds), *Literature and Nation in the Middle East*, Edinburgh: Edinburgh University Press, pp. 1–15.

Suleiman, Yasir (2006b), 'The Nation Speaks: On the Poetics of Nationalist Literature', in Yasir Suleiman and Ibrahim Muhawi (eds), *Literature and Nation in the Middle East*, Edinburgh: Edinburgh University Press, pp. 208–31.

Suleiman, Yasir (2011), *Arabic, Self and Identity: A Study in Conflict and Displacement*, New York: Oxford University Press.

Suleiman, Yasir, and Ibrahim Muhawi, eds (2006), *Literature and Nation in the Middle East*, Edinburgh: Edinburgh University Press.

Taha, Ibrahim (2002), *The Palestinian Novel: A Communication Study*, London: Routledge.

Tessler, Mark A. (1977), 'Israel's Arabs and the Palestinian Problem', *The Middle East Journal* 31 (3): 313–29.

Tipps, Dean C. (1973), 'Modernization Theory and the Comparative Study of Societies: A Critical Perspective', *Comparative Studies in Society and History* 15 (2): 199–226.

Tiryakian, Edward A. (1992a), 'Dialectics of Modernity: Reenchantment and Dedifferentiation as Counterprocesses', in Hans Haferkamp and Neil J. Smelser (eds), *Social Change and Modernity*, Berkeley, LA: University of California Press, pp. 79–95.

Tiryakian, Edward A. (1992b), 'From Modernization to Globalization', *Journal for the Scientific Study of Religion* 31 (3): 304–10.

Tuan, Yi-Fu (1991), 'Language and the Making of Place: A Narrative-Descriptive Approach', *Annals of the Association of American Geographers* 81 (4): 684–96.

Turner, Victor (1975), 'Symbolic Studies', *Annual Review of Anthropology* 4 (1): 145–61.

al-Usta, Adel (1992), *Jews in Palestinian Literature between 1913 and 1987* [Arabic: *Al-Yahud fi-l-Adab al-Falastini 1913–1987*], Jerusalem: Ittihad al-Kuttab al-Falastinyin fi-l-Diffa al-Gharbiyya wa-Qita' Ghazza.

al-Usta, Adel (2002), *Critical Issues and Phenomena in the Palestinian Novel* [Arabic: *Qadaya wa-Zawahir Naqdiyya fi-l-Riwaya al-Falastiniyya*], Acre: Mu'assasat al-Aswar.

Van Soest, Dorothy, and Shirley Bryant (1995), 'Violence Reconceptualized for Social Work: The Urban Dilemma', *Social Work* 40 (4): 549–57.

Wagner, Tamara S. (2004), *Longing: Narratives of Nostalgia in the British Novel, 1740–1890*, Lewisburg, PA: Bucknell University Press.

Walder, Dennis (2011), *Postcolonial Nostalgias: Writing, Representation and Memory*, Routledge Research in Postcolonial Literatures 31, New York: Routledge.

Weaver, Alain Epp (2007), 'Remembering the Nakba in Hebrew: Return Visits as the Performance of a Binational Future', *Holy Land Studies* 6 (2): 125–44.

Yaqub, Nadia G. (2007), *Pens, Swords, and the Springs of Art: The Oral Poetry Dueling of Palestinian Weddings in Galilee*, Leiden; Boston: Brill.

Yiftachel, Oren (1992), 'The Arab Minority in Israel and Its Relations with the Jewish Majority: A Review Essay', *Studies in Comparative International Development* 27 (2): 57–83.

Young, Robert (2001), *Postcolonialism: An Historical Introduction*, Oxford; Malden, MA: Blackwell Publishers.

Zahavi, Dan (2004), 'First-Person Thoughts and Embodied Self-Awareness: Some Reflections on the Relation between Recent Analytical Philosophy and Phenomenology', *Phenomenology and the Cognitive Sciences* 1 (1): 7–26.

Zreik, Raef (2004), 'Palestine, Apartheid, and the Rights Discourse', *Journal of Palestine Studies* 34 (1): 68–80.

INDEX

1948 War, 1, 12, 15, 18, 20–3, 33–4, 48, 50, 54, 57, 59, 106, 114, 123, 130, 141, 144, 146, 148, 150, 160, 170, 198, 208
1967 War, 12, 17, 84–5, 108–9, 113–14, 116

Abbasi, Mahmud, 10, 55
Al-Hamishiyy, 183–5, 200
alienation, 50, 53, 64, 89–93, 96–7, 130, 133, 139, 180–6, 188–9, 195, 200–1, 203–4, 210
Al-Juththa al-Majhula, 69, 70, 71–4, 76, 79, 81–2, 84, 86–7, 90–2, 94–8, 104, 132–3, 135, 173, 212
Al-Qadiyya Raqam 13, 82, 92
Al-Qasim, Samih, 99, 102, 105, 175, 210
Al-Sura al-Akhira fi-l-Album, 99, 100
Al-Waqa'i' al-Ghariba fi Ikhtifa' Sa'id Abi-l-Nahs al-Mutasha'il, 98, 114–21, 123, 125–9, 131–2, 167
anomie, 81–4, 89, 91–2, 97, 132, 145
Asiyy al-Dam', 149, 150, 152–4, 158
attenuation, 24–7, 29, 33, 109
Awja' al-Bilad al-Muqaddasa, 146, 148, 150, 158, 170

Baydas, Riyad, 183
Bit-hun, 23–5, 27, 54

canon (canonisation; literary canon), 10–12, 119, 211
collectivisation, 145–6, 150, 155, 164, 173–5, 177, 180, 182, 200, 210
colonial studies, 7
colonialism, 7–8, 58, 166
counteraction novels, 69–70, 91–3, 95–7, 100, 132–4, 186, 210, 212
counter-erasure, 69, 92–6, 120, 133–4, 152, 209–10

Darih al-Hasna', 92, 98
dark humour, 101–2
Dhakirat al-Ayyam, 144–5, 155, 166
dialogism (and un-dialogism), 95–6
differentiation, 13, 69–71, 75, 78–9, 81, 83, 87–8, 91, 97, 132, 145, 150, 152, 167, 170, 173, 185, 200, 209–10
discontinuity, 68, 150–1, 155, 157, 162, 167, 172, 174, 176, 200
disenchantment, 98
disenchantment novels, 134
doubly contradictory identity, 99, 105, 107, 111, 113–15, 125, 134, 162, 175, 188, 198, 209–10

El-Asmar, Fouzi, 57, 108, 109
erasure, 3, 7, 48–50, 63–4, 67, 69–70, 91, 93–7, 120, 122, 133–4, 151, 154–6, 162–4, 166, 173–6, 181–2, 184, 186–7, 191–2, 200

evolution, 2–3, 10–11, 17–18, 32, 68, 123–5, 127–9, 139, 142, 175, 208–9, 213

Fanon, Frantz, 63–4
Farhat Farhat, 82
Fayyad, Tawfiq, 116–18
First Intifada, 12–13, 139–40, 151
folklore, 141, 143, 148, 150–1, 159–62, 165–7, 184, 201
folklorification, 141, 143, 146, 148, 159, 162, 164, 167

Habiby, Emile, 114–20, 122–8, 130–2, 134, 158, 159–61, 167, 184, 210
Hazim Ya'ud Hadha-l-Masa', 189, 196, 199, 200
Hijazi, Abd al-Rahman, 70
Hsaysi, Majid, 82
Hubb 'Abir al-Qarrat, 70, 85, 86, 88–91, 94, 96–7, 132–3, 212
Hubb bila Ghad, 55

Ibrahim, Hanna, 146
Ikhtayya, 98, 126–32, 134, 141, 158, 160, 167, 184, 207
Ila al-Jahim Ayyuha al-Laylak, 98, 105–6, 108–9, 110–12, 114, 175
In a New Light, 56–60, 63–4, 67, 209
individualisation, 13, 71, 75, 76–9, 86, 132–3, 145, 185
Intifada novels, 141, 151, 164–7, 170–4, 176–7, 180–1, 187–8, 190, 199–202

Kafr Qasim, 54
Kanafani, Ghassan, 8, 56, 114, 212
Kana'na, Mahmud, 37, 55
Kashua, Sayyed, 184–5, 187
Khuri, Salim, 98, 103, 213
Kibbutz, 35, 37–43, 45–8, 55, 57–8, 60–1, 153–4
Kiwan, Suhil, 149

Let It Be Morning, 184–8, 200

Majmu'at Akka, 778, 115–18
Mansour, Atallah, 32, 34–6, 46–7, 56, 57, 60, 64, 67, 108, 209, 213
memory, 18, 21, 23, 33, 55, 59, 63, 106–7, 122, 131, 134, 142–6, 162–4, 166, 190–2, 209–10.
methodology, 2, 6, 9, 210
military rule, 12, 15–17, 23–4, 26–8, 32, 51, 53, 55, 62, 108–9, 174, 208
modernisation, 3, 5, 7–8, 12–13, 17, 29, 30–2, 34, 36–45, 48, 50–62, 64, 65, 67–70, 73–4, 76, 80–1, 83–5, 88–9, 91, 96–8, 103, 131–4, 152–7, 159, 162, 179, 185–6, 209, 212–13
 and academia, 31
modernisation novels, 8, 29, 32, 38, 50–6, 60–1, 64, 77, 89, 92, 96, 99–100, 109, 131, 133, 153–4, 212
monologic discourse, 95
Mu'ammar, Tawfiq, 17–29, 33–4, 38, 47, 54–5, 59, 62, 109, 208–9
Mudhakkarat Laji' aw Hayfa fi-l-Ma'raka, 17, 18, 20–1, 23–5, 33
Muhammad Khalid, Khalid, 87

Nakba, 1, 12, 14–15, 20, 107, 113, 115, 125, 141, 143, 146, 148, 150–2, 159, 161–4, 167, 170–1, 174–5, 181, 190, 200, 209
Nasir, Yusif, 92
nostalgic-folkloric novels, 141–6, 148–52, 154–5, 158, 161, 163, 164, 166–7, 169–72, 175–7, 181, 190, 201
novels of perplexity (/perplexity novels), 180, 182–4, 186, 189, 198–202

Palestinian literature, 8–11, 137, 167, 177, 202–3, 211, 212
Palestinian refugees, 16, 25, 48, 106–7, 144, 146, 160–2, 185, 195, 199
perplexity novels *see* novels of perplexity
postcolonial theory, 6
postmodernisation, 57, 64, 68

Qalb fi Qarya, 37–9, 41–3, 45–8, 53, 55, 153

rationalisation, 69, 97–8, 103–4
resistance literature, 8, 212
Ruh fi-l-Butaqa, 98, 103–5, 213

Said, Edward, 8–9, 47, 58, 60
Salama, Kamal, 70
Second Intifada, 13, 139
settler colonialism, 7
Siraj al-Ghula, 159, 184
stranger ('concept', Georg Simmel), 46

Tannus, Jiryis, 144–5, 155, 166–7, 174, 199

Uda, Nabil, 189, 198
un-erasure, 120, 122, 127, 152, 162

violence, 49, 84, 92–3, 187–8

Wa-Baqiyat Samira, 32, 34, 36

Yad al-Qadar, 166–7, 174–6, 199

EU representative:
Easy Access System Europe
Mustamäe tee 50, 10621 Tallinn, Estonia
Gpsr.requests@easproject.com

www.ingramcontent.com/pod-product-compliance
Lightning Source LLC
Chambersburg PA
CBHW070347240426
43671CB00013BA/2426
9781474459280